TAPESTRY

POWER
THROUGH THE
WRITTEN WORD

TAPESTRY

The **Tapestry** program of language
materials is based on the concepts
presented in *The Tapestry Of
Language Learning: The Individual
in the Communicative Classroom* by
Robin C. Scarcella &
Rebecca L. Oxford.

❖

Each title in this program focuses on:

❖

Individual learner strategies and
instruction

❖

The relatedness of skills

❖

Ongoing self-assessment

❖

Authentic material as input

❖

Theme-based learning linked to task-
based instruction

❖

Attention to all aspects of
communicative competence

✦ TAPESTRY

POWER THROUGH THE WRITTEN WORD

Robin C. Scarcella

Heinle & Heinle Publishers
A Division of Wadsworth, Inc.
Boston, Massachusetts, 02116, USA

The publication of *Power Through the Written Word* was directed by the members of the Heinle & Heinle ESL Publishing Team:

David C. Lee, Editorial Director
Susan Mraz, Marketing Manager
Lisa McLaughlin, Production Editor

Also participating in the publication of this program were:

Publisher: Stanley J. Galek
Editorial Production Manager: Elizabeth Holthaus
Assistant Editor: Kenneth Mattsson
Manufacturing Coordinator: Mary Beth Lynch
Full Service Project Manager/Compositor: Monotype Composition Company
Interior Design: Maureen Lauran
Cover Design: Maureen Lauran

Manufactured in the United States of America.

ISBN: 0-8384-4668-X

Heinle & Heinle Publishers is a division of Wadsworth, Inc.

10 9 8 7 6 5 4 3 2 1

To my son,
Chris

WELCOME TO TAPESTRY

*E*nter the world of Tapestry! Language learning can be seen as an ever-developing tapestry woven with many threads and colors. The elements of the tapestry are related to different language skills like listening and speaking, reading and writing; the characteristics of the teachers; the desires, needs, and backgrounds of the students; and the general second language development process. When all these elements are working together harmoniously, the result is a colorful, continuously growing tapestry of language competence of which the student and the teacher can be proud.

This volume is part of the Tapestry program for students of English as a second language (ESL) at levels from beginning to "bridge" (which follows the advanced level and prepares students to enter regular postsecondary programs along with native English speakers). Tapestry levels include:

Beginning
Low Intermediate
High Intermediate
Low Advanced
High Advanced
Bridge

Because the Tapestry Program provides a unified theoretical and pedagogical foundation for all its components, you can optimally use the Tapestry student books in a coordinated fashion as an entire curriculum of materials. (They will be published from 1993 to 1995, with further editions likely thereafter.) Alternatively, you can decide to use just certain Tapestry volumes, depending on your specific needs.

Tapestry is primarily designed for ESL students at postsecondary institutions in North America. Some want to learn ESL for academic or career advancement, others for social and personal reasons. Tapestry builds directly on all these motivations. Tapestry stimulates learners to do their best. It enables learners to use English naturally and to develop fluency as well as accuracy.

Tapestry Principles

The following principles underlie the instruction provided in all of the components of the Tapestry program.

EMPOWERING LEARNERS

Language learners in Tapestry classrooms are active and increasingly responsible for developing their English language skills and related cultural abilities. This self-direction leads to better, more rapid learning. Some cultures virtually train their students to be passive in the classroom, but Tapestry weans them from passivity by providing exceptionally high-interest materials, colorful and motivating activities, personalized self-reflection tasks, peer tutoring and other forms of cooperative learning, and powerful learning strategies to boost self-direction in learning.

The empowerment of learners creates refreshing new roles for teachers, too. The teacher serves as facilitator, co-communicator, diagnostician, guide, and helper. Teachers are set free to be more creative at the same time their students become more autonomous learners.

HELPING STUDENTS IMPROVE THEIR LEARNING STRATEGIES

Learning strategies are the behaviors or steps an individual uses to enhance his or her learning. Examples are taking notes, practicing, finding a conversation partner, analyzing words, using background knowledge, and controlling anxiety. Hundreds of such strategies have been identified. Successful language learners use language learning strategies that are most effective for them given their particular learning styles, and they put them together smoothly to fit the needs of a given language task. On the other hand, the learning strategies of less successful learners are a desperate grab-bag of ill-matched techniques.

All learners need to know a wide range of learning strategies. All learners need systematic practice in choosing and applying strategies that are relevant for various learning needs. Tapestry is one of the only ESL programs that overtly weaves a comprehensive set of learning strategies into language activities in all its volumes. These learning strategies are arranged in six broad categories throughout the Tapestry books:

Forming concepts	Managing your learning
Personalizing	Understanding and using emotions
Remembering new material	Overcoming limitations

The most useful strategies are sometimes repeated and flagged with a note, "It Works! Learning Strategy . . ." to remind students to use a learning strategy they have already encountered. This recycling reinforces the value of learning strategies and provides greater practice.

RECOGNIZING AND HANDLING LEARNING STYLES EFFECTIVELY

Learners have different learning styles (for instance, visual, auditory, hands-on; reflective, impulsive; analytic, global; extroverted, introverted; closure-oriented, open). Particularly in an ESL setting, where students come from vastly different cultural backgrounds, learning style differences abound and can cause "style conflicts."

Unlike most language instruction materials, Tapestry provides exciting activities specifically tailored to the needs of students with a large range of learning styles. You can use any Tapestry volume with the confidence that the activities and materials are intentionally geared for many different styles. Insights from the latest educational and psychological research undergird this style-nourishing variety.

OFFERING AUTHENTIC, MEANINGFUL COMMUNICATION

Students need to encounter language that provides authentic, meaningful communication. They must be involved in real-life communication tasks that cause them to *want* and *need* to read, write, speak, and listen to English. Moreover, the tasks—to be most effective—must be arranged around themes relevant to learners.

Themes like family relationships, survival in the educational system, personal health, friendships in a new country, political changes, and protection of the environment are all valuable to ESL learners. Tapestry focuses on topics like these. In every Tapestry volume, you will see specific content drawn from very broad areas such as home life, science and technology, business, humanities, social sciences, global issues, and multiculturalism. All the themes are real and important, and they are fashioned into language tasks that students enjoy.

At the advanced level, Tapestry also includes special books each focused on a single broad theme. For instance, there are two books on business English, two on English for science and technology, and two on academic communication and study skills.

UNDERSTANDING AND VALUING DIFFERENT CULTURES

Many ESL books and programs focus completely on the "new" culture, that is, the culture which the students are entering. The implicit message is that ESL students should just learn about this target culture, and there is no need to understand their own culture better or to find out about the cultures of their international classmates. To some ESL students, this makes them feel their own culture is not valued in the new country.

Tapestry is designed to provide a clear and understandable entry into North American culture. Nevertheless, the Tapestry Program values *all* the cultures found in the ESL classroom. Tapestry students have constant opportunities to become "culturally fluent" in North American culture while they are learning English, but they also have the chance to think about the cultures of their classmates and even understand their home culture from different perspectives.

INTEGRATING THE LANGUAGE SKILLS

Communication in a language is not restricted to one skill or another. ESL students are typically expected to learn (to a greater or lesser degree) all four language skills: reading, writing, speaking, and listening. They are also expected to develop strong grammatical competence, as well as becoming socioculturally sensitive and knowing what to do when they encounter a "language barrier."

Research shows that multi-skill learning is more effective than isolated-skill learning, because related activities in several skills provide reinforcement and refresh the learner's memory. Therefore, Tapestry integrates all the skills. A given Tapestry volume might highlight one skill, such as reading, but all other skills are also included to support and strengthen overall language development.

However, many intensive ESL programs are divided into classes labeled according to one skill (Reading Comprehension Class) or at most two skills (Listening/Speaking Class or Oral Communication Class). The volumes in the Tapestry Program can easily be used to fit this traditional format, because each volume clearly identifies its highlighted or central skill(s).

Grammar is interwoven into all Tapestry volumes. However, there is also a separate reference book for students, *The Tapestry Grammar,* and a Grammar Strand composed of grammar "work-out" books at each of the levels in the Tapestry Program.

Other Features of the Tapestry Program

PILOT SITES

It is not enough to provide volumes full of appealing tasks and beautiful pictures. Users deserve to know that the materials have been pilot-tested. In many ESL series, pilot testing takes place at only a few sites or even just in the classroom of the author. In contrast, Heinle & Heinle Publishers have developed a network of Tapestry Pilot Test Sites throughout North America. At this time, there are approximately 40 such sites, although the number grows weekly. These sites try out the materials and provide suggestions for revisions. They are all actively engaged in making Tapestry the best program possible.

AN OVERALL GUIDEBOOK

To offer coherence to the entire Tapestry Program and especially to offer support for teachers who want to understand the principles and practice of Tapestry, we have written a book entitled, *The Tapestry of Language Learning: The Individual in the Communicative Classroom* (Scarcella and Oxford, published in 1992 by Heinle & Heinle).

A Last Word

We are pleased to welcome you to Tapestry! We use the Tapestry principles every day, and we hope these principles—and all the books in the Tapestry Program—provide you the same strength, confidence, and joy that they give us. We look forward to comments from both teachers and students who use any part of the Tapestry Program.

Rebecca L. Oxford
University of Alabama
Tuscaloosa, Alabama

Robin C. Scarcella
University of California at Irvine
Irvine, California

PREFACE

*P*ower through the Written Word is a composition text designed for high-intermediate learners of English as a Second Language. Although primarily designed for international students, it is also appropriate for permanent residents of the United States.Instructors have flexibility in their use of this book since they may choose which chapters to use, and within each chapter, the lessons and activities to use.

The focus of this thematically-based text is power. There are four chapters: Personal Power, Power through Force, Power and the Environment, and Power through the Written Word.

Chapter Organization

Each chapter has the following design: an introduction, three lessons, and essay and self-evaluation activities.

INTRODUCTION

The introduction contains Needs Analysis and Goal Setting activities and survey tasks. In the Needs Analysis and Goal Setting section of the introduction, students are asked to provide a detailed description of their own language needs as well as assess their goals. They can then refer back to their goals throughout the chapter.

The final section of the introduction contains cooperative learning and survey activities. These are designed to motivate learners, interest them in the theme, and activate their previous knowledge. The learners refer back to the survey data throughout their lessons.

LESSONS

Following the introduction are three lessons which contain key readings from a variety of genres and sources. The readings have been chosen to stimulate students to investigate an issue from a variety of perspectives and to appeal to learners from different cultures and academic disciplines. Included are business and science readings as well as political and social science readings. Readings are preceded by a section entitled *About the Reading,* which contains background information about the reading. Sections entitled *Before you Read* and *While you Read* include prereading and reading activities. Comprehension activities follow each reading in a section entitled *Comprehension Workout.* To further facilitate learner comprehension, some of the readings have been glossed.*

After the *Comprehension Workout* is a section entitled *Listening.* This section introduces the students to the audiotaped stories and essays which accompany each chapter. The audio-tapes provide learners with additional exposure to the features of English needed to develop their writing proficiency. Multiple exposure to audio-taped readings on a single topic serves to recycle vocabulary words, grammatical structures, and discourse features previously presented in the lesson readings. The audiotapes also help the students gain additional perspectives of the lesson theme which they discuss in their journals.

Each lesson also contains one or two *Grammar Explanations,* presentations of key grammatical features which stem from an analysis of actual student writing and an examination of the primary grammatical difficulties facing students when completing specific writing tasks. They include count and noncount nouns, comparatives, relative clauses, verb tense, subject/verb agreement, pronoun reference, passives, parallel structures, and sentence fragments and run-ons. The *Grammar Practices* which follow the *Grammar Explanations* help students build the grammatical proficiency needed to complete accompanying writing tasks. *Grammar Explanations* and *Grammar Practices* are designed in such a way that they do not interfere with the composing process and allow the students to focus on the theme of power, rather than on language forms. Included in each chapter are also *Editing Practices* based on the grammatical and mechanical errors students actually make when completing the text's writing tasks.

Along with grammar, punctuation is emphasized in each lesson because it is highly teachable and enhances writing. Students are taught to use periods, commas, semicolons, colons, and quotation marks in *Punctuation Explanations* and *Punctuation Practices.*

Vocabulary is presented in each lesson through reading and writing activities as well as on audiotapes. Within each chapter, thematically related count and noncount nouns are presented. Learners are also encouraged to learn new words from the readings which are of personal interest to them. Because students are invested in these words, they are likely to study and to remember them.

---

*The following abbreviations for grammatical parts of speech are used in the gloss:

noun	(n.)
verb	(v.)
adjective	(adj.)
adverb	(adv.)
preposition	(prep.)

While grammar, punctuation, and vocabulary are important aspects of writing proficiency, they are not the only ones. Another important section of the lessons is entitled *Gaining Writing Competence.* Although students are not given formulas for writing specific genres, useful guidelines and suggestions are provided in this section. The various rhetorical features presented include: cohesive devices; techniques for developing audience awareness and purpose; and suggestions for writing introductions, bodies, and conclusions as well as guidelines for writing summaries, reports, narratives, letters, comparison-contrast essays, and persuasive essays. The presentation of each of the major rhetorical features listed above is recycled in a different way in each chapter. Accompanying the presentation of rhetorical features is a section entitled *Gaining Writing Practice.* In this section, students receive practice using the rhetorical features presented.

Students need numerous opportunities to write and to vary the type of writing they produce. Each lesson offers students a variety of writing tasks. In *Quick Writes*—short, in-class writing activities—students write quickly without going through all stages of the writing process. These writing activities encourage students to react quickly to ideas presented by classmates or the readings and to develop writing fluency. Within each chapter, *Quick Write* sections focus on two or more of the following writing types: definitions, narratives, summaries, comparison-contrast essays, reports, and persuasive essays.

Because a key component of *Power through the Written Word* is the composing process, each lesson also contains *Writing Tasks* which take students step-by-step through this process. In "prewriting activities," students are taught to gather and organize ideas. In "revising activities," students are provided with revision checklists and peer revising forms. They are taught to add, delete, move, and connect ideas as well as develop attention-grabbing introductions, strong thesis statements, effective conclusions, and audience awareness. In "editing activities," students are taught to correct grammatical errors as well as mechanical ones (involving spelling and punctuation). Through these activities, students are helped to select those prewriting, revising, and editing techniques and strategies which are most useful to them in specific circumstances. Within each chapter, *Writing Task* sections focus on two or more of the following writing types: definitions, narratives, summaries, comparison-contrast essays, reports, and persuasive essays. Within each chapter, students gain practice writing all these writing types in either *Quick Writes* or *Writing Tasks.*

ESSAY AND SELF–EVALUATIONS

Following the three lessons is a concluding section entitled *Essay Assignment.* This section contains the chapter's essay assignment and unifies all activities in the chapter. Ideas from journal entries, readings, *Quick Writes,* and *Writing tasks* are used as the basis of the essay assignment, and the activities presented in the previous lessons (including such sections as *Grammar Explanations, Punctuation Explanations,* and *Gaining Writing Practice*) prepare students for the assignment. In this multidraft assignment, students are given suggestions for gathering and focussing their ideas in prewriting activities, revising the organization and content of their essays in revising activities, and correcting grammatical and mechanical errors in editing activities. In addition, sample papers are included so that students can examine their peers' writing and learn by example. In concluding the chapter, students evaluate their learning experience in a section entitled *Self-Assessment*.

Power through the Written Word is designed to appeal to a variety of learning styles. For instance, grammatical and rhetorical rules are presented both deductively and inductively. Presentations of language features are designed to appeal to visual and auditory learners. Sections entitled *Test Analysis* are provided for analytical learners. A section called *Using a Language Learning Log* is designed for reflexive learners. Cooperative learning activities appear throughout the text.

The book also meets the needs of students of different cultural backgrounds. It is sensitive to the strengths learners form diverse cultures bring with them to the writing task and builds on these strengths. In addition, it includes information designed to address the difficulties learners from diverse cultures might encounter when acquiring writing proficiency in a second language.

Power through the Written Word provides learners with the proficiency needed to write well. In so doing, learners empower themselves and others— through the written word.

Acknowledgments

Dave Lee and Ken Mattsson of Heinle & Heinle deserve special thanks. I will always be indebted to Dave Lee for his professional advice and thorough editing; he encouraged me to work long hours to produce a book worthy of the Tapestry Program and provided me with the feedback I needed to complete it. Ken Mattsson's orchestration of the testing of the materials and the reviews was also extremely helpful.

In addition, I wish to thank those reviewers who provided insightful comments on previous drafts of this book. Among the persons I wish to express my special appreciation are Laurie Blass, Linda Robinson Fellag (University of Houston-Downtown), Barbara Gaffney (University of New Orleans), Helen Harper (New Uork University), Glenda Hayley (University of Miami), Brian Hickey (Manhattanville College), Martha Low (University of Oregon), and Sandra McKay (San Francisco State University), who read earlier versions of the manuscript and provided valuable comments. Thanks also go to the students of Ann Gambaro and Judy Graves (both of Eurocenters Alexandria), Colette Green (ICPR Junior College), Linda Robinson Fellag (University of Houston–Downtown), and Colleen Hildebrand and Susan Proctor (both of the University of California, Irvine) for testing the materials in their classrooms.

Above all, I am indebted to colleagues associated with the *Tapestry* project, specifically Sandra McKay of San Francisco State University, and, most especially, Rebecca Oxford, who gave freely of her time and energy and shared her knowledge of learning strategies throughout the book's development.

Finally, I am grateful to the ESL faculty (Colleen Hildebrand and Susan Proctor) and the ESL students at UCI who shaped the development of this book and who empowered me through their own writing. The following students were particularly helpful: Cam Tu Tran, Kosuke Harada, Ruben Sanchez, and Hyun Do Lee.

Robin Scarcella
University of California, Irvine

To the Student

Power through the Written Word is designed to help you gain the writing skills that you need to succeed in academic situations. There are four chapters: Personal Power, Power through Force, Power and the Environment, and Power through the Written Word. each chapter is characterized by the following features:

- cooperative learning exercises;
- needs analysis and goal setting;
- editing exercises based on actual student grammatical and mechanical errors;
- presentation of key grammatical features;
- explicit instruction of a variety of learning strategies;
- diverse writing tasks, including: summaries, narratives, comparison-contrasts, persuasive essays, reports, letters, and journal writing;
- essay assignments with authentic samples of essays, as well as prewriting activities, revising activities, and editing activities; and
- language learning logs.

Throughout this book, you will be using the composing process, which has been modified to meet your needs. To learn the process, you need practice in all of its stages, including prewriting, drafting, revising, and editing. Here is a description of this important process and its stages.

The Composing Process

PREWRITING

Prewriting involves finding a topic, finding out about the topic, and thinking about it. Prewriting helps you to think of ideas, refine them, and organize them. In addition, prewriting helps you shape your writing to the needs of particular audiences and the purpose of the writing task. This unit will give you many opportunities to gather ideas before writing. Ideas will come form articles, essays, short stories, and other reading materials.

DRAFTING

Drafting involves writing the words down which express the ideas. Once you have gathered your ideas, you need to write them down. This text will give you some practical strategies and guidelines for shaping your ideas and will encourage you to focus on what you are trying to say.

REVISING

In revising, you rewrite what you have written and delete, substitute, add, and reorganize. In the revision stage, you reconsider the content and organization of your writing and make whatever revisions that you feel appropriate. In this text, you will be participating in numerous peer reviews. In these reviews, you will read and comment on your classmates' writing. These reviews offer you reactions from real readers who provide different perspectives. Such reviews help you become aware of your readers.

EDITING

After you get your ideas on paper and organize them exactly as you like, it is time to edit. Editing means proofreading. This is the final stage of the writing process. When you edit your essay, you correct all your grammatical, spelling, and punctuation mistakes. In other words, you polish up your writing.

A WORD OF CAUTION

Most good writers do not always follow the various stages outlined above (prewriting, writing, revising, and editing) in a rigid order. Rather, they go back and forth between the various stages. Writing is a messy process for most writers—not the "plan-write-rewrite" process which many traditional textbooks describe.

Journal Writing

In addition to using the composing process while you use this book, you will also keep a special kind of journal. In this journal, you will write two types of journal entries. In Free Topic Entries, you will write about anything you like. For example, you may use these entries to describe a particular idea that you thought of or read about or to discuss a particularly interesting experience or person. In

Audiotape Entries, you will respond to the audiotapes which correspond to this unit. Keep the following guidelines in mind when writing your journal:

- Write at least one entry each day.
- Your journal is for you. Do not be overly concerned with grammar or style. Your goal should be to get your ideas down. Your journal will not be checked for grammar.
- Use about half of your journal entries to react to any topic that you like. Use the other half to respond to the audiotapes.

FREE TOPIC ENTRIES

In Free Topic Entries, you write about your own ideas. It will be more interesting if you avoid writing lists of events. Rather than describing everything you did in a day, it is better to write about a specific idea that struck you or something you read about.

AUDIOTAPE ENTRIES

In Audiotape Entries, you write about your reaction to the audiotapes which supplement the unit. Find a phrase, sentence, or idea from the audiotapes which you find particularly noteworthy. Copy it at the top of your page. Skip a line. Then, write a one or two paragraph reaction to this sentence or idea.

Enjoy writing in your journal and completing the writing assignments in this book. I hope that you will use writing purposefully so that you can react effectively to the world around you and, most importantly, gain power—through the written word.

TEACHING APPROACH

Consistent with the Tapestry approach, *Power through the Written Word* is designed to help learners develop writing proficiency both inside and outside the language classroom.

Another unique aspect of the book is the needs analysis, goal setting, language learning logs, and self-assessment instruments. You will be encouraged to assess your needs, identify your goals, and measure the attainment of these goals through language learning logs and self-assessment instruments. You will also be encouraged to reflect on your learning process through Quick Writes.

CONTENTS

2 *Power through Force 81*

SUMMARY OF LESSON 2: REASONS FOR WAR

LESSON 3: FORCE IN RESPONSE TO INJUSTICE

SUMMARY OF LESSON 3: FORCE IN RESPONSE TO INJUSTICE

WRITING ASSIGNMENT FOR CHAPTER 2

3 Power and the Environment 147

INTRODUCTION

LESSON 1: PERSPECTIVES OF POLLUTION

SUMMARY OF LESSON 1: PERSPECTIVES OF POLLUTION

4 *Power through the Written Word* 209

SUMMARY OF LESSON 1: PERSPECTIVES OF GOOD WRITING

LESSON 2: THE LANGUAGE OF DECEPTION

SUMMARY OF LESSON 2: THE LANGUAGE OF DECEPTION

LESSON 3: EMPOWERMENT THROUGH THE WRITTEN WORD

SUMMARY OF LESSON 3: EMPOWERMENT THROUGH THE WRITTEN WORD

WRITING ASSIGNMENT FOR CHAPTER 4

Personal Power

Power corrupts. Absolute power corrupts absolutely.

Necessity and opportunity make a weakling powerful.

All things are obedient to wealth.

INTRODUCTION

In this chapter, you will read about other people's ideas about power. In addition, you will collect survey data concerning your classmates' views of power and explore your own personal opinions about it. Some of the questions you will consider in this unit include:

- What is power?
- What are several different types of power?
- What is meant by *personal power*?
- Does the notion of personal power vary across cultures?
- How does a person obtain personal power?
- Does power necessarily corrupt?
- What are the characteristics of powerful people?

Your main task is to contribute an essay to a class reader. All the activities in this chapter will prepare you for this task. Your contribution will be an essay pertaining to one aspect of your own experience with power. Specific assignments for this essay are given on pages 75–79.

Needs Analysis and Goal Setting

Before you start the lessons in this unit, find out what your own learning needs, preferences, and goals are.

SELF-EVALUATION OF LEARNING ACTIVITIES

First, check (✓) the boxes below which apply to you.

ACTIVITY	I LIKE	IT'S OKAY	I DON'T LIKE
Reading poems	——	——	——
Reading articles	——	——	——
Reacting to audiotapes in a journal	——	——	——
Doing grammar exercises	——	——	——
Doing vocabulary exercises	——	——	——
Doing group work	——	——	——
Collecting and analyzing survey data	——	——	——
Writing definitions	——	——	——
Writing letters	——	——	——

ACTIVITY	I LIKE	IT'S OKAY	I DON'T LIKE
Writing summaries	_____	_____	_____
Writing stories	_____	_____	_____
Writing reactions to stories	_____	_____	_____
Writing essays	_____	_____	_____
Interviewing my classmates	_____	_____	_____

Next, to help you set goals for learning to write better, find out about your writing goals. Number the goals below from 1 to 18—with 1 as your most important goal and 18 as your least important goal. When you set goals, you gain power over your own learning process.

SELF-DIAGNOSIS OF WRITING GOALS

My goals are:

1. Vocabulary

   _____ to improve my vocabulary

2. Grammar

   _____ to improve my use of count and noncount nouns

   _____ to improve my use of verb tenses

   _____ to avoid sentence fragments

3. Punctuation

   _____ to improve my use of commas

   _____ to improve my use of quotation marks

4. Rhetoric

   A. Organization and Unity

   _____ to improve the organization of my writing

   _____ to use effective transitions between sentences and paragraphs

   _____ to write strong thesis statements

   B. Types of Writing

   _____ to learn how to write a definition

   _____ to learn how to write a summary

   _____ to learn how to write a letter of advice

_____ to learn how to write a reaction to a story

_____ to learn how to write an essay in which I compare and contrast

_____ to learn how to write a persuasive essay

C. The Composing Process

_____ to learn how to gather ideas and focus on them in my writing

_____ to learn how to revise my writing for organization and content

_____ to gain editing skills

Now that you have identified your own language learning goals, find out about your classmates' goals. Divide into small groups. Try to identify five major language learning goals which are shared by all the members of your group.

Cooperative Learning

NUMBERED HEADS TOGETHER

Divide up into teams of four. Number off within groups (*one, two, three,* or *four*). Discuss each of the questions below. Make sure that everyone on your team knows the answers. Your team will have five minutes to discuss each question and to come up with an answer. Your teacher will call a number from one to four. Only students with that number can raise their hands if they have the answer.

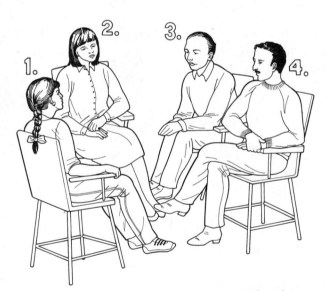

Question 1: What are ten characteristics of powerful people?

Question 2: What are five ways that powerful people control others?

Question 3: What are three different definitions of power?

Question 4: Who are five of the most powerful people in the world?

Question 5: In the United States, a person is often considered powerful on the basis of wealth, while in other cultures a person is often considered powerful on the basis of education or kindness, regardless of wealth. In what ways does the notion of power vary across cultures?

Survey

Survey your classmates to see what they think of power. Each student in the class should complete the survey below.

POWER SURVEY

Directions: Fill in the blanks with a "T" if the statement is true or an "F" if the statement is false.

GENDER: MALE _____   FEMALE _____

_____ 1. Power is easily achieved.

_____ 2. Tall people are more powerful than short people.

_____ 3. Independent people are more powerful than dependent people.

_____ 4. Shy people are more powerful than outgoing people.

_____ 5. In order to gain power, one must be healthy.

_____ 6. Males are more powerful than females.

_____ 7. Educated people are likely to be powerful.

_____ 8. People with authority are powerful.

_____ 9. Powerful people can make a positive difference in others' lives.

_____ 10. People aged fifty to seventy have more power than people aged twenty to forty.

_____ 11. People in powerful positions suffer from more anxiety than people who are not in these positions.

_____ 12. People can buy power with money.

_____ 13. Spiritual or religious people are powerful.

_____ 14. People with power do not need to obey laws.

_____ 15. Power always involves controlling other individuals.

_____ 16. All wealthy people are powerful.

_____ 17. Educated people who are poor are more powerful than uneducated people who are wealthy.

_____ 18. Powerful people are always competent.

_____ 19. Powerful people believe in themselves.

_____ 20. Power corrupts.

> ## Threads
>
> **The purpose of getting power is to be able to give it away.**
>
> Aneurin Bevan
> 1897–1960

As a class, analyze the results of the survey on the chalkboard. Compile all student responses. Did your classmates respond to the survey in the same way that you did? Have a class discussion in which you identify and explain major patterns in the data. (For instance, were there any items in which all students responded with "true" or "false"? Why do you think this might be the case?) Write down notes from this class discussion. You will use these notes in writing activities throughout this chapter.

LESSON 1: WHAT IS POWER?

Overview

In this lesson, you will define the word *power*. In addition, you will write stories about powerful people and describe your own personal power.

About the Reading

To help you define the term *power*, read what others have to say about it. The words marked with gloss marks (°) are defined in the vocabulary section after the readings. The definitions will help you understand the readings.

BEFORE YOU READ

Let's figure out what this reading is all about. Read the title and look at the picture. Considering the picture and subtitles, how do you think different people define the term *personal power*?

WHILE YOU READ

Read the passage quickly the first time and try to identify the general ideas. While you read, try to focus on the main points of the reading. It is difficult to react to a reading before you understand it. Do not attempt to understand and react to the passage in a single read. Reading the passage quickly two or three times is more enjoyable and results in more efficient reading than reading the passage very slowly just one time. After you have read the passage a first time, reread the passage again. Answer these questions:

1. Do you agree or disagree with what others say?
2. To what extent do you believe that you have personal power?
3. How does the notion of personal power vary across cultures?

Reading: Excerpts from Interviews with Powerful Persons

PERSONAL POWER

Here's what Beth Milwid says:

A friend who I worked with once told me that I was a very powerful person. I asked him, "How can you say that? You know what my level is in the company."

My friend replied, "No, you don't understand. I'm not talking about authority. I'm talking about personal power." He really made me take a look at what kind of power plays a role in success.

Others had told me that I'm viewed as being somewhat powerful here—but my friend made me understand what being powerful really means. He was suggesting that power comes from inside a person. It is an ability to lead, to communicate with all kinds of people, and to believe in oneself and to act on one's beliefs. I now realize that personal power is often confused with authority. If I had to choose between personal power and authority, I would choose personal power."

Source: Adapted from Beth Milwid, 1990. *Working with Men: Professional Women Talk about Power, Sexuality, and Ethics*. Kingsport, Tennessee: Beyond Words Publishing Inc., p. 129.

INITIATIVE AND RESOURCEFULNESS

Here's what Marguirite Aguirre (manager) says about initiative° and resourcefulness:°

"How did I obtain power? By taking initiative and using my resourcefulness. If there is a problem or a job to do, I don't wait for someone else to take care of it. I seize the initiative and do whatever I need to do to solve the problem or get the job done."

COMPETENCE

Hank Woodward (computer consultant) thinks competence is an important part of obtaining power. He explains:

"You want to know how I obtain power? By being competent. The only thing that gains a person power is being right. Others want the correct answer, and I give it to them. The bottom line is *be competent*. Do your best job. You make friends when you consistently pull through. Competence is highly prized in the United States. Just be very good at what you do and put your nose to the grindstone."°

PERFORMANCE

Stephen Covey argues:

"Power is the ability to act and the strength to accomplish something. People don't care whether you are competent or not. What counts is whether you perform well when the performance is required."

Source: Adapted from Stephen R. Covey, 1989. *The Seven Habits of Highly Effective People*. New York: Simon & Schuster, p. 109.

SELF-PROMOTION

Sandra O'Neilly (politician) has a different view of what it takes to obtain power. She thinks self-promotion is an essential means of obtaining it. She argues:

"The key to getting power is promoting oneself. I'm not talking about promoting myself on my job. I'm talking about promoting myself in everything I do. I obtain power by going out of the way to be visible. I make sure that everyone sees my best attributes.° I show myself in the best light possible. When I give a talk, I make elaborate° preparations. My primary concern is not the content of my speech. Rather, it is my appearance and the effect I have on the audience. I define myself, and I make sure that no one else defines me. I advertise my abilities, and I make sure that I get everyone's attention."

CONFIDENCE

Katie Gonzalez (physician) believes that conviction° leads to power. Here's what she says about it:

"Conviction buys me power. I have such strong beliefs that I'm 100% sure of what I'm talking about. When giving my opinions, I state them in a way that shows I firmly believe in what I am saying. I avoid the words 'I think.' Instead, I say, 'This is the way it is.'"

SELF-ESTEEM

Many argue that a person's power is built upon self-esteem°—the type of esteem which is developed at a very early age.

When Margaret Mead, a famous anthropologist,° was just a young child, she memorized numerous poems. These poems may have been the foundation of her own personal power. At the age of four, her grandmother taught her the verse below. It is possible that this poem led to the development of Mead's personal power.°

> I'm sitting alone by the fire
> Dressed just as I came from the dance,
> In a gown, Frog, even you would admire—
> It cost a cool thousand in France.
> I'm bediamonded out of all reason,°
> My hair is done up in a queue,°
> In short, sir, the belle of the season,°
> Is wasting an hour on you.

(Note that most of her life Mead was able to convince both men and women that she herself was a powerful person, "the belle of the season.")

HARD WORK AND LUCK

J. Paul Getty supposedly had a different formula for power. He allegedly said:

"Formula for power: Rise early, work hard, strike oil."

Threads

Kathleen Lindsay of South Africa published 904 novels before her death in 1973.

VOCABULARY

initiative (n.)	the act of taking action by oneself without others' influence
resourcefulness (n.)	the ability to do well in a variety of situations, often includes the ability to substitute an object in the absence of the usual object
to put your nose to the grindstone (v.)	(idiom) to work hard
self-promotion (n.)	the act of raising or improving one's own position
attribute (n.)	characteristic
elaborate (adj.)	done very carefully, with great detail
conviction (n.)	belief
self-esteem (n.)	confidence and satisfaction in oneself
anthropologist (n.)	a person who studies anthropology, the science of humankind
personal power (n.)	the strength of the individual
bediamoned (adj.)	covered with diamonds
out of all reason (p.p.)	(infrequently used slang) an unreasonably large quantity
queue (n.)	a particular hairstyle in which the hair is pinned on top of the head in a long bun
belle of the season (n.)	(*French*) most remarkable, beautiful woman of the times

Comprehension Workout

EXERCISE 1

Find a partner. With your partner, fill in the chart below. If necessary, reread the excerpts on pages 7–8.

PERSON	CHARACTERISTICS OF POWERFUL INDIVIDUALS
Beth Milwid	*ability to communicate, ability to believe in oneself*
Marguirite Aguirre	_____
Hank Woodward	_____
Stephen R. Covey	_____
Sandra O'Neilly	_____
Katie Gonzalez	_____
Margaret Mead	_____
J. Paul Getty	_____

EXERCISE 2

First in small groups and then as a class, discuss the following questions:

1. Consider the quotations on pages 7–8. Do you admire the people for what they said? Is there anyone who you would not admire?
2. Do you want power? What kind? How much?
3. If you don't want power, what do you want?
4. Who are the powerful persons in your culture? Are these individuals admired? Why? What kinds of power do these persons have?

Listening

Listen to the audiotaped stories at home. The stories are about the characteristics of some very powerful individuals. They focus on humanitarian and business leaders.

BEFORE YOU LISTEN

Consider this strategy:

LEARNING STRATEGY

Forming Concepts: Listening with a purpose helps you predict the language that you will hear, and this improves your listening comprehension.

WHILE YOU LISTEN

As you listen to the stories, ask yourself why each story was written.

AFTER YOU LISTEN

React to the stories in your journal. If you are having difficulty reacting to the stories, consider the following questions on page 11.

1. Focus on the content of the stories. Which sentences reflect the authors' purposes?
2. Were there any parts of stories which you particularly liked? Why?
3. Were there any parts of the stories which bothered you? Why?
4. Concentrate on the characteristics of the individuals discussed in the stories. Find places in the stories which discuss these characteristics.

Punctuation Explanation

PUNCTUATION WITH APPOSITIVES

Explanation: In the Quick Write activity on page 12, you will describe different people's views of power. First, find out about appositives, which are useful in describing people. Appositives make your writing look sophisticated and are easy to use.

APPOSITIVES

A noun or noun phrase that immediately follows another noun and renames that noun is called an appositive. An appositive explains or defines the noun it follows and is generally set off by commas as in the following example.

George Bush, the former president of the United States, is a powerful person.

(George Bush = the former president of the United States)

Punctuation Practice: Appositives

EXERCISE 3

Decide if these sentences contain appositives. If they do, circle the appositives and set them off with commas. Follow the example given below.

EXAMPLE: John F. Kennedy, former president of the United States, once said, "I don't get angry. I get even."

1. J. Paul Getty the wealthy owner of the Getty Museum in Los Angeles thought that power came from luck.
2. As a young child, Margaret Mead a well-known anthropologist had to memorize verses which may have developed her self-esteem.
3. Stephen R. Covey author of *The Seven Habits of Highly Effective People* believes that powerful people accomplish important goals.
4. Meg Davis is the president of the Hewler Packaging Company and the vice-president of the Kyler Shelter for the Homeless.
5. Katie Gonzalez a hard-working physician believes that power is gained through strong conviction.
6. According to Sandra O'Neilly a politician from Chicago power can only be obtained through self-promotion.

7. Donald Douglas is the powerful manager who has made his company so successful.
8. Hank Woodward a computer consultant argues that competence is highly prized in the United States.
9. Is initiative an important characteristic of powerful people? "You bet!" says Marguirite Aguirre manager of a large chemical plant in Albany.
10. "If I had to choose between personal power and authority, I would choose personal power," states Beth Milwid author of *Working with Men: Professional Women Talk about Power, Sexuality, and Ethics*.

Add two of your own sentences which use appositives:

11. _____

12. _____

Optional Quick Write

Write one or two paragraphs about some ways in which views of power vary across cultures. You may want to describe how in some cultures a poor person who is well-educated is seen as powerful, while in other cultures a wealthy person with no education is seen as powerful. Your purpose is to inform. You are writing for your instructor.

Quick Write

DESCRIBING OTHERS' VIEWS OF POWER

Write a one paragraph description in which you discuss two of the views on pages 7–8. Make sure that you use appositives to identify the people who you discuss. Your purpose is to explore your own ideas. You are mainly writing for yourself.

BEFORE YOU WRITE

Consider this strategy:

LEARNING STRATEGY

Remembering New Material: Using English language rules helps you learn them.

WRITE

As you write, try to use the rules about appositives which you just learned. It is not enough just to study rules. You need to use these rules to remember and apply them effectively.

Quick Write

REPORTING SURVEY DATA

By now you have formed some strong opinions about power. What do your classmates think about it? Write a one or two paragraph report pertaining to what you have learned from the survey on page 5. Focus on one or two findings from the survey data which surprised you. Your purpose is to inform others of your classmates' views of power. Imagine that a group of native English-speaking peers will read your report.

BEFORE YOU WRITE

As a class, review your notes on the total class results of the survey. Compile all the results on the chalkboard by the first-language background of the students. When you are done, have a class discussion in which you answer the following questions:

1. Do students from some cultures view power differently than students from other cultures?
2. What characteristics do all students agree contribute to the making of a powerful person?

Divide into small groups and discuss the findings. Find two trends in the data which surprised you. Were there wide differences in opinion?

WRITE

You are now ready to write. In one or two paragraphs, describe two interesting findings from the survey data which surprised you.

AFTER YOU WRITE

LEARNING STRATEGY

Managing Your Learning: Objectively critiquing your own writing helps you improve it.

Objectively critique the report which you have just written. How did you do? What did you learn? The key to effective self-criticism is detachment. Try to be like another person as you read your paper to make changes. This can be difficult at first, but it makes a big difference when you critique your own written work. Reading aloud helps. From as objective a point of view as possible, what did you like about your own writing?

If you wrote something that you felt good about, dwell upon it for a while. Let it sink in before moving on to what needs improvement.

Optional Quick Write

Use the survey on page 5 to find out what native English-speaking Americans think about power. Give the survey to five native English-speaking Americans. Then, compile the results. When you are finished, write one or two paragraphs about two interesting findings from the survey data. Your purpose is to inform. You are writing for your instructor and your classmates.

Grammar Explanation

COUNT AND NONCOUNT NOUNS FOR ABSTRACT IDEAS

Explanation: In the next writing activity, you will write an extended definition of the word *power*. Knowing how to use count and noncount nouns correctly will help you complete this task successfully.

COUNT AND NONCOUNT NOUNS

Count nouns describe something that we can count. They have both singular and plural forms.

SINGULAR FORM	PLURAL FORM
an ability of a powerful person	*five abilities* of a powerful person
a characteristic of a powerful person	*three characteristics* of a powerful person
an opinion about a powerful person	*two opinions* about a powerful person

Noncount nouns describe something that we cannot count in a specific context in English.

EXAMPLES

power	Hitler had power.
credibility	Nixon had little credibility.
creativity	Gloria's creativity had no limits.
self-promotion	Self-promotion is unacceptable in some countries.
self-esteem	His self-esteem was very low.

1. Noncount nouns:
   - have no plural form
   - are never used with *a* or *an*
   - are used with the singular (third person singular) verb form, as in the sentence, *Power corrupts*.
   - are used with singular pronoun and singular possessive pronoun forms (*it, its*)

2. Some nouns are noncount in one context and count in another context. Consider these examples:

   John has a lot of <u>authority</u>. (noncount noun)
   but
   He is an <u>authority</u> on Shakespeare. (count noun)

   Mária has a lot of <u>success</u>. (noncount noun)
   but
   Her <u>successes</u> are many. (count noun)

3. *Many* or *a lot of* is used with count nouns.
Much or *a lot of* is used with noncount nouns.
Much is often used with negative statements and questions.
A lot of can be used with any type of statement or question.

count noun   How <u>many</u> quarters does she have?

noncount noun   How <u>much</u> wealth does she have?

(For further information about countable and uncountable nouns, refer to your grammar workout book.) Some noncount nouns which are frequently used in most contexts include:

NONCOUNT NOUNS		
advice	fun	love
aggression	gossip	luck
authority	happiness	peace
beauty	health	poetry
bravery	help	potential
competence	ignorance	poverty
confidence	information	progress
control	initiative	resourcefulness
corruption	intellect	self-esteem
cowardice	intelligence	self-promotion
education	justice	stupidity
entertainment	knowledge	wealth
experience	laughter	violence

LEARNING STRATEGY

Remembering New Material: Teaching others language rules helps you remember them.

Cooperative Learning—Each One/Teach One

COUNT AND NONCOUNT NOUNS

Teach each other language rules. Find a partner with whom you have not worked before. Study the grammar explanation above. Make sure that your partner understands the explanation. When you are finished studying, do the grammar and editing activities on the following pages.

Grammar Practice: Count and Noncount Nouns

EXERCISE 4

Circle the correct word in parentheses. Follow the example given.

Income ((is) are) necessary.

The following passage was written by José Lara, a freshman at UCI.

PERSONAL POWER
José Lara

These factors are essential to building personal power: knowledge, wealth, health, mental well-being, morals, and luck. Knowledge (is, are) important in the lives of powerful people. Without knowledge, people lack information. Such information (help, helps) them obtain valuable resources. These resources (provide, provides) the foundation of the powerful individual's financial well-being.

Wealth (is, are) also essential to obtaining personal power. Without sufficient money, individuals must depend on others. Dependency, after all, (is, are) not a characteristic of the wealthy. The poor can never obtain personal power in the United States. They are dependent on too many people. They are not free to live where they want or do as they like.

In addition to wealth, physical health is important to gaining personal power. Health, of course, (is, are) something which cannot be purchased.

Mental well-being is also an essential ingredient of personal power. Powerful individuals (is, are) always psychologically balanced; they are normal. This is because mental well-being is the foundation of self-esteem and (lead, leads) to motivation.

Motivation is central to personal power. It (provide, provides) individuals with the courage that they need to succeed in life.

In addition to motivation, morality is necessary for obtaining personal power. Those with personal power are able to

distinguish good from evil and lead others compassionately. For these individuals, power never (corrupt, corrupts). They are responsible to others for they know that responsibility (is, are) an important part of personal power.

Perhaps most importantly, to obtain personal power, one must have luck. Luck (is, are) an essential factor underlying personal power, one which (lead, leads) to knowledge, wealth, health, mental well-being, and morals.

Editing Practice: Count and Noncount Nouns

EXERCISE 5

The exercise below contains *five* errors involving noncount nouns. In the incorrect sentences, noncount nouns incorrectly end in *s*. Read the passage and make appropriate corrections. (If you have difficulty doing this exercise, refer to your grammar workout book.)

STUDENT WRITING SAMPLE

A desire for power is basic to men and women. However, powers is often considered a bad characteristic. It is often confused with violences and aggressions. Most people do not want to admit that they want power, which is why they never get it. Those who do get power often try to gain it secretly. Some politicians openly desire power. However, most Americans feel that power leads to corruptions. They believe that power corrupts and absolute power corrupts absolutely.

Power, nevertheless, does not always lead to evil. Power is an essential component of happiness which can result in creativities, fulfillment, and enjoyment.—M.V.

Writing Task: Defining "Power"

In a paragraph or two, write your own definition of the word *power*. Your purpose is to inform others. Your classmates will read your writing.

BEFORE YOU WRITE

Read the student writing sample below.

STUDENT WRITING SAMPLE

What is power? Power is control. There are many different kinds of power—physical, emotional, and mental. Physical power represents bodily strength. Weight-lifters have control over their bodies. They can move heavy objects. Emotional power represents control of emotions. A person who has emotional power does not often show strong emotion in difficult times. Mental strength represents intellect. An intellectual has the power to reason logically and effectively. When resolving problems, people should draw on whatever types of power that they have.—T.N.

Study the guidelines below.

GUIDELINES FOR WRITING DEFINITIONS

A definition identifies a word as a member of a specific group and gives enough information about the word to distinguish it from other words. A good definition always provides more than a statement of what is in the dictionary.

- Do not include either the word that you are defining or a form of that word in your own definition. (For instance, do not state, "Power is what powerful people have.)
- Distinguish the word from other words by using synonyms, antonyms, or examples.
- If appropriate, provide a description of the origin of the term.
- Go beyond the dictionary meaning of the term. Do not use the dictionary as the only source of explanation of the term.

QUESTIONS TO ASK WHEN WRITING DEFINITIONS

What is X?

What is X composed of?

Where did X come from?

What are the characteristics of X?

USEFUL WORDS

is	Power <u>is</u> authority. It is. . .
means	Power <u>means</u> authority.
by that I mean	Power is authority. <u>By that I mean</u>, power involves controlling others.

EXAMPLES OF DEFINITIONS (NOT EXTENDED)

1. **Self-esteem**
   Self-esteem is very important in the language classroom. We define self-esteem as self-judgment of worth, based on feelings of efficacy—a sense of interacting effectively with one's own environment. Low self-esteem is obvious in statements like, "I sure feel stupid." High self-esteem is found in comments such as, "I feel so good about what I just did." Self-esteem influences motivation and attitudes, and vice versa.[1]

2. **Money**
   The dictionary defines money as "anything customarily used as a medium of exchange and measure of value, such as sheep, wampum, gold dust, etc." Most Americans have a good idea of what money is in our society—bills, coins, and checks.
   Money is useful because it facilitates transactions. Just think of how society would be if people had to barter for everything—that is, exchange goods for goods. In economies based on a barter system, people spend tremendous amounts of time and effort making transactions. They waste much potential output by engaging in barter transactions instead of using money.[2]

---

[1]Robin Scarcella and Rebecca Oxford. 1992. *The Tapestry of Language Learning.* Boston: Heinle & Heinle, p. 57.

[2]Steven L. Mandell, Scott S. Cowen, and Roger Leroy Miller. 1961. *Introduction to Basic Business: Concepts and Applications.* Minneapolis: West Publishing Company.

WRITING AN EXTENDED DEFINITION

You can write an effective extended definition of power by explaining what it is, what its characteristics are, where it can be found, who uses it, what it is used for, what it does, and what your opinion of it is.

QUESTIONS TO ASK WHEN EXTENDING YOUR DEFINITION

How is X similar to or different from Y?

What does X feel like?

What does X do?

Who does X affect?

Is X good or bad? Why?

Who influences X?

What are the conditions which create X?

Where can X be found?

What is my personal opinion of X?

(For examples of extended definitions, refer to the student sample on page 17.)

Use the prewriting technique of "cubing" as a quick means of extending your definition of power. This technique will help you gather ideas. In cubing, you write about all six sides of the cube. You spend about five minutes on each side. The sides are:

1.	Describing *power*	Use your senses to examine the color, size, and shape of power; Try to feel, smell, touch, and hear *power*.
2.	Comparing *power* to something else	Compare *power* with something else (a lion? weakness? writing?).
3.	Associating—bringing to mind similar or dissimilar	Associate *power* with something similar or dissimilar.
4.	Analyzing something	Analyze the composition of *power*; describe what it is part of.
5.	Applying the concept	Describe how *power* can be used.
6.	Arguing for or against *power*	Argue for or against *power*, and give reasons for taking your position.

WRITE

Write the first draft of your entire definition (from beginning to end) in one sitting. Concentrate on getting your meaning across, not on using correct language forms.

WHILE YOU ARE WRITING

Consider this strategy:

LEARNING STRATEGY

Overcoming Limitations: When you are having difficulty expressing a particular thought, try expressing it in a simple sentence.

When you cannot express your ideas easily, try expressing them in simple sentences. You can always revise your sentences later.

REVISE YOUR FIRST DRAFT

The following Revision Questionnaire will help you revise your first draft. Answer the questions below. Then use the answers to guide your revision.

REVISION QUESTIONNAIRE

1. In composing your draft, what was the biggest problem that you experienced?

   _____

   _____

2. What changes do you intend to make?

   _____

   _____

3. If you had something to add to this essay, what would it be?

   _____

   _____

EDIT YOUR DRAFT

When you have finished revising your draft, edit it carefully. Review your writing and correct your grammatical mistakes. Limit the number of errors you correct. The editing checklist below will help you identify and correct grammatical mistakes.

EDITING CHECKLIST

_____ 1. I checked each noun to see if it was count or noncount and whether it was in the appropriate form.

_____ 2. I used subject/verb agreement correctly.

_____ 3. If I used appositives, I used them appropriately and set them off with commas.

SHARE YOUR WRITING

Share your writing in small groups of students. Take turns reading your writing aloud to the students in your group and leading the group in a discussion about your writing. These questions will be helpful in your discussion:

1. How does my view of power differ from yours?
2. How does my view of power differ form those views discussed in the reading passage on pages 7-8?
3. Do you agree with my perspective of power? Why?

Quick Write

WRITING A REACTION TO A STORY

Write a one or two paragraph reaction to one of the audiotaped stories about people who obtained power. Your purpose is to explore your own ideas. You are writing for your instructor and yourself.

BEFORE YOU WRITE

Consider this strategy:

LEARNING STRATEGY

Personalizing: Retelling stories to your friends and giving personal reactions are good ways to practice English.

Practice retelling the audiotaped stories which correspond to this unit. Think about the stories and retell one of them to a classmate. Your classmate should then react to the story in some way.

1. Think about the stories.
2. Pair with a classmate.
3. Retell one of the audiotaped stories.
4. Ask your partner to react to the story. Your partner may want to use some of the useful expressions on page 22.

EXPRESSIONS OF OPINION

In my opinion, . . .
I think that. . .
I believe that. . .
I (completely) agree/disagree with. . .
I am certain that. . .
I am convinced that. . .
There is no question that. . .

5. Reverse roles with your partner. This time your partner will share a story and you will react to it.

WRITE

Write your own one or two paragraph reaction to one of the stories. Use some of the expressions of opinion from the list above.

AFTER YOU WRITE

Reflect on your own writing. What did you learn from this Quick Write activity?

LEARNING STRATEGY

Managing Your Learning: Keeping track of your own progress in acquiring a second language enables you to pinpoint areas in which you need to improve.

Using a Language Learning Log

1. Vocabulary

   Write down as many new words from the lesson as you can remember.

   _____

   _____

   _____

2. Grammar

   Note examples of any grammatical structures from the lesson learned or reviewed. Write a brief explanation of the grammar points that they illustrate.

   _____

   _____

3. Punctuation

   Briefly describe any punctuation rules that you learned.

   _____

   _____

   _____

4. Techniques for Gaining Writing Competence

   List any new techniques for writing improvement that you learned. (Such techniques might include those for writing interesting introductions and conclusions, and those for composing different types of writing such as letters and essays.)

   _____

   _____

   _____

Threads

In 1989, the Sony Corporation bought Columbia Pictures for $3.47 trillion.

5. Learning Strategies

   Describe briefly any new learning strategies that you learned.

   _____

   _____

   _____

6. Areas that Need More Work

   Note here any areas that you are still trying to improve. Try to be as specific as possible.

   _____

   _____

   _____

   How many learning objectives have you been able to accomplish? (Refer to page 3; also, consider the strategy below.)

LEARNING STRATEGY

Managing Your Learning: Establishing your own action plans helps you accomplish your language learning objectives.

Quick Write

Write one paragraph in which you describe your plan to accomplish your language learning objectives. Your plan might include learning a specific number of vocabulary words each week, talking to native English speakers and visiting your teachers in their office.

In this lesson, you have explored the notion of personal power. You have written definitions, reported survey data, and reacted to stories. In the next lesson, you will read about the lives of other powerful people. This will help you sharpen your definition of personal power yet further.

QUICK REFERENCE TO LEARNING STRATEGIES

Forming Concepts: Listening with a Purpose (p. 10)

Remembering New Material: Using English Language Rules (p. 12)

Managing Your Learning: Objectively Critiquing Your Own Writing (p 13.)

Remembering New Material: Teaching Others Language Rules (p.15)

Overcoming Limitations: Using Simple Sentences (p. 20)

Personalizing: Retelling Stories and Personal Reactions in English (p. 21)

Managing Your Learning: Keeping Track of Your Progress (p. 22)

Managing Your Learning: Making Action Plans (p. 23)

Overview

In this lesson, you will learn about the lives of various types of powerful persons. You will also write summaries of these individuals' lives, descriptions of a classmate's experience with power, and new definitions of the term *power*.

About the Reading

The following excerpts describe Nobel Peace Prize winners. These winners are chosen primarily for humanitarian reasons. They have a special kind of power.

ALFRED BERNHARD NOBEL

Alfred Bernhard Nobel (1833-1896) founded the Nobel Prize Foundation in 1899. He was the Swedish chemist whose invention of dynamite made him a wealthy man. He financed the Nobel Peace Prize Foundation with the millions of dollars that nations paid him for his dynamite. When he first created dynamite, he believed that his invention would force the world to give up warfare forever. He erroneously believed that dynamite was so powerful an explosive that no one would dare use it as a weapon. It is ironic that the man who established the Nobel Peace Price Foundation created an invention that made mass killings not only possible but also efficient. Dynamite has killed millions of people and destroyed billions of dollars worth of property. It is said that when Nobel approached old age, he felt guilty about the deaths his dynamite had caused and, guilt-stricken, he established the Nobel Peace Prize Foundation. He wanted to make up for some of the harm his dynamite caused.

The Nobel Peace Prize is awarded by a committee of five people elected by the Norwegian Parliament. Many of the people who receive this prize risked their lives to promote peace. The biographical sketches of the Nobel Peace Prize winners below describe some of the events which shaped their lives.

AS YOU READ

Remember what you have learned about reading from Lesson 1; look for the authors' main points. Several quick readings for understanding is more effective than a slow, careful reading for details. These questions will help you understand the main ideas:

1. What are the sources of the Nobel Prize winners' personal power?
2. What are the characteristics of each of these persons and how did these characteristics lead to their empowerment?

Reading: Nobel Peace Prize Winners

MOTHER TERESA OF CALCUTTA (1911–   )

Servant of the poor and sick and dying
Awarded the Nobel Peace Prize in 1979

Quiet, almost timid by nature, Mother Teresa is internationally known for her work in relieving the suffering of the poor, sick, and dying. This small, stooped° old woman is loved and admired for her noble character, her selfless dedication to social work, and her tireless work for the poor.

When she received the Nobel Peace Prize, she was surrounded by the rich, the talented, and the powerful. They came dressed in their elegant gowns and tuxedos. Dressed in a faded° blue sari and worn sandals, Mother Teresa accepted the Nobel Peace Prize from the hand of the King of Norway.

Recalling Mother Teresa's acceptance of this award, Robert Fulghum, a Unitarian minister and author, states:

> No shah or president or king or general or scientist or cartel or oil company or ayatollah holds the key to as much power as she has. None is as rich. For hers is the invincible weapon against the evils of this earth: the caring heart. And hers are the everlasting riches of this life: the wealth of the compassionate spirit.[1]

Mother Teresa, who was born on August 27, 1919 in Albania, grew up in Yugoslavia. There she attended a local government school. As a young student, she became a member of a Catholic association for children. She was only twelve years old when she began taking care of young children. Even at that age, she knew that she wanted to advance respect for those without power and dedicate her life to helping them. At the age of eighteen, she entered the order of the Sisters of Our Lady of Loreto. She taught in the order's convent school in Calcutta, India, until September 10, 1946, when her heart told her that she should go to live among the poor, the sick, and the dying.

In February 1948, Mother Teresa was granted special permission from the Vatican to leave the convent "in order to spend herself in the service of the poor and the needy in the slums° of Calcutta, and gather around her some companions ready to undertake° the work." On August 16, 1948, she took off the religious clothes of the Loreto nun and put on a cheap, simple, white sari with a blue border, a small cross pinned to the left shoulder, and sandals. She began the new service by bringing dying people from the streets into a room in a home at Kalighat where they could die in peace and with dignity. In her words, "We have picked up from the streets of Calcutta 54,000 people, and 23,000-something have died in that one room (at Kalighat)."[2]

Mother Teresa has since established many homes for the dying, orphanages for the hundreds of sick, unwanted, or abandoned children, schools for these children, and leper° clinics. She says, "Any work of love brings a person face to face with God."

In 1959, she founded a Roman Catholic order—the Missionaries of Charity. In this order, over 4,000 sisters, brothers, and co-workers have committed° themselves to serving the poor in 102 countries, including the United States. The order runs 468 shelters for the homeless, sick, and dying.[3]

In describing Mother Teresa's special kind of power, Robert Fulghum writes, ". . .while I wrestle° with frustration about the impotence° of the individual, she goes right on changing the world. While I wish for more power and resources, she uses her power and resources to do what she can at the moment."

Mother Teresa's message is simply stated in her own words: "We can do no great things—only small things with great love."

[1]Robert Fulghum. 1988. *All I Really Need to Know I Learned in Kindergarten*. Random House, Inc.
[2]Interview. "A pencil in the hand of God." *Time*, December 4, 1989, p. 11.
[3]George W. Cornell. "Mother Teresa, 'saint of gutters,' contrasts with churchly splendor." *Orange County Register*. Saturday, August 15, 1992, E8.

VOCABULARY

stooped (adj.)	the quality of standing or walking with bad posture; not standing up straight
faded (adj.)	the quality of losing color
slum (n.)	a city area characterized by very poor housing
to undertake (v.)	to do (something)
leper (n.)	a person who has leprosy, a fatal disease characterized by deformities
committed (adj.)	characterized by doing something enthusiastically despite problems
to wrestle (v.)	to fight
impotence (n.)	the quality of being without power

ALBERT SCHWEITZER (1875–1965)

Alsatian minister, musician, philosopher, doctor, and medical missionary
Awarded the Nobel Peace Prize in 1952 for his service to humanity

Albert Schweitzer is known throughout the world for his missionary service to humanity and reverence° for all life—plant, animal, and human. Like Mother Teresa, Schweitzer worked tirelessly for those without power.

He was born on January 14, 1875, in Kayersburg, Alsace (which was, at that time, a part of Germany). He was a sensitive young boy—sensitive to nature, to music, and to the feelings of those around him. He excelled in his academic studies and in music.

At the age of twenty-one, young Schweitzer began to question his right to have such a fortunate life without doing something in return for those less fortunate. He made a secret promise to himself that he would continue studying and living for himself until he was thirty; then, for the rest of his life, he would only serve those weaker than himself.

Like his father, Schweitzer became a protestant minister. By the age of thirty, he had also established himself as an author and a lecturer. He also had become a talented musician and an authority on Johann Sebastian Bach. In addition to all this, he served as the director of a religious college in Strasbourg, Alsace. He preached the gospel° of love through both his deeds° and words.

While serving as a minister, Schweitzer learned of the great shortage of physicians in the Congo area of Africa. Africans in this region were dying needlessly because of the poor health care that they received. At the age of thirty, Schweitzer decided to become a doctor to help those in Africa who needed medical attention for their survival. Although his family and friends were dismayed by his decision, he went to the University of Strasbourg to pursue a degree in medicine.

Six years later, Schweitzer finished medical school and passed his medical exams. He then completed a year of internship at a hospital where he studied tropical medicine. At the age of thirty-seven, he was finally ready to begin helping the sick in the African Congo. Before he left for Gabon, in French Equatorial Africa, Schweitzer married Helen Bresslau, the daughter of a university professor. She had taken a nursing course so that she could assist him in Africa.

Dr. and Mrs. Schweitzer left for West Africa on Easter Day, 1913. Their mission was to establish a hospital at the Lambarene Mission in Africa. With them, they brought boxes of equipment and medicine which were donated by friends. When the Schweitzers arrived in West Africa, patients came to them from great distances. These patients suffered from a variety of diseases and ailments, including sleeping sickness, malaria, heart trouble, dysentery, leprosy, and injuries from accidents. The Schweitzers had no choice but to treat these patients from an old henhouse. A short time later, however, with the help of their African friends, the Schweitzers built a new hospital with many small houses. There, in the hospital village, the African people could live with their families until they were well.

World War I interrupted the Schweitzer's humanitarian° service to the medically needy. Since the Schweitzers were German citizens in a French colony in Africa, they were sent to a prison camp in France. In 1924, Dr. Schweitzer was finally able to return to Lambarene to rebuild the hospital. Mrs. Schweitzer remained behind in Europe with their young daughter, Renna.

When Mrs. Schweitzer returned to Africa in 1929, she hardly recognized the hospital at Lambarene. It was very different from the beginning days when she and Dr. Schweitzer treated patients in the henhouse. The hospital had been remodeled° and now included a well-equipped operating room and a large staff of well-trained doctors and nurses.

Schweitzer, often speaking of his "reverence for life," believed that no man should kill any other living creature. He even protected the insects which at times invaded his hospital.

In 1952, Schweitzer was awarded the Nobel Peace Prize. In a sense, the world had finally come to recognize the greatness of Schweitzer's personal power. When he accepted this award, he stated, ". . . humanitarianism is the origin of all progress toward some higher existence. Inspired° by humanitarianism, we are true to ourselves and capable of creating. Inspired by a contrary° spirit, we are unfaithful to ourselves and fall prey° to all manner of error."

When Schweitzer was ninety years old, he died. The date was September 4, 1965. Schweitzer did not die a wealthy man, but he had never desired wealth. He was buried next to his wife in a simple grave at Lambarene.

Schweitzer promoted a philosophy termed "the reverence for life." In one of his books, *Out of My Life and Thought,* he explained this philosophy:

A man is ethical° only when life, as such, is sacred to him, that of plants and animals as well as that of his fellow men, and when he devotes himself helpfully to all life that is in need of help.

VOCABULARY

reverence (n.)	adoration, love, or worship
gospel (n.)	message that is considered true
deed (n.)	action
humanitarian (adj.)	the quality of being concerned about the well-being of others
remodeled (adj.)	the quality of being changed and improved
inspired (adj.)	the characteristic of being motivated
contrary (adj.)	opposing or negative
to fall prey to (v.)	(*idiom*) to become a victim of (the enemy)
ethical (adj.)	relating to good standards of behavior

THE DALAI LAMA (1935–)

Tibetan Buddhist monk, spiritual and political leader of the Tibetan Government in Exile

Awarded the Nobel Prize for Peace in 1989 for his dedication to justice

During the period 1949–1950, the People's Republic of China invaded the country of Tibet. The Dalai Lama remained as spiritual and political leader of Tibet for the decade following the Chinese invasion.° He lived in his country and ruled gently. However, the Chinese who took over his country began to treat the Tibetans cruelly. As the cruelty increased, the Dalai Lama discovered that he could help his country more if he escaped from Tibet and lived in exile in India than if he remained in Tibet. Today, he resides in Dharamsala, India, where he continues to struggle to obtain justice for his nation. He is famous throughout the world for his spiritual leadership and pacifist° views.

The Dalai Lama was born on July 6, 1935 in the small village of Takster. At the time, he was named Llamo Thorndup. His parents leased land and farmed it by themselves. The Tibetans believe that Dalai Lama is the reincarnation° of each of the previous thirteen Dalai Lamas of Tibet and is spiritually connected to the Buddha himself. When Llamo Thorndup was not quite three years old, the thirteenth Dalai Lama died. The Tibetan Government sent a search party to look for the new incarnation° of the Dalai Lama. This search party discovered Llamo Thorndup by a series of miraculous and spiritual events. Members of the party took Llamo Thorndup to the Potala palace, the seat of the Tibetan government. There, he became the new Dalai Lama, the spiritual and political leader of the Tibetan people. Like all previous Dalai Lamas, he devoted himself to spiritual studies and became a monk.

When the Chinese Communists invaded Tibet, many of the Tibetan people wanted to rebel. However, the Dalai Lama encouraged the rebel fighters to put down their arms and to resist the Chinese invaders peacefully. The Dalai Lama's efforts to peacefully resist the People's Republic of China were unsuccessful. The People's Liberation Army sent 80,000 soldiers into Tibet where they set up their own Chinese government.

Although Mao promised the Dalai Lama that the Chinese would not place many restrictions on the freedoms the Tibetan people enjoyed, Mao broke his promise. As the Dalai Lama explains:

Far from leaving [the Tibetan] people be, they [the Chinese] had begun to press ahead unilaterally° with all kinds of "reform." New taxes were imposed on houses, and land, and cattle, and, to add insult to injury, the contents of the monasteries were also assessed for tax. Large estates were confiscated° and the land redistributed by the local Chinese cadres. . . . Landowners were publicly arraigned and punished for "crimes against the people." To my horror, some were even put to death. Simultaneously, the Chinese authorities began to round up the many thousands of nomad farmers who roamed these fertile regions. To our new masters, nomadism was repugnant as it smacked of barbarism.[1]

By 1956, Chinese oppression of Tibetans had increased significantly. Monasteries had been bombed, and women and children were mercilessly tortured° and executed.° Monks and nuns were abused and imprisoned. Finally, the Dalai Lama realized that the lives of all those Tibetans who were fighting against the Chinese were endangered. The sheer number of soldiers in the People's Liberation Army made a successful battle impossible. The Dalai Lama escaped to India. He hoped that he could obtain more support for his nation outside it than he had inside it.

From India, the Dalai Lama organized massive rescue efforts for the over 100,000 Tibetan refugees° who escaped Chinese oppression.° He helped provide these refugees with shelter, food, education, medical supplies, and jobs. Simultaneously,° he worked to obtain political recognition for the Tibet Government in Exile. In 1989, he was awarded the Nobel Peace Prize for his efforts to obtain justice.

[1]Tenzin Gyatso, the Fourteenth Dalai Lama of Tibet. 1990. *Freedom from Exile; The Autobiography of the Dalai Lama.* New York: Harper Collins, p. 104.

VOCABULARY

invasion (n.)	the act of taking over a country against the desires of the people who live there
pacifist (adj.)	a person who is against war or violence
reincarnation (n.)	being reborn in a different body
incarnation (n.)	the union of spirit and body
unilaterally (adv.)	doing something without considering the other person's views
to confiscate (v.)	to take away
to torture (v.)	to punish by causing extreme pain
to execute (v.)	to kill
refugee (n.)	a person who leaves his or her country to find safety
oppression (n.)	cruel use of power
simultaneously (adv.)	at the same time

Comprehension Workout

EXERCISE 6

Write lines for each of the three Nobel Peace Prize winners about whom you just read. Fill in the chart on page 31. Follow the examples given.

MOTHER TERESA

Year	Event
1919	_Mother Teresa was born on August 27, 1919 in Albania._
1931	
1946	
1948	
1959	
1979	
1990	

ALBERT SCHWEITZER

Year	Event
1875	_Albert Schweitzer was born on January 14, 1875, in Kayersburg, Alsace (which was, at that time, a part of Germany.)_
1913	
1924	
1952	
1965	

THE DALAI LAMA

Year	Event
1935	
1949	
1956	
1989	

Threads

Power is the ultimate aphrodisiac.

Henry Kissinger

Writing Task: Extending Your Definition of Power

Write a paragraph in which you explore the notion of power as it is exemplified in *one* of the Nobel Prize winners' lives. Your purpose is to explore your own ideas. Your paragraph is for yourself.

BEFORE YOU WRITE

In small groups of students, discuss the following questions:

1. What three characteristics do Mother Teresa, Albert Schweitzer, and the Dalai Lama share?
2. Would your group classify Mother Teresa, Albert Schweitzer, and the Dalai Lama as powerful individuals? Why or why not?
3. Would Mother Teresa, Albert Schweitzer, and the Dalai Lama be considered powerful in your cultures?
4. Do you think Americans value the work of humanitarian leaders? Why do you think this?
5. Do you think people from all cultural backgrounds value humanitarian work equally? Why?

WRITE

Write your paragraph.

AFTER YOU WRITE

Consider this strategy:

LEARNING STRATEGY

Forming Concepts: Study your classmates' writing to get ideas to improve your own writing.

Read your paragraphs aloud in small groups. Take notes on your classmates' ideas. If something a classmate has written strikes you as particularly interesting or noteworthy, write it down.

REVISE YOUR PARAGRAPH

Make any changes that you like to the organization and content of your paragraph. Feel free to borrow your classmates' ideas.

EDIT YOUR PARAGRAPH

Edit your paragraph carefully. Correct the grammatical errors that you made.

Listening

One famous humanitarian leader not described above was Martin Luther King, Jr. Listen to the audiotaped story about his life and his famous speech, "I Have a Dream," at home.

BEFORE YOU LISTEN

Consider this strategy:

LEARNING STRATEGY

Personalizing: Exploring your own ideas before you listen to a story helps you relate to the ideas in the story, and this improves your listening comprehension.

To help you explore your own ideas, consider what you already know about Martin Luther King, Jr.

1. What race was Martin Luther King, Jr.?
2. What part of the United States was Martin Luther King, Jr. from?
3. What was Martin Luther King, Jr.'s job?
4. What did Martin Luther King, Jr. do to try to improve the living conditions of African-Americans in the United States?

AFTER YOU LISTEN

React to Martin Luther King, Jr.'s speech in your journal. If you are having difficulty reacting to the audiotape, consider the following questions.

1. Focus on the content of Martin Luther King, Jr.'s speech. Which part did you like the most? Why?
2. Was there any part of Martin Luther King, Jr.'s speech which bothered you? Why?
3. Focus on the introduction and conclusion of Martin Luther King, Jr.'s speech. How did he drive home his main point in the introduction and the conclusion?

Writing Task: Writing a Summary

Write two or three paragraphs in which you summarize the main events in one of the lives of the Nobel Peace Prize winners discussed in this lesson (Mother Teresa, Albert Schweitzer, the Dalai Lama, or Martin Luther King, Jr.). Imagine that you are writing this summary for a group of college students who do not know anything about Nobel Peace Prize winners and who have not read the reading selections above or listened to the audiotape which accompanies this lesson.

BEFORE YOU WRITE

Read the guidelines below.

PRACTICAL GUIDELINES FOR SUMMARIZING THE IMPORTANT EVENTS IN A PERSON'S LIFE

A summary is a short statement or condensation of the most important ideas in a piece of writing. The main goal of a summary is to provide a useful and objective account of the content of a piece of writing. Here are some guidelines for summarizing biographical writing.

- Discuss the events chronologically. It is important to discuss life events in the order in which they occur.
- Be sure that your summary is complete. Make sure that you have included all the significant events.
- Do not write your own opinion about the individual's life. Try to keep the writer's account of the individual's life.
- Keep your audience in mind. If your audience does not know much about the person's life, you will have to provide the audience with useful background information.
- Use your own words and grammatical structures.
- Use time expressions to provide smooth transitions within your summary. These expressions include:

TIME EXPRESSIONS

in 1984, in 1934, etc.	afterward
first, second, etc.	simultaneously
next	finally
subsequently	later
then	prior to
after that	

Note: Be careful not to begin all of your sentences with these words.

Review the reading selection that you would like to summarize. Underline the main ideas. Then, on a clean sheet of paper, jot down some of the important achievements of the individual whom you are describing.

WRITE

Write your summary. To prevent using the writer's words in your summary, do not look back at the reading when you write it.

WHILE YOU WRITE

Refer to your notes as well as the time line you made earlier. (Refer to page 31.)

AFTER YOU WRITE

Use this Revision Checklist.

REVISION CHECKLIST

_____ 1. I have discussed the main events in the individual's life in chronological order.

_____ 2. My summary is complete. I have included all the main points of the reading selection.

_____ 3. I have not included unimportant details.

_____ 4. I have excluded my own opinion about the individual's life.

_____ 5. I have provided the audience with necessary background information about the individual.

_____ 6. I have used my own words and grammatical structures.

_____ 7. I have used time expressions to clarify when events occur.

REWRITE YOUR SUMMARY

Refer back to the reading if necessary.

AFTER YOU REWRITE YOUR SUMMARY

Exchange summaries with a classmate who wrote about the same person. With your classmate, answer the following questions:

1. Did both of you discuss the same events in this person's life? Which events did you leave out?
2. Did both of you discuss the events in the same order?
3. Should any details in your summaries be deleted? Why?
4. Could any parts of the summaries be rewritten so that they sound more like your own words?

REVISE YOUR SUMMARY AGAIN

Consider this strategy:

LEARNING STRATEGY

Overcoming Limitations: Asking native English writers helps you improve your writing by providing you with valuable feedback and assisting you to perfect your skills.

Use this strategy when you are in the editing stage of your writing.

Ask a native English writer to identify your grammar and punctuation errors, to correct them, to explain the corrections given, to provide you with alternative ways of expressing yourself, and to pinpoint both your strengths and weaknesses as a writer.

EDIT YOUR SUMMARY

With the help of a native English writer, edit your summary carefully.

Punctuation Explanation

QUOTATIONS

Explanation: When you write about the lives of people, you may want to use quotations.

INTRODUCING QUOTED MATERIAL AND AVOIDING "DROPPED QUOTATIONS"

INTRODUCING QUOTED MATERIAL

Direct quotations of someone else's words, whether written or spoken, must always be in quotation marks. The quoted material is always repeated exactly, word for word.

QUOTING SENTENCES

In 1: If a quotation is introduced with an expression such as "he wrote," or if it is followed by such an expression, a comma is needed.

1. Mark Twain wrote, "It is curious that physical courage should be so common in the world, and moral courage so rare."

Threads

Lee Kuan Yew was Prime Minister of Singapore for 31 years before resigning in November, 1990.

QUOTING INTERRUPTED SENTENCES

In 2: If a quoted sentence is interrupted by words such as "wrote Mark Twain," set off the explanatory words with commas. If a question mark is used, place it inside the quotation marks.

2. "What's the use you learning to do right," wrote Mark Twain, "when it's troublesome to do right and ain't no trouble to do wrong, and the wages is just the same?"*

DROPPED QUOTATIONS

Avoid *dropped quotations*. Dropped quotations are those which are introduced without any warning. To avoid surprising your reader when you use quotations, use *signal phrases* in your writing which prepare your reader for what is to come. Signal phrases often include the author's name and appropriate background information.

DROPPED QUOTATION

"In recognition of his varied and significant writings, in which he champions humanitarian ideals and freedom of thought," he was awarded the Nobel Prize in Literature.

QUOTATION WITH SIGNAL PHRASE

The King of Norway is responsible for awarding the Nobel Prize in Literature. As he was handing the award to Naguib Mahfouz, the famous Egyptian writer, he stated that Mahfouz was being awarded the prize "in recognition of his varied and significant writings, in which he champions humanitarian ideals and freedom of thought."

1. To avoid repetition and monotony, change your signal phrases, as in these examples:

> In the words of Albert Einstein, ". . ."
> The Dalai Lama has noted, ". . ."
> Martin Luther King, Jr. answered these objections with the following analysis: ". . ."
> As Pearl S. Buck argued, ". . ."
> Naguib Mahfouz, the famous Egyptian writer, claims, ". . ."
> Paul Anthony Samuelson offers an odd argument for this view: ". . ."
> Irene Joliot-Curie, a dedicated chemist, emphasized, ". . ."

When the signal phrase includes a verb, it is important to choose one that is effective. Vary your use of signal phrases, but be aware that the words below are not interchangeable; they have different meanings. Choose an appropriate verb, such as the ones in the list on page 38.

---

*The quotation from *Huckleberry Finn* is ungrammatical. *Ain't* means *is not*. *Wages* refers to *salary*.

SIGNAL PHRASES			
acknowledges	comments	endorses	reasons
adds	compares	grants	refutes
admits	confirms	illustrates	rejects
agrees	contends	implies	reports
argues	declares	insists	responds
asserts	denies	notes	suggests
believes	disputes	observes	thinks
claims	emphasizes	points out	writes

2. It is unnecessary to quote the entire sentence from a source. You may quote only a word or expression, but make sure that when you put this word or expression in your own sentence, your sentence is grammatically correct.

> For George Bullucks, the single variable underlying power is "people appeal," the ability to influence others by personal charm or charisma.

3. To shorten a quoted passage, you can use ellipses (three periods with spaces between) to show that you have left out words. The sentences that remain must be grammatically correct.

> Milton Friedman, an American economist, argues against uniform governmental regulations: "At any moment in time, by imposing uniform standards in housing, or nutrition, or clothing, the government could undoubtedly improve the level of living of many individuals. . . . But in the process, government would replace progress by stagnation."

As seen in the example above, when you want to omit a full sentence or more, use a period before the three ellipsis dots.

4. For long quotations, quotation marks are deleted. When you quote more than four typed lines, you should set off the quotation by indenting it ten spaces from the left margin. Indent every line. Use the normal right margin and single-space. Long quotations should be introduced by a sentence which contains background information about the quotations. Quotation marks are unnecessary because the indented format tells readers that the quotation appears word for word.

When Naguib Mahfouz was asked about the importance of his winning the Nobel Prize to Egypt and the Arab world, he replied:

> It's given me for the first time in my life the feeling that my literature could be on the international level. Egypt and the Arab world also get the Nobel Prize with me. I believe that from now on the international doors have opened and in the future, literate people will look for Arab literature, and Arab literature deserves the recognition.

5. Whenever you use quotations, you need to provide a complete citation of the source. In other words, you need to explain to the reader who said or

wrote the words, where the words appeared, and when. When you write for an academic audience, you usually provide the complete reference at the end of your writing so that the readers can locate the source. Since various fields have specific guidelines for writing references, make sure to request these guidelines from your instructor.

Punctuation Practice: Quotations

EXERCISE 7

Fill in the blanks with an appropriate verb. Since there is more than one correct answer for the items, you will need to correct your answers with your teacher.

1. The President _____ convincingly that the people must allow her to control all aspects of their lives.

2. Marguirite Aguirre _____, "I obtained power by taking initiative and using my resourcefulness."

3. Hank Woodward, a nationally known computer consultant, thinks competence is an important part of obtaining power. He _____: "You want to know how I obtain power? By being competent."

4. Covey convincingly _____: "Power is the ability to act and the strength to accomplish something."

5. Sandra O'Neilly has a different view of what it takes to obtain power. She _____: "The key to getting power is promoting oneself. I obtain power by going out of the way to be visible. I make sure that everyone sees my credentials."

6. One physician, Katie Gonzalez, believes that conviction leads to power. Here's what she _____: "Confidence buys me power. I have such strong beliefs that I'm 100% sure of what I'm talking about."

7. Margaret Mead, a famous anthropologist, _____, "Self-esteem is a critical component of personal power."

8. J. Paul Getty allegedly _____, "Formula for power: Rise early, work hard, strike oil."

9. Lee _____, "When President Park died, the Korean people lost a powerful leader."

10. "Power comes from within," _____ Geraldine Woods.

Grammar Explanation

SIMPLE PRESENT AND PAST VERB TENSES

Explanation: Summarizing the events of an individual's life often involves using simple present and past tense verbs appropriately. The following information will help you review these two tenses. This lesson provides general guidelines for using the present and past tenses.

THE SIMPLE PRESENT

We use the simple present to express relatively simple time relations, such as:

an action occurring regularly
Mother Teresa <u>works</u> each day.

an action occurring at the time of the writing
Bill Clinton <u>is</u> the president.

a general truth
The moon <u>revolves</u> around the earth.

a condition which is not repeated, but which is always true
Humanitarians <u>are</u> unselfish.

We often use simple present verbs with these words:

today	every day, week, month, year
always	once a week, month, year
often	occasionally
frequently	seldom
usually	rarely
sometimes	never

The simple present is also used with nonaction verbs to show that something is happening now.

NONACTION VERB

I	<u>remember</u>	when my grandmother died.
I	<u>seem</u>	to have forgotten my book.
I	<u>hear</u>	that you will be going to Japan soon.

Nonaction verbs are also called *stative* verbs.

NONACTION (STATIVE) VERBS

Appearance	Perception	Preference/Desire
appear	hear	hate
seem	sound	like
consist	see	love
cost	smell	need
equal	taste	prefer
look	feel	want
	desire	
	approve	
	appreciate	
	mind	

Possession	Inclusion	Thoughts
belong	comprise	believe
have	consist	feel (think, believe)
own	contain	understand
possess	include	doubt
		guess (suppose)
		imagine
		mean (signify)
		recognize
		remember
		understand
		perceive

THE SIMPLE PAST TENSE

1. We use the simple past tense to write about an event or action which began and ended at a definite time in the past or to describe a series of past events in chronological order.

In 1: The simple past indicates that an event or action began and ended at a definite period in the past.

1. Mother Teresa <u>worked</u> in Calcutta.

In 2: The simple past indicates that a series of events began and ended in the past.

2. The Dalai Lama <u>escaped</u> to India, <u>organized</u> refugee camps, and <u>helped</u> the Tibetan rebels.

2. We often use the past tense with a specific time reference such as *six months ago, last March, in 1985, when we first met,* etc. However, an

expression of time may not be given in the sentence as in the examples below.

EXAMPLES   **a.** John, being somewhat immature, <u>saw</u> *Batman Returns* three times.

        b. President Park's death <u>marked</u> the beginning of a new era in the politics of South Korea.

3. When the action of a clause which begins with <u>when</u> happens in the past, the action in the "<u>when</u> clause" occurs first.

EXAMPLES   **a.** When Mother Teresa <u>established</u> the mission, she helped many people.

        b. When Mother Teresa <u>received</u> the Nobel Peace Prize, many people in the audience cried.

Grammar Practice

EXERCISE 8: SIMPLE PRESENT AND PAST VERB TENSES

The following passage was written by Akram Safadi, a graduate student in economics at the University of California.

Fill in the blanks with the correct form of the verb given in the parentheses.

TRUMP'S RISE TO THE TOP

Akram Safadi

Donald J. Trump is an enterprising° billionaire who lives in New York City. He is an extraordinary businessman who combines hard work with competence.

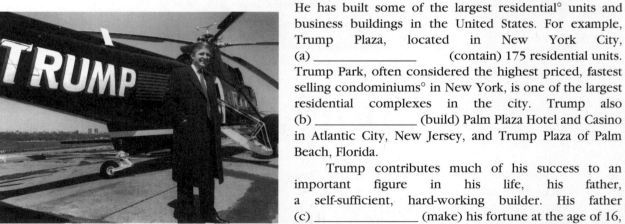

Donald J. Trump, New York's young billionaire and real estate developer.

He has built some of the largest residential° units and business buildings in the United States. For example, Trump Plaza, located in New York City, (a) _____ (contain) 175 residential units. Trump Park, often considered the highest priced, fastest selling condominiums° in New York, is one of the largest residential complexes in the city. Trump also (b) _____ (build) Palm Plaza Hotel and Casino in Atlantic City, New Jersey, and Trump Plaza of Palm Beach, Florida.

Trump contributes much of his success to an important figure in his life, his father, a self-sufficient, hard-working builder. His father (c) _____ (make) his fortune at the age of 16, when he built a two-car frame garage. Since middle-class people (d) _____ (be) just beginning to purchase cars and had homes without attached garages in those days, Trump's father (e) _____ (grow) wealthy.

Trump also (f) _____ (attribute) his success to his education. As a child he went to Catholic elementary and secondary schools. His education was furthered at the Wharton School of Finance at the University of Pennsylvania.

There, Trump (g) _____ (establish) valuable connections with people who would later help him.

Trump also attributes his success to his aggression. As a child, he (h) _____ (be) very aggressive. Later, this aggression helped him negotiate large business deals. Once, when Trump was just a small boy, he was playing blocks with his brother. He (i) _____ (run out) of blocks and asked his brother if he could have some of his. His brother (j) _____ (agree) on the condition that Trump later return the blocks. However, after Trump built his block construction, he (k) _____ (like) the way that it looked so much, that he (l) _____ (glue) the entire block construction together. His brother never did get his blocks back. On another occasion, when Trump (m) _____ (be) only in the second grade, he (n) _____ (become) angry with his music teacher because he thought the teacher didn't know anything about music. Trump (o) _____ (punch) the teacher in the eye.

Trump also attributes his success as a real estate° developer to his ability to identify good deals and make them effectively. For Trump, this ability (p) _____ (be) one in which people are born with. Intelligence (q) _____ (be) important, according to Trump, but business ability is essential. In discussing his particular style of deal-making, Trump (r) _____ (state):

> My style of deal-making is quite simple and straightforward. I aim very high, and then just keep pushing, and pushing and pushing to get what I'm after. Sometimes I settle for less than I sought, but in most cases I still end up with what I want. (Trump 1987, pg. 45)

Although Trump has been criticized for his recent business failures and divorce from Ivana Trump, he remains one of the wealthiest individuals in the United States. He (s) _____ (continue) to work from the early morning into the late hours of the evenings. Like it or not, he is one of the United States' most enterprising businessmen.

Trump, Donald J. with Tony Schwartz, 1987. *Trump: The Art of the Deal.* New York: Warner Books, Inc.

VOCABULARY

enterprising (adj.)	characterized by independence, energy, and creativity
residential (adj.)	housing
condominium (n.)	a type of housing shared by two or more owners
real estate (n.)	property in buildings and land

Threads

The world's richest man, Yoshiaki Tsutsumi, is head of Seibu Railway Group of Japan. Estimated worth: $16 billion.

Gaining Writing Competence

WRITING A SUMMARY

In the Quick Write activity on page 44, you will write a summary. These guidelines will help you.

GUIDELINES FOR WRITING A SUMMARY

1. Make sure that you have a general understanding of the reading passage that you are asked to summarize. Read it more than once if necessary.
2. Make sure that you understand the author's main ideas. Highlighting or underlining main ideas and taking notes is helpful.
3. Avoid plagiarizing by using your own words.
4. Make sure that you do not copy the writer's writing style. Use your own.
5. Follow your own organization of ideas; do not organize the ideas in the same way as the original reading.
6. Avoid giving your own personal opinions about the reading.
7. Do not include minor details and other unimportant information. Include only the author's main ideas and major supporting details.
8. Always begin by identifying the title of the passage which you are summarizing and the name of the author who wrote the passage.

EXAMPLES   In a recent article in the *Times*, entitled "Gaining Personal Power," Hank Beckett argues . . .

Tom Sawyer, a novel written by Mark Twain, tells about . . .

Quick Write

MORE PRACTICE WRITING SUMMARIES

Write a one paragraph summary of the reading passage about Trump on page 42. You are writing for the general public. Your purpose is to inform.

Gaining Writing Competence

THESIS STATEMENTS

Explanation: In the previous writing activities, you looked at the lives of world leaders. Many of us recognize these people as powerful. However, individuals need not receive worldwide recognition to have personal power. All individuals have experienced personal power of some type. In the writing task which follows, you will describe your classmates' experiences with power. The information below will help you.

THESIS STATEMENTS

The main idea of a piece of writing can often be stated in a single sentence which often, though not always, appears in the opening paragraph. This sentence is called the thesis statement. Such a statement prepares the reader for the text which follows and takes the reader and writer in a specific direction. It helps the reader identify the writer's main point. It is a good idea to develop a thesis statement early on in the writing process. You can jot it down on a piece of paper and reformulate it later when you revise your writing.

What is a good thesis statement?

1. *Specificity:* A good thesis statement says something specific about a topic. It is not too general.*
2. *Grammaticality:* A good thesis statement is expressed in complete, grammatical sentences.
3. *Focus:* A good thesis focuses the reader's attention on the author's main idea and prepares the reader for the writing which follows.
4. *Writer's Attitude:* A good thesis statement often, though not always, expresses the writer's attitude toward a topic.

Note: Stories do not always contain thesis statements. This is because their main ideas might be so subtle that it is difficult to state them in thesis statements. When omitting a thesis statement in a story, use an introduction which suggests the purpose of the story and the direction it will take.

*Note, however, that a good thesis must be specific, but not too specific. Because a good thesis prepares readers for facts and details which support it, it itself cannot be a fact. It must always require development.

Gaining Writing Practice

EXERCISE 9: THESIS STATEMENTS

The student essay below contains an appropriate thesis statement. It is underlined. Read the essay and answer these questions:

1. Why is the thesis statement considered an appropriate one?
2. What are the characteristics of a good thesis as it is demonstrated in the essay below?
3. What is the connection between the thesis statement and the body paragraphs in this essay?

CHIN

Personal power often stems from self-confidence, however self-confidence is not always built easily. The road to self-confidence was a difficult one for Chin, a shy, quiet boy who lacked self-esteem. He found self-confidence through success in two activities: doing well in karate lessons and playing the drums.

When Chin was just a child, he was often harassed by a neighborhood bully. One day, his parents decided to send Chin to Karate school to learn fighting techniques. These techniques helped him to defeat the bully who had tormented him so. His self-esteem was greatly enhanced through his victory.

However, Chin's newly discovered power did not help him to gain complete self-confidence. In high school, he had neither the confidence to make new friends nor receive good grades. He felt so lonely that he often cried himself to sleep at night. His loneliness drove him to take up a hobby, playing the drums to amuse himself. He passed hour after hour playing his drums alone in his bedroom.

Then one day, Chin tried out for the school band. He was accepted. He felt good about his accomplishment and this led to an increase in his self-esteem. As he gained confidence in himself, his shyness diminished and he began to make friends. As he became more extroverted, he grew more popular at school. He found himself surrounded with friends at all times. At the golden age of "18," he had discovered his own personal power.

Chin's power led him to many other accomplishments. His parents saw his excellent social skills, and asked him to work in their family-owned business, a one-hour photo lab which is situated in Seoul. Chin gained experience in the field of photography while simultaneously learning to manage a business and earning good money.

One accomplishment led to another. In addition to his newly acquired business success, Chin encountered academic success. His grades improved to such an extent that others began to count on him for tutoring. Chin quickly became one of the best students at his high school.

Practicing karate and the drums has become two of Chin's favorite pastimes. While these two activities no longer bring him a sense of immediate success, he contributes his personal power to these activities.—L.C.

Gaining Writing Practice

EXERCISE 10: THESIS STATEMENTS

Study the thesis statements below. Check (✓) the ones that are good and revise those that you think are weak.

_____ **1.** Fifty-two percent of all Americans do not want to lead others.

_____ **2.** Power allowed Kim to gain power.

_____ **3.** When I first arrived in the United States, I used my own personal power to overcome my communication difficulties.

_____ **4.** In general, there are numerous people with power in this world.

_____ **5.** To obtain personal power, one must have wealth, education, and luck.

_____ **6.** Power is like a knife hanging on a string; one mistake and all one's power is drained away.

Writing Task: Interviews—Writing Descriptions of a Classmate's Life

In the previous tasks, you explored personal power in the lives of famous individuals. However, personal power resides in all of us. In this task, you will examine the personal power of one of your classmates. You will write a one page description of this power as exemplified in your classmate's life. Your writing is for your instructor and your classmates. Your purpose is to inform and to entertain.

BEFORE YOU WRITE

Interview someone sitting near you. Take five minutes to ask questions and jot down notes about your classmate's life before reversing roles for another five minutes. Focus on interesting events in your classmate's life which made her or him feel powerful.

After you finish this interview, take an additional fifteen minutes to organize a rough draft from your notes.

REWRITE YOUR ROUGH DRAFT

You are ready to rewrite your rough draft. And while you are rewriting, consider this strategy:

LEARNING STRATEGY

Managing Your Learning: Focusing on your thesis statement prevents you from wandering off the topic (digressing).

To focus on your thesis statement, write it on an index card and glance at the card from time to time as you are writing.

AFTER YOU REWRITE YOUR ROUGH DRAFT

Read your writing to your partner for reactions and suggestions so that misconceptions can be corrected and information can be added or deleted. Create a vivid, yet accurate account of your partner's life. Make sure that you include a strong thesis statement.

REWRITE YOUR DRAFT

Revise your papers. Focus on an event which affected your classmate in a positive way.

EDIT YOUR ESSAY

Consider this strategy:

LEARNING STRATEGY

Managing Your Learning: Using a checklist to correct written errors helps you during the editing stage.

When you are satisfied with your revised essay, use the Editing Checklist to correct your grammatical and mechanical (spelling and punctuation) mistakes. You will need to reread your essay several times, concentrating on correcting one mistake at a time.

EDITING CHECKLIST

1. Find the Verbs

_____ Do the verbs agree with their subjects?

_____ Are the verbs in the correct tense for the context in which they occur? If you are unsure, ask a native speaker for help.

2. Find the Nouns

_____ Are nouns preceded by definite or indefinite articles where required? If you are unsure, ask a native speaker to help you.

3. Correct the Punctuation

_____ Are periods, commas, and quotation marks used appropriately?

4. Correct the Spelling

_____ Are the words spelled correctly? If you are unsure, check the spelling by looking the words up in a dictionary.

AFTER YOU EDIT YOUR ESSAY

Consider this strategy:

LEARNING STRATEGY

Understanding and Using Emotions: Commenting on your classmates' writing strengths increases your classmates' desire to write.

Take turns reading your finished papers. After your classmates read their papers, comment on the positive aspects of their writing.

Quick Write

REDEFINING THE WORD *POWER*

Earlier, you were asked to define the word *power*. (Refer to page 17.) Now that you have read about humanitarian and political leaders and have written about the personal power of your classmates, your views of power may have changed. Redefine the term *power* in one or two paragraphs. Your purpose is to inform, and your audience is your instructor.

Using A Language Learning Log

1. Vocabulary

Write down as many new words from the lesson as you can remember.

_____

_____

_____

2. Grammar

Note examples of any grammatical structures from the lesson learned or reviewed. Write a brief explanation of the grammar points that they illustrate.

_____

_____

_____

3. Punctuation

Briefly describe any punctuation rules that you learned.

_____

_____

_____

4. Techniques for Gaining Writing Competence

List any new techniques for gaining writing competence that you learned. (Such techniques might include those for writing a strong thesis statement, those for writing interesting introductions and conclusions, and those for composing different types of writing such as letters and essays.)

IT WORKS!
Learning Strategy:
Keeping Track of
Your Progress

_____

_____

_____

5. Learning Strategies

Describe briefly any new learning strategies that you learned.

_____

_____

_____

6. Areas that Need More Work

Note here any areas that you are still trying to improve. Try to be as specific as possible.

_____

_____

_____

In this lesson, you have identified who is powerful, and you have examined those events in the lives of famous people which led to personal power. You have also explored the notion of personal power in relation to less famous people, specifically one of your classmates. This exploration enabled you to redefine the word *power*. The focus of the next lessons is a different, though related, topic: power and gender.

QUICK REFERENCE TO LEARNING STRATEGIES

Forming Concepts: Study Your Classmates' Writing (p. 32)

Personalizing: Exploring Your Own Ideas (p. 33)

Overcoming Limitations: Asking Native English Writers for Help (p. 36)

Managing Your Learning: Focusing on Your Thesis Statement (p. 47)

Managing Your Learning: Using a Checklist (p. 47)

Understanding and Using Emotions: Commenting on Your Classmates' Writing Strengths (p. 48)

Overview

In this lesson, you will examine whether women can be powerful. The roles of men and women vary across cultures. In some cultures, women are considered very powerful. They hold the most important government positions and control the wealth. In many cultures today, however, women are not viewed as powerful. In some countries, rather than controlling others, others control them. To clarify your thoughts on the topic of power and gender, you will write a persuasive essay, a reaction paper, a comparison-contrast essay, and a report on the survey data collected earlier.

About the Reading

Judy Syfers was born in San Francisco in 1937. She received her B.A. degree from the University of Iowa in 1960. Although she wanted to attend graduate school, she never did. Her male professors talked her out of it. The essay that follows originally appeared in the first issue of *Ms.* magazine, a liberal women's magazine. In this essay, Syfers argues that she would like to have a wife who would take care of her personal needs.

Threads

In 1980, Vigdis Finnbogadottir of Iceland became the first woman to be an elected head of state.

BEFORE YOU READ

Consider this strategy:

LEARNING STRATEGY

Forming Concepts: Exploring your knowledge of and opinion about the topic of the reading helps you to better understand the reading.

Before you read Syfers's essay, consider what you already know about the topic and examine your personal opinions about it. These questions will help you.

1. Should the wife take care of all of her husband's needs? Why?
2. How does the role of wife vary across cultures?
3. Would you like a wife or husband to pick up after you?
4. What chores would you not allow others to do for you?

WHILE YOU READ

First, read Syfers's essay quickly to discover her most important ideas. As you read, you will find that you do not know all of the words. Guess the meanings of these new words, skip over them, or refer to the vocabulary gloss at the end of the reading. (The words in the vocabulary section are marked with a degree symbol (°) in the reading.) You do not need to understand every single word to understand Syfers's main ideas. Remember what you learned in Lessons 1 and 2: It is better to read over an essay several times quickly and to enjoy it than to read it slowly word for word.

READING: WHY I WANT A WIFE

Judy Syfers

1   I belong to that classification of people known as wives. I am A Wife. And, not altogether incidentally, I am a mother.

2   Not too long ago a male friend of mine appeared on the scene fresh from a recent divorce. He had one child who is, of course, with his ex-wife. He is looking for another wife. As I thought about him while I was ironing one evening, it suddenly occurred to me that I, too, would like to have a wife. Why do I want a wife?

3   I would like to go back to school so that I can become economically independent, support myself, and, if need be, support those dependent upon me. I want a wife who will work and send me to school. And while I am going to school I want a wife to take care of my children. I want a wife to keep track of the children's doctor and dentist appointments. And to keep track of mine, too. I want a wife to make sure my children eat properly and are kept clean. I want a wife who will wash the children's clothes and keep them mended. I want a wife who is a good nurturant° attendant° to my children, who arranges for their schooling, makes sure that they have an adequate social life with their peers, takes them to the park, the zoo, etc. I want a wife who takes care of the children when they are sick, a wife who arranges to be around when the children need special care, because, of course, I cannot miss classes at school. My wife must arrange to lose time at work and not lose the job. It may mean a small cut° in my wife's income from time to time, but I guess I can tolerate that. Needless to say, my wife will arrange and pay for the care of the children while my wife is working.

4   I want a wife who will take care of "my" physical needs. I want a wife who will keep my house clean. A wife who will pick up after my children, a wife who will pick up after me. I want a wife who will keep my clothes clean, ironed, mended, replaced when need be, and who will see to it that my personal things are kept in their proper place so that I can find what I need the minute I need it. I want a wife who cooks the meals, a wife who is a good cook. I want a wife who will plan the menus, do the necessary shopping, prepare the meals, serve them pleasantly, and then do the cleaning up while I do my studying. I want a wife who will care for me when I am sick and sympathize° with my pain and loss of time from school. I want a wife to go along when our family takes a vacation so that someone can continue to care for me and my children when I need a rest and a change of scene.

5   I want a wife who will not bother me with rambling° complaints about a wife's duties. But I want a wife who will listen to me when I feel the need to explain a rather difficult point I have come across in my course studies. And I want a wife who will type my papers when I have written them.

6   I want a wife who will take care of the details of my social life. When my wife and I are invited out by friends, I want a wife who will take care of the

babysitting arrangements. When I meet people at school that I like and want to entertain, I want a wife who will have the house clean, will prepare a special meal, serve it to me and my friends, and not interrupt when I talk about things that interest me and my friends. I want a wife who will have arranged that the children are fed and ready for bed before my guests arrive so that the children do not bother us. I want a wife who takes care of the needs of my guests so that they feel comfortable, who makes sure that they have an ashtray, that they are passed the hors d'oeuvres,° that they are offered a second helping of food, that their wine glasses are replenished° when necessary, that their coffee is served to them as they like it . And I want a wife who knows that sometimes I need a night out by myself.

7   I want a wife who is sensitive to my sexual needs, a wife who makes love passionately and eagerly when I feel like it, a wife who makes sure that I am satisfied. And, of course, I want a wife who will not demand sexual attention from me when I am not in the mood° for it. I want a wife who assumes complete responsibility for birth control, because I do not want more children. I want a wife who will remain sexually faithful to me so that I do not have to clutter up° my intellectual life with jealousies. And I want a wife who understands that "my" sexual needs may entail° more than strict adherence° to monogamy.° I must, after all, be able to relate to people as fully as possible.

8   If, by chance, I find another person more suitable as a wife than the wife I already have, I want the liberty to replace my wife with another one. Naturally, I will expect a fresh, new life; my wife will take the children and be solely responsible for them so that I am left free.

9   When I am through with school and have a job, I want my wife to quit working and remain at home so that my wife can more fully and completely take care of a wife's duties.

10   My God, who "wouldn't" want a wife?

Source: Judy Syfers, "Why I Want a Wife," from *Ms.,* Vol. 1 (December 31, 1971). Reprinted with the permission of the author.

VOCABULARY GLOSS

The definitions given below will help you understand Syfers's essay. Numbers in the parenthesis to the right of the word refer to the paragraph in which the word appears. Not all words that you do not understand are glossed. Either skip over the words that you do not understand, or guess the meanings from the context in which they occur.

nurturant (3) (adj.)	soothing in quality
attendant (3) (n.)	one who takes care of another
cut (3) (n.)	reduction or decrease
to sympathize (4) (v.)	to share in suffering or pain
rambling (5) (adj.)	state of talking for along time in a wandering fashion
hors d'oeuvres (6) (n.)	food served before dinner as an appetizer
to replenish (6) (v.)	to refill (a glass)
mood (7) (n.)	a state of mind or attitude
to clutter up (7) (v.)	to cover with things
to entail (7) (v.)	to involve
adherence (7) (n.)	steady and faithful attachment
monogamy (7) (n.)	the practice of marrying only once in a lifetime

Comprehension Workout

EXERCISE 11

Try to find a partner who comes from your same cultural background. With your partner, write the answers to the following questions.

1. Reading between the lines of Syfers's essay, what can you assume about the roles of husbands and wives in the culture Syfers describes?
2. What are your own culture's norms regarding husbands and wives?
3. What is each of your own individual opinions?

EXERCISE 12

The following questions refer directly to Syfers's essay. Refer to the paragraph (¶) numbers for the answers.

1. Should both husband and wife have jobs? (¶3 and ¶9)
2. Who should do the housework? (¶3-¶4)
3. Do husband and wife serve each other? Themselves? (¶4)
4. Who entertains guests? (¶6)
5. Are both husband and wife expected to be monogamous? (¶7)
6. Is divorce acceptable? For what reasons? Is it common? (¶8)
7. Who keeps the children in case of divorce? (¶8)

Cooperative Learning

NUMBERED HEADS TOGETHER

Divide into groups. It is best to sit in a circle for this activity if possible. Within your groups, number yourselves from one to four. Remember your number. You will have fifteen minutes to answer the four questions below. At the end of fifteen minutes, your instructor will call out the number of one of the questions and a number from one to four. For example, your instructor may call out "Question Number 2, Student 1." This means that those students who have the number 1 should raise their hands to answer Question 2 . If you do not know the answer when your number is called, ask your group to help you.

Question 1: What are ten reasons Judy Syfers says that she wants a wife?

Question 2: What are ten activities that many wives do that servants also do?

Question 3: In writing this essay, Judy Syfers is trying to break many stereotypes. Stereotypes are generalizations about groups of people which may or may not be true. Often stereotypes damage the people who are stereotyped. A stereotype about women is that they talk a lot. A stereotype about Californians is that they are always late. How are wives stereotyped in the United States?

Question 4: How are wives stereotyped in three different cultures?

Threads

In 1990, 58.4% of married women in the U.S. were working or looking for work.

U.S. Bureau of Labor Statistics

Quick Write

REPORTING QUESTIONNAIRE DATA

Syfers's essay was published in 1971. Do you think her points are still true today? Use the questionnaire below to find out. Then, write a one or two paragraph report in which you discuss your findings. You are writing this report for the general public. Your purpose is to inform. Ask two Americans—one man and one woman—to read Syfers's essay, "Why I Want a Wife." Next, ask each of them to complete the following questionnaire.

Questionnaire

Background information about the Americans

_____   _____   _____

Gender   Age   Education Completed

                                                    _____

Approximate income (if the subject cares to say)

_____

Marital Status (married, single, divorced)

Questions

1. Do you think Syfers's points are still true today?

   _____

   _____

2. Why or why not?

   _____

   _____

Bring the results of the questionnaire to class and compile the results with all your classmates. Analyze the results on the chalkboard. Then, as a class discuss the Americans' responses to Question 2. Try to explain the responses.

WRITE

Put pen to paper (or hands to keyboard) and write about the class findings.

Listening

Listen to Martin Luther King, Jr.'s audiotaped speech at home again.

BEFORE YOU LISTEN

Before you listen to the speech, think about King's struggle to help African-Americans* receive equal rights in the United States. In what ways is the struggle of African-Americans similar to the struggle of women?

WHILE YOU LISTEN

Write a list of the phrases and sentences which Martin Luther King, Jr. uses repeatedly to express the unequal treatment which African-Americans have received in the United States. Try to determine why King uses repetition as frequently as he does.

AFTER YOU LISTEN

Write a one paragraph reaction to Martin Luther King, Jr.'s speech.

Gaining Writing Competence

LEXICAL COHESION

Explanation: In the essay which you just read, Syfers repeats the phrase "I want a wife" again and again. She does this for two reasons: to make her essay unified and to avoid using feminine pronouns that would define her "wife" as necessarily being a female. Clearly, she "overuses" this expression to make a point about gender. In the audiotape which you just listened to, Martin Luther King, Jr. gave a persuasive speech in which he, like Syfers, repeated vocabulary words very effectively. In the writing task which follows you will write a persuasive essay in which you explain why you want (or do not want) a woman to pick up after you. You will need to know how to write cohesively so that your writing "flows" and your sentences link together smoothly. The activities that follow will help you gain this knowledge. One way to get your writing "to flow" is through *lexical* cohesion. You have already heard how King used this kind of cohesion. Some writers achieve lexical cohesion by repeating key vocabulary words again and again. Other writers use related vocabulary words. Yet other writers state the same thing in different words. They use synonyms or paraphrases to do this. Effective writers use all three types of lexical cohesion listed on page 57.

---

*Today, many blacks are proud of both their African and their American heritages. They use the term *African-American* instead of *black* to express their pride. The term *Negro* is considered a discriminatory term.

1. **Repeat key vocabulary words again and again.**
   <u>I want a wife</u> who will take care of the details of my social life. When my wife and I are invited out by friends, <u>I want a wife</u> who will take care of the babysitting arrangements. When I meet people at school that I like and want to entertain, <u>I want a wife</u> who will have the house clean, will prepare a special meal, serve it to me and my friends, and not interrupt when I talk about things that interest me and my friends.

2. **Use related vocabulary words.**
   I belong to that classification of people known as <u>wives</u>. I am A <u>Wife</u>.

3. **Say the same thing in different words.**
   <u>I want a wife who is a good nurturant attendant to my children</u>, who arranges for their schooling, makes sure that they have an adequate social life with their peers, takes them to the park, the zoo, etc. <u>I want a wife who takes care of the children</u> when they are sick, a wife who arranges to be around when the children need special care, because, of course, I cannot miss classes at school.

LEARNING STRATEGY

Forming Concepts: Analyzing good writing enables you to discover the techniques used by expert writers.

Gaining Writing Practice: Lexical Cohesion

EXERCISE 13

Find a partner who sits close to you. Analyze the use of lexical cohesion in Judy Syfers's essay. When you have finished, report your findings from this analysis to the class.

EXERCISE 14

Practice using lexical cohesion. Write one paragraph explaining why you want something (a dog, cat, car, personal computer, secretary, or friend). You are writing for your instructor and yourself. Your purpose is to experiment with lexical cohesion.

Gaining Writing Competence: Text Analysis

PARAGRAPH TRANSITIONS

Explanation: When writing your persuasive essay, you will want to make sure that there are smooth transitions between paragraphs. These transitions satisfy the reader's subconscious desire for unity and organization. In "I Want a Wife," Judy Syfers relies on different techniques to make the relationships between paragraphs clear. She shows the transitions or relationships between paragraphs in the six different ways listed on page 58:

1. by repeating key words
2. by using words which are related in meaning and/or form
3. by restating ideas in different words
4. by repeating ideas which are related in meaning
5. by using transitional words and phrases
6. by raising questions and answering them

The exercise below will help you understand the use of these techniques.

EXERCISE 15

Analyze the ways that Judy Syfers provides smooth transitions between paragraphs. You will need to examine the last sentence in each paragraph and the first sentence in the next paragraph. Try to determine how these two sentences are connected. Note that in some cases Syfers uses lexical cohesion, while in other cases she does not. Follow these examples.

Paragraphs one and two: Syfers uses two words, *mother* and *divorce* which are loosely related in meaning to the category, *family*.

Paragraphs two and three: Paragraph two asks a question. Paragraph three answers a question.

Paragraphs three and four: _____

_____

Paragraphs four and five: _____

_____

Paragraphs five and six: _____

_____

Paragraphs six and seven: _____

_____

Paragraphs seven and eight: _____

_____

Paragraphs eight and nine: _____

_____

Paragraphs nine and ten: _____

_____

Writing Task

WRITING A PERSUASIVE ESSAY

Write a one to two page essay in which you explain why you want (or do not want) a woman to pick up after you. The readers are your classmates. Your purpose is to persuade them that you are correct. Don't forget to repeat key vocabulary words again and again, use related words and synonyms, and paraphrase key ideas. Also, provide smooth transitions between paragraphs.

BEFORE YOU WRITE

Read the guidelines for writing a persuasive essay.

GUIDELINES FOR WRITING A PERSUASIVE ESSAY

Perhaps you have a particular theory, hypothesis, opinion, attitude, solution, or idea that you want to convince your readers of. You can write a persuasive essay to get your readers to agree with you.

1. Focus on one idea about which you can make a strong case or argument.

    EXAMPLES: Wives are unnecessary. Husbands can prevent their wives from having fun. Wives do most of the housework.

2. Focus on an idea with two arguments, one *for* something and one *against* something. (See examples above.)
3. Do not focus on general statements of fact.
4. Highlight the main idea of your persuasive essay in some way. You can highlight it by:
   • stating it clearly
   • stating it forcefully
   • giving good reasons for supporting it

ORGANIZATION OF THE PERSUASIVE ESSAY

FIRST PARAGRAPH

Your first paragraph normally states your reason for writing. It should capture your reader's interest and reflect your attitude.

MIDDLE PARAGRAPHS/THE BODY

Your middle paragraphs contain your arguments in favor of your case as well as your counterarguments. They state your facts and statistics in a logical sequence.

LAST PARAGRAPH

In the last paragraph, emphasize your main point. If you want the reader to take action, now is the time to ask for it. Leave a forceful impression on the reader. Make the summation of your arguments very brief and pointed. Persuasive essays do not call for a word-for-word repetition of what you have stated previously.

USEFUL EXPRESSIONS TO SHOW STRONG BELIEF	
I support/I reject the idea that	I support the idea that wives are necessary. I reject the idea that wives are necessary.
I am certain that	I am certain that wives are necessary.
I am convinced that	I am convinced that wives are necessary.
There is no question that	There is no question that wives are necessary.
In my opinion, . . .	In my opinion, wives are necessary.
Undoubtedly, . . .	Undoubtedly, wives are necessary.

Consider this strategy:

LEARNING STRATEGY

Personalizing: Shaping your writing topic to your own personal interests helps you to overcome limitations and communicate more effectively.

Dear authors! Suit your topic to your strength
And ponder well your subject
And its length

—Lord Byron

If you do not like the essay topic, change it a bit. For example, instead of describing why you want a woman to pick up after you, describe why you want a man to pick up after you. Or, narrow the topic in such a way that you identify a specific person (such as your mother, a good friend, your husband or wife) who you want to pick up after you. You can change the topic significantly if you link your new topic to the original one by stating something like, "I'm a student and while I don't need a woman to pick after me, I do need a woman to type my papers." (Note that if you choose a topic which is too different than the one assigned, you may be penalized. Check with your instructor whenever in doubt!)

Take out a piece of paper and write a list of all the chores that you have to do. Then, circle the ones that you do not like doing yourself. Next, underline the chores that you would like someone else to do.

WRITE

Try to write your entire essay in one sitting. This will help you generate your ideas and organize them. Concentrate on expressing your ideas. Do not worry about your grammar.

WHILE YOU ARE WRITING YOUR FIRST DRAFT

Consider this strategy:

LEARNING STRATEGY

Overcoming Limitations: When you can't think of what to write in English, write it in your native language so you can avoid "writer's block"—not being able to write further.

Don't worry about falling back on your native language. You can always go back over your writing later. At that time, you can paraphrase what you want to say in English, use a native English speaker to help you express yourself, or use your bilingual dictionary to translate a word or phrase.

This strategy is particularly useful when you are getting your ideas together or writing the first draft of your essay.

REVISE

You are ready to begin the revision process. Exchange papers with a partner. Read your papers aloud to one another. When you have finished, complete the Peer Response Form for both papers. Then, use the Peer Response Form to revise your essay.

PEER RESPONSE FORM

1. Does the author of the persuasive essay focus on one idea? Is the idea stated clearly? Is the idea stated forcefully?
2. Does the author of the persuasive essay present a strong case or argument for the case? Does the author provide good reasons for supporting his or her case or argument?
3. Does the author use lexical cohesion appropriately?
4. Does the author use smooth transitions between paragraphs? Between which paragraphs could better transitions be made?
5. What suggestion can you make for improving this essay?
6. What was your favorite part of this essay?

EDIT YOUR ESSAY

Consider this strategy:

LEARNING STRATEGY

Overcoming Limitations: Resources such as dictionaries, thesauruses, and grammar reference books can help you express yourself accurately and precisely, and can push you past your current limits.

Use a dictionary to correct your spelling errors. Use a thesaurus to find more vivid, expressive vocabulary words. Use your grammar reference book to improve the grammatical accuracy of your sentences. Read the strategy below.

LEARNING STRATEGY

Understanding and Using Emotions: Rewarding yourself for using English encourages you to use it more.

Give yourself a reward for finishing a writing assignment. Give yourself something that you really value. A new pen? A visit to your friend's house? A swim? A bike ride? A quiet walk? A good movie?

LEARNING STRATEGY

Managing Your Learning: At the editing stage, put all your ideas on paper, and organize them the way you want them.

Additional Reading

Explanation: The additional reading selection below will provide you with more information about gender and power. After reading it, you will respond to it in writing.

About the Reading

Women who have struggled against subtle forms of discrimination are often able to achieve power. In the following excerpt from Gloria Steinem's volume, *Revolution from Within,* a woman successfully finds power in a prison. This woman was imprisoned for prostitution. To help you understand the story, some of the words have been glossed.

WHILE YOU READ

As you read the story, ask yourself the questions listed below.

1. What did the woman do wrong?
2. Is it fair to jail prostitutes but not their customers?
3. Steinem seems to think that the woman in her story was discriminated against. Why?
4. How is prostitution viewed in the United States and in other cultures?
5. How did the woman in the story eventually obtain power?

EXCERPTS FROM *REVOLUTION FROM WITHIN*

Gloria Steinem

1   A woman explained that she had first seen *Ms.* magazine in a Michigan prison when she was serving time for prostitution. After reading an issue or two, she began to wonder: "Why am I in prison, but my customer and my pimp° are not? If prostitution is a crime, why is the seller arrested—but not the buyer?"

2   Remembering a movie about a prisoner who had read law books and become his own advocate,° the woman went to the prison library. In her state, she was told, only men's prisons had law books. Made more rebellious by this news, she organized a few other women prisoners to protest. When the state's criminal-code° books finally arrived, she began reading, and soon she was answering questions for other prisoners about their problems of regaining custody° of children put in foster homes,° or of getting children job training to support themselves. Once out of prison, she went to a local women's law firm for a clerical job. Knowing motivation when they saw it, they hired her.

3   To make an extraordinary story short, she passed a high school equivalency° exam,° entered college at night, and gradually moved from filing, to secretarial, and then to paralegal° work. Some years later, she finished law school itself.

Source: Gloria Steinem, 1991. *Revolution from Within: A Book of Self-Esteem.* Boston: Little, Brown and Company, p. 14.

VOCABULARY GLOSS

The definitions given below will improve your comprehension of the story. Note the glossed words in the reading passage. Numbers in the parenthesis to the right of the word refer to the paragraph in which the word appears. Not all words that you do not understand are glossed. Guess the meanings of those words in the reading selection which you do not understand.

pimp (1) (n.)	a man who hires prostitutes to work for him and who finds the prostitutes clients
advocate (2) (n.)	one that promotes the cause of another
criminal-code (2) (adj.)	law
custody (2) (n.)	the immediate responsibility for and authority of
foster homes (2) (n.)	homes which provide the care for children that their parents are unable or unwilling to provide
high school equivalency exam (3) (n.)	a test which gives credit for work not completed in high school
paralegal (3) (n.)	one who helps a lawyer; a lawyer's assistant

Comprehension Workout

EXERCISE 16

Fill in the blanks with a "T" if the statement is true or an "F" if the statement is false. Write the number of the paragraph (¶) which includes information to support your answer if the answer is explicitly stated in the story.

_____ **1.** The woman described by Steinem was serving time in prison for stealing money. (¶ ___)

_____ **2.** While in prison, the woman read *Time* magazine. (¶ ___)

_____ **3.** The woman decided that she was unfairly punished. (¶ ___)

_____ **4.** The woman wanted to become her own legal advocate. (inference)

_____ **5.** The woman was happy because there were no law books in her prison. (¶ ___)

_____ **6.** While in prison, the woman organized a protest. (¶ ___)

_____ **7.** Because of the woman's protests, her prison received criminal-code books. (inference)

_____ **8.** The woman provided other women with legal advice. (¶ ___)

_____ **9.** Once out of prison, the woman studied business management. (¶ ___)

_____ **10.** Today, the woman is a practicing attorney. (inference)

Quick Write

WRITING A REACTION PAPER

Write a one page reaction paper. React to the story. You are writing for your classmates. The purpose is to persuade them to accept your perspective of the story. Express your opinion strongly.

BEFORE YOU WRITE

Discuss the following questions in small groups.

1. Why was the woman in the story arrested? What did she do wrong?
2. In the United States, prostitution is illegal. Would the woman have been arrested in a different country? Why?
3. How is prostitution viewed in the United States? How is it viewed in other countries?
4. Is it fair to jail prostitutes but not their pimps or customers?
5. Was the woman in the story discriminated against? Why?
6. Did the woman in the story eventually obtain power? How?

7. Steinem fails to provide the reader with much information about the woman in the story. Which of the following words do you *think* might best describe her? If there are any words that your group does not know, ask your instructor to explain them to you.

assertive	energetic
cautious	ethical
compassionate	lethargic
competent	outgoing
confident	rebellious
courageous	resourceful
creative	shy
critical	self-conscious
diligent	self-pitying

WRITE

You are now ready to write your reaction.

Grammar Explanation

DEFINITE ARTICLES

Explanation: Many ESL students complain that they have difficulty using the definite article *the* correctly. Here are some very general guidelines for definite article use.

1. Normally, use *the* before nouns that have been previously mentioned.
   This lesson focuses on <u>grammar</u>. <u>The grammar</u> is not hard.
   I saw some <u>women</u>. <u>The women</u> were participating in a demonstration.
2. *The* is often used with *heavy nouns*. Heavy nouns are ones which have many modifiers.
   Some men discriminate against women. The women <u>who they discriminate against</u> are often young.
   The <u>intelligent</u> women <u>with the notebooks</u> received the worst treatment.
3. *The* is never used with plural count nouns (such as *books*) when you are making a generalization.
   Specific: <u>The books</u> that are written by Steinem are good.
   General: <u>Books</u> are good.

Editing Practice: Definite Articles

EXERCISE 17

The following reading passage has many grammatical inaccuracies relating to the absence of definite articles where required. *Twelve* articles are incorrectly omitted. Alone or with a partner, edit the passage.

About the Reading

In this reading, Melvin Tumin discusses the work of the anthropologist, Margaret Mead. Mead's studies of the Arapesh, a tribal community in Papua, New Guinea, show that men and women in Arapesh culture in the 1930s held very different roles than men and women in the United States.

READING: THE ARAPESH

Melvin Tumin

1   Arapesh life is organized around the way that women and men, physically different and possessing different abilities, share a common adventure. This adventure is primarily maternal, loving, and directed away from self toward needs of next generation. In Arapesh culture, women and men do different things for same reasons. It is a culture in which men are not expected to have one set of motives and women another.

2   **Who Does What.** When the Arapesh are questioned about the division of labor, they answer: cooking everyday food, bringing firewood and water, weaving, and carrying—these are women's work. Cooking ceremonial food, carrying pigs and heavy logs, housebuilding, sewing the material for the roofs of huts, clearing and building fences, carving, hunting, and growing sweet potatoes—these are men's work. Making ornaments and care of children—these are the work of both men and women. If the wife's task is more import ant at moment than the husband's, if there are no greens for evening meal, or a leg of meat must be carried to neighbors in next village—the husband stays home and takes care of baby.

3   **Arapesh Attitudes Toward Children.** The Arapesh regard both women and men as naturally gentle, sensitive, and cooperative. Adults of both sexes are willing and able to consider their own needs as less important than needs of those who are younger and weaker—and receive satisfaction from doing so. They are delighted in part of parenthood that we consider to be especially maternal—loving care for little child and selfless delight in that child's progress toward maturity.

Source: Adapted from Melvin M. Tumin. 1980. *Foundations in Social Studies: Male and Female in Today's World.* Harcourt Brace Jovanovich, Inc., reprinted by permission of the publisher. "The Arapesh" is an adaptation originally based on material from *Sex and Temperament in Three Primitive Societies* by Margaret Mead, copyright 1935, 1950, 1963 by Margaret Mead, reprinted by permission of William Morrow & Co., Inc.

Gaining Writing Competence

MAKING COMPARISONS AND CONTRASTS

Explanation: In the next writing activity, you will write a comparison-contrast essay in which you describe the advantages and disadvantages of being a woman. The following information will help you to write this essay.

COMPARISONS AND CONTRASTS

When you write about the similarities of two objects, people, or ideas, you are making a comparison. When you write about their differences, you are making a contrast.

1. In order to compare two things, these things must be logically equivalent.

   Incorrect: The work that women do is comparable to men.

   work   ≠   men

   Correct: The work that women do is comparable to that of men.

   work   =   that . . .

   Correct: The work that women do is comparable to men's.

   work   =   men's

2. Take about the same amount of writing space for discussing X as you do when you discuss Y. Also, discuss the same characteristics of X and Y when you compare them.

   Incorrect: Slaves have no liberty. They do not have the freedom to say what they want, to attend the Church of their choice, to raise their children as they like. They must do as their masters direct. Similarly, wives lack freedom.

   Correct: Slaves have no liberty. They do not have the freedom to say what they want, to attend the Church of their choice, to raise their children as they like. They must do as their masters direct. Similarly, wives lack freedom. Like slaves, they have no freedom to speak what is on their minds. In addition, they have no religious freedom, since they must attend the religious institute of their husband. Moreover, like slaves, they must do whatever their masters—that is, their husbands—demand.

THE BLOCK STYLE AND THE POINT-BY-POINT STYLE

Although you can organize a comparison-contrast essay in several different ways, there are two major ones: the block style and the point-by-point style.

BLOCK STYLE

The block style looks like this.

Situation A
Point 1
Point 2
Point 3

Situation B
Point 1
Point 2
Point 3

EXAMPLE: John is better than Henry. He is smart, honest, and hard-working. In contrast, Henry is stupid, dishonest, and lazy. Not surprisingly, I'd rather know John than Henry.

In the *block style,* the characteristics of one person are contrasted with the characteristics of another.

THE POINT-BY-POINT STYLE

The point-by-point style looks like this.

Situation A	Situation B
Point 1	Point 1
Point 2	Point 2
Point 3	Point 3

In the *point-by-point style,* two types of people are contrasted first in terms of one point and then in terms of another.

EXAMPLE: John is better than Henry. He is smart, while Henry is stupid. John is honest, while Henry is dishonest. John is hard-working, while Henry is lazy. Not surprisingly, I'd rather know John than Henry.

Useful Expressions for Writing Comparison-Contrast Essays

TRANSITION WORDS

Comparisons	Contrasts
and	on the other hand
moreover	in contrast
furthermore	but
similarly	however
in the same vein	by contrast
also	whereas
too	

COMPARISONS	EXAMPLES

1. (Both) X and Y are <u>the same</u>.
           alike
           similar
           comparable

Men and women are similar.

2. X and Y have   <u>many similarities</u>.
             much in common

Men and women have many
   similarities.

3. X is the same as Y.
   X is similar to Y.
   X resembles Y.

A man is the same as a woman.

4. X is as _____ as Y.

A man is as hard-working as a woman.

5. X and Y <u>share</u>   many   <u>similarities</u>.
        have   characteristics

Men and women share
   many characteristics.

6. <u>One</u> similarity   <u>is</u> . . .
   Another   concerns
   Yet another

One similarity concerns work.
Another similarity concerns happiness.
Yet another similarity concerns liberty.

CONTRASTS	EXAMPLES

1. X and Y differ.

Men and women differ.

2. There are many differences
   between X and Y.

There are many differences between
   men and women.

3. X and Y are very different.

Men and women are very different.

4. X and Y have many different
   <u>characteristics</u>
   traits

Men and women have many
   different characteristics.

5. X and Y are <u>different</u>.
          dissimilar

Men and women are dissimilar.

6. X differs from Y.

Men differ from women.

7. X is more/less/-er than Y.

Men are lazier than women.

8. <u>One</u>   difference   <u>is</u> . . .
   Another   concerns

Yet another

One difference concerns work habits.
Another difference concerns
   competence.
Yet another difference concerns
   attitude.

Writing Task

WRITING A COMPARISON-CONTRAST ESSAY

In a short essay, of approximately one page in length, compare and contrast the advantages and disadvantages of being a woman. You are writing this essay for your classmates. Your purpose is to write an analytical, objective essay in which you provide an accurate account of the advantages and disadvantages of being a woman.

BEFORE YOU BEGIN

Consider this strategy:

LEARNING STRATEGY

Forming Concepts: Guessing the characteristics of the readers of your writing helps you write effectively.

Before beginning your writing, guess the characteristics of your readers. Complete the Audience Profile below.

AUDIENCE PROFILE

1. Who is going to read my writing?
2. What are these readers interested in?
3. What could I write to make them want to read my writing?
4. What are their beliefs? For instance, are they politically conservative or liberal? Do they believe that males and females are equal, or do they believe that one of the genders is more "powerful" than the other?
5. How old are they?
6. What is their gender?
7. What is their ethnicity?
8. How formal do I need to be?
9. How polite should I be?

Find a partner. Fill in the chart below. Then, discuss what you intend to write.

ADVANTAGES OF BEING A WOMAN	DISADVANTAGES OF BEING A WOMAN
1. At school	
a. _____	_____
2. At work	
a. _____	_____

b. _____   _____

c. _____   _____

3. At home

a. _____   _____

b. _____   _____

c. _____   _____

4. In leadership positions

a. _____   _____

b. _____   _____

c. _____   _____

WRITE YOUR FIRST DRAFT

While you are writing, if you find you have difficulty with this assignment, review the guidelines for writing comparison-contrast essays. (See also pages 67–69.)

AFTER YOU WRITE YOUR FIRST DRAFT

Read your essays to each other. Divide into groups of about six students. It is best for all the students in a group to sit in a circle for this activity. You should take your name off the top of your essay if you want to remain anonymous. You have five minutes to read and respond to a classmate's essay, underline your favorite section, put a question in the margin of one part of the essay that is unclear, and jot down any interesting ideas on a sheet of scratch paper.

The teacher will give you five minutes to read and respond to a classmate's essay. At the end of the five-minute period, exchange papers with another student. If you are sitting in a circle, pass papers to the right. (If you are sitting in rows, pass papers to the person who sits in front of you. The person sitting in the front of the row can take his or her essay to the person at the end of the row.) Continue exchanging essays until you have read and responded to all the essays written by the students in your group.

REVISE YOUR ESSAY

When you revise your essay, use your notes from this activity. Make any changes to the content or organization of your own essay that you like. The Revision Checklist below may be helpful in this stage of the writing process.

REVISION CHECKLIST

_____ **1.** My essay contains an interesting introduction which makes the reader want to read the rest of my essay.

_____ **2.** My thesis statement is stated clearly and is easy to understand.

_____ **3.** I have written just as much about the advantages of being a woman as I have about the disadvantages.

_____ **4.** There are smooth transitions between my paragraphs.

_____ **5.** I have used different ways to make my writing unified.

_____ **6.** A conclusion effectively ends my essay.

EDIT

When you have finished revising your writing, consider this strategy:

LEARNING STRATEGY

Managing Your Learning: Identifying major grammar problems helps you overcome these problems.

List your three major grammar problems below.

1. _____

2. _____

3. _____

Read your writing aloud three times. Edit your essay as you do this. First, focus on one of your grammar mistakes, and try to correct mistakes of that type. Then, focus on the second type of grammar mistake and try to correct mistakes of that type. Then, focus on the third type of grammar mistake and try to correct that type of error.

Quick Write

REPORTING SURVEY DATA

In this lesson, you examined power and gender. Through the reading and writing activities, you investigated the treatment of women. In this Quick Write activity, you will consider one aspect of power and gender not previously addressed: male and female views of power. Write a two paragraph report in which you compare and contrast the way the males in your class answered the survey questions given on page 5 and the way the females in your class answered these questions. Your audience is that part of the general public which is interested in statistics. Your purpose is to inform.

BEFORE YOU WRITE

As a class, analyze the data on the chalkboard. This time, compare the way the females and males answered the survey questions. Your instructor will write the words "female response" on the right side of the chalkboard and "male response" on the left and will record the responses. After the responses are recorded, discuss them as a class. You will need to take out a clean sheet of paper. Copy down the results so that you can refer to them when you write. Divide up into small groups of the same gender to discuss the results. As a group, try to identify two or three major differences in the ways in which the males and females responded. Discuss your findings with the class.

WRITE

You are ready to write your report.

REWRITE

Rewrite your report.

Using a Language Learning Log

1. Vocabulary
Write down as many new words from the lesson as you can remember.

_____

_____

_____

2. Grammar

Note examples of any grammatical structures from the lesson learned or reviewed. Write a brief explanation of the grammar points that they illustrate.

_____

_____

_____

3. Punctuation

Write down any new punctuation rules that you learned.

_____

_____

_____

IT WORKS!
Learning Strategy:
Keeping Track of
Your Progress

4. Techniques for Gaining Writing Competence

List any new composition techniques that you learned. (Such techniques might include those for making your writing cohesive; writing interesting introductions, bodies, and conclusions; and composing different types of writing effectively.)

_____

_____

_____

5. Learning Strategies

Briefly describe any new learning strategies that you have applied in your writing.

_____

_____

_____

6. Areas that Need More Work

Note here in brief form any areas that you are still trying to improve. Try to be as specific as possible.

_____

_____

_____

SUMMARY OF LESSON 3: CAN WOMEN BE POWERFUL?

This lesson has focused on power and gender. The tasks involved writing a persuasive essay, reacting to a reading, composing a comparison-contrast essay, and reporting survey data. All of the activities in this lesson were designed to help you complete the writing assignment on pages 75-76.

QUICK REFERENCE TO LEARNING STRATEGIES

Forming Concepts: Exploring Your Knowledge of and Opinions about a Topic (p. 51)

Forming Concepts: Analyzing Good Writing to Discover Techniques (p. 57)

Personalizing: Shaping the Writing Assignment Topic to Your Own Interests (p. 60)

Overcoming Limitations: Switching to Your Native Language (p. 61)

Overcoming Limitations: Using Resources (p. 62)

Understanding and Using Emotions: Using Rewards (p. 62)

Managing Your Learning: Organizing Your Ideas (p. 62)

Forming Concepts: Making Inferences About Your Readers (p. 70)

Managing Your Learning: Identifying Major Grammar Problems (p. 72)

Description of Writing Assignment

Write an essay about your own experience with power. Your essay should be one to two double-spaced, typed pages or two to three double-spaced handwritten pages. You may want to describe a specific situation in which you felt powerful. Your audience for this particular topic is that part of the general public who is interested in people, and your purpose is to entertain them.

PREWRITING ACTIVITIES

GUIDED DISCUSSION

It is helpful to discuss your ideas before you write your essay. Find a partner and tell each other about the essay that you plan to write. The following questions may be helpful:

1. What does personal power mean?
2. How can personal power be described?
3. What are the component parts of personal power?
4. How did I obtain personal power?
5. What are the causes of my power?
6. What did I do with my power?
7. How can actions which resulted from my power affect others?
8. What is a story which involves my use of personal power?
9. What is my personal response to my own power?
10. What is the value of personal power?

BRAINSTORMING

Brainstorming involves thinking quickly so as to give as many different ideas as possible about a given topic. It is an especially good way to generate ideas and to get ideas organized before you start a writing assignment. Find a partner with whom you have not worked before. Generate as many ideas about the topic as you can.

FAST WRITING

After you brainstorm, you may want to use *fast writing,* a technique writers use to develop their ideas and relate them quickly. Because speed is important in this activity, it is best to limit your writing to twenty minutes. Follow the directions below.

DIRECTIONS FOR FAST WRITING

1. Focus on ideas, not on grammar.
2. Write as quickly as you can and do not stop writing.
3. Do not bother to correct any mistakes that you make.
4. If you can't think of a word you need, use another one or write in your native language.
5. When you are finished with your essay, use a dictionary or rely on your teachers to help you replace translated or incorrect words with correct English words.

REVISING ACTIVITIES

Once you have written your first draft, you can read what you wrote and make any changes that you like. When revising your essay, concentrate on improving the organization and content of your writing. Use the following Peer Review Sheet and Response Form to provide your peers with encouragement and constructive criticism.

PEER REVIEW SHEET

Reviewers: _____

Paper which is being reviewed: _____

Describe the best part of this essay.

_____

Does the author define "power" or any other terms which require definition?

_____

Is the thesis clearly stated?

_____

Is the introduction interesting?

_____

Is the main idea of each paragraph clear?

_____

Are there any details which do not belong in the essay?

_____

Did the author provide enough examples from his or her own experience or from
    the reading?

_____

Is the conclusion effective?

_____

How can the author improve this essay? Give the author specific suggestions.

_____

_____

Response Form

I agree with the following comments:

_____

These are the changes I want to make in response to the reviewers' suggestions:

_____

I disagree with the following comments:

_____

I need help with the following parts of the essay:

_____ introduction

_____ thesis

_____ body

_____ conclusion

_____ vocabulary

_____ transitions

_____ content

_____ grammar

_____ other (please describe):

From Lebauer, R. 1985. Class Observation, UCI.

When you give your teacher your final paper, tear out this page and submit it with your paper.

EDITING ACTIVITY

Use a checklist when you edit your final essay. Before turning in your final essay, check the following points.

CHECKLIST

Content and Organization

_____ **1.** My thesis is clearly stated.

_____ **2.** I define "power" and other terms requiring definitions.

_____ **3.** The main idea of each paragraph is clear.

_____ **4.** Each paragraph supports my thesis statement.

_____ **5.** I provide enough examples from my own experience or from the reading.

_____ **6.** My conclusion is effective.

_____ **7.** I have responded to my peers' suggestions.

Language

Grammar

_____ **1.** I have corrected verb tense mistakes.

_____ **2.** I have corrected mistakes involving count and noncount nouns.

_____ **3.** I have corrected mistakes involving definite and indefinite articles.

_____ **4.** I have corrected mistakes involving pronouns.

Vocabulary

_____ **1.** I have avoided using the same words again and again.

_____ **2.** I have avoided using such slang expressions as "guy," "you know," and "kid."

_____ **3.** I have used vivid, colorful words and have avoided using very general words such as "thing" and "nice."

SHARING YOUR WRITING

In small groups, choose those writings which best illustrate what you have learned in this chapter. Then, share them with the rest of the class and your teacher.

Power through Force

A just war is better than an unjust peace.

Better lean peace than fat victory.

Broken bones set well become stronger.

INTRODUCTION

In the last unit, you examined various views of personal power. In this unit, you will learn about a different type of power: that which is gained through force. As you complete the writing assignments for this unit, try to determine your own views of force and violence. Is violence ever justified? Can violence be used to obtain power?

Your main task will be to contribute to a collection of class readings. Your contribution to the collection of readings will be an essay which compares two types of violence. Specific essay assignments are given on pages 143–145.

Needs Analysis and Goal Setting

Before you start this unit, find out about your own learning needs, preferences, and goals.

SELF-EVALUATION OF LEARNING ACTIVITIES

First, check the boxes below which apply to you.

ACTIVITY	I LIKE	IT'S OKAY	I DON'T LIKE
Reading stories	___	___	___
Reading essays	___	___	___
Reacting to audiotapes in a journal	___	___	___
Doing grammar exercises	___	___	___
Doing group work	___	___	___
Collecting and analyzing survey data	___	___	___
Analyzing the organization of stories and essays	___	___	___
Writing definitions	___	___	___
Writing summaries	___	___	___
Writing letters	___	___	___
Writing stories	___	___	___
Writing persuasive essays	___	___	___
Writing essays in which you compare and contrast	___	___	___
Reporting survey data	___	___	___

Next, identify your goals for this unit. Complete the self-diagnosis of writing goals below. Number the goals below from 1 to 11 with 1 as your most important goal and 11 as your least important goal. When you set goals, you gain power over your own learning process.

SELF-DIAGNOSIS OF WRITING GOALS

My goals are:

_____ to write cohesive essays (ones which stick together)

_____ to write an interesting introduction

_____ to improve my grammar

_____ to improve my vocabulary

_____ to improve my punctuation

_____ to learn how to write a definition

_____ to learn how to write a summary

_____ to learn how to write a story

_____ to learn how to write a formal business letter

_____ to learn how to write a paragraph to compare and contrast

_____ to learn how to write a persuasive essay

Cooperative Learning

NUMBERED HEADS TOGETHER

Divide up into teams of four. Number off within groups (one, two, three, or four). Discuss each question carefully. Make sure that everyone in your group knows the answer. Your team will have five minutes per question to discuss the answer to one of the questions. Your instructor will call out the number of a question. After five minutes, your instructor will call out a number from one to four. Only students with that number can raise their hand if they have the answer.

Question 1: What are five types of physical violence?

Question 2: In what specific situations, if any, is war justifiable?

Question 3: What are five reasons that nations fight against each other?

Question 4: What are two different ways to prevent nations from engaging in war against each other?

Question 5: Does the notion of violence vary across cultures? In answering this question, you may want to consider whether some cultures tolerate acts of aggression more than others.

Survey

How do your classmates feel about war? Do they justify war in all circumstances or only in some circumstances? Do they believe that "all is fair in love and war," or do they think that some types of warfare (including the use of poison or viruses as weapons) should be prohibited? Find out how your classmates feel. Later, you will be asked to write a brief report of the findings. Complete the survey below. Fill in the blanks with "T" if you believe the statement is true and with "F" if you believe that the statement is false.

SURVEY: ATTITUDES TOWARDS PHYSICAL VIOLENCE

Feelings about Physical Violence

_____ 1. I would like to fight in a war.

_____ 2. I want my children to fight in a war.

_____ 3. I think war is honorable.

_____ 4. A battlefield is an interesting place.

_____ 5. War is terrifying.

Reasons for Physical Violence

_____ 6. A good reason to fight others is to obtain power over them.

_____ 7. I would never kill anyone under any circumstances.

_____ 8. It is okay to kill another person who wants to take away my freedom of speech.

_____ 9. I want my country to fight against any nation that threatens to take away my country's natural resources.

_____ 10. It is okay to kill someone who tries to take away my house.

_____ 11. It is okay to kill someone who steals something from me.

_____ 12. Anyone who kills my mother or father should be killed.

_____ 13. Defending other nations from Fascist nations is a good reason for war.

_____ 14. Defending one's country (not necessarily one's own property) is a justifiable reason for a war.

_____ 15. International conflicts between countries should be settled in international courtrooms, not on the battlefield.

Weapons

_____ 16. Poison should be used in war.

_____ 17. Nuclear weapons are good.

_____ 18. Viruses are good weapons which should be used in warfare.

_____ 19. It is good for children to play with war toys.

_____ 20. Civilians should be allowed to carry guns.

As a class, tally all of the students' responses to the items on the chalkboard. Then, compile the results. If possible, try to identify several major findings from your class survey. Take notes. You will be using them throughout this chapter. When you have finished analyzing the data, discuss possible reasons for the results.

LESSON 1: IMPRESSIONS OF WAR

Overview

The focus of this particular lesson is impressions of war. You will study the sights and sounds of war as well as the emotions associated with war. You will write a personal letter which describes the sights and sounds of war and expresses feelings as well as a short essay in which you compare and contrast the feelings of two different kinds of soldiers. The final writing assignment is a report on the survey data collected earlier.

About the Reading

The following excerpts came from interviews with soldiers.

WHILE YOU READ

As you read the excerpts, try to imagine the sights, sounds, and feelings associated with war.

Reading: The Sights, Sounds, and Feelings of War Excerpts from Interviews with Soldiers

WAR SMELLS EVIL

Hank Warner, a veteran of the Vietnam War, believes that war actually smells evil.

"When I remember the Vietnam War I think of the stench of dying soldiers. I remember the evil smells which rose from the fields where we hid. I remember the jungle with its different, sweeter smells which contrasted sharply with the evil smells of war."

THE SIGHTS OF WAR VIOLENCE ARE INHUMANE

Elie Wiesel was only sixteen when he was taken from his home and placed in a Jewish ghetto with his mother, father, and three sisters. From there, his family and he were deported to the Nazi concentration camp in Auschwitz,

Poland. He watched as the friends he knew died of illness and starvation, and others were killed in the gas chambers. When accepting the Nobel Peace Prize in 1986, he stated:

"I swore never to be silent whenever and wherever human beings endure suffering and humiliation. We must always take sides. Neutrality helps the oppressor, never the victim. Sometimes we must interfere. When human lives are endangered, when human dignity is in jeopardy, national borders and sensitivities become irrelevant. Wherever men or women are persecuted because of their race, religion, or political views, that place must—at that moment—become the center of the universe."

THE SIGHTS OF THE BATTLEFIELD CAN BE SERENE

Martha Hammer, a sergeant in the Marine Corps, speaks of the serenity of the battlefield in Kuwait.

"I looked over the battlefield. All was silent. I heard the comforting sounds of my friends speaking in low whispers. I gazed around. For miles around, I viewed gentle slopes and flat desert."

SOLDIERS FEEL EXCITED WHEN THE FIGHT BEGINS

José Rodriguez, a soldier from El Salvador, speaks of his excitement.

"For several days we waited for the fight to begin. Our nerves were on edge. We argued with one another, we lost our tempers easily, and we laughed for no reason. Then, when the fight began, we entered it enthusiastically. We were excited. We looked forward to crushing the enemy."

WAR SWEEPS EVERYTHING ASIDE

Naguib Mahfouz, a famous Arab novelist and winner of the Nobel Prize for Literature, states that war destroys the noble-minded.

"The innermost parts of the earth burst open, and it [violence] sweeps everything aside. Even noble-mindedness has its breathing choked."

THE LONGING FOR POWER MAKES PEOPLE LOSE THEIR REASON

Oscar Arias Sanchez, winner of the Nobel Peace Prize in 1987 for his role in securing peace in Costa Rica, argues that the desire for power drives people crazy.

"How ironic for peacemaking efforts to discover that hatred is stronger than love; that the longing to achieve power through military victories makes so many men lose their reason, forget all shame, and betray history."

VIOLENCE IS DEHUMANIZING

Desmond Mpilo Tutu, the South African politician who fought against apartheid and won the Nobel Peace Prize in 1984, claims that violence is dehumanizing.

"Perhaps oppression dehumanizes the oppressor as much as, if not more than, the oppressed. We need each other to become truly free, to become human. We can be human only in fellowship, in community, in *koinonia*, in peace."

Comprehension Workout

EXERCISE 20

Find a partner. Use the reading excerpts above as well as your own imagination. Discuss your lists with the class.

1. List three smells of the battlefield.
2. List three beautiful sights of the battlefield.
3. List three ugly sights of the battlefield.
4. List two emotions shared by soldiers before the fighting begins.
5. List two emotions shared by soldiers after the fighting begins.

Quick Write

WRITING ABOUT YOUR PERSONAL OPINION

Write a paragraph discussing whether it is possible that people from some cultures view the sights, smells, and feelings associated with war differently than people from other cultures. Your audience is yourself. Your purpose is to explore your own ideas.

Additional Reading

ABOUT THE READING

Naguib Mahfouz, the author of the story below, is a famous Arabic novelist who was awarded the Nobel Prize for Literature in 1988. Today, he lives in the Cairo suburb of Agouza. In this story, he uses dialog to portray the feelings associated with war. The story focuses on the feelings of Egyptians who experienced war during the 1940s.

Optional
Quick Write

Writing about Your
Personal Opinion: Write
a one paragraph reaction
to any of the quotes on
pages 85–86. Your
audience is yourself.
Your purpose is to
explore your own ideas.

BEFORE YOU READ

Try to imagine what it would be like to live in a war zone and face possible death. Answer these questions:

1. What would average citizens feel like? How would they go about their daily chores?
2. What would citizens see?
3. Are citizens innocent victims of war?

AS YOU READ

As you read through the story the first time, try to understand the organization of the story. Keep in mind the following questions, as they will help you figure out the way in which the story is developed.

1. Who are the main characters in the story? Identify these characters:
   Salama
   Mahmoud
   Amna
   Dahroug
2. Where does the story take place?
3. When does the story take place?
4. What exciting event happens in the story?
5. How does the story end?

Threads

The Memorial Day holiday was started in America in 1868 by General John A. Logan to honor the dead of the American Civil War (1861–1865).

A FUGITIVE FROM JUSTICE

Naguib Mahfouz

1   "The German army has invaded Polish territory. . ."
2   The news burst forth from the radio jammed in an aperture° in the wall of the sole room still standing in the ruins, and made its way beyond the boundaries of the vast Khafeer area.
3   "Quiet!" shouted Dahroug sharply. "Listen, the lot of you!"
4   The boy and his three sisters stopped making a noise. When they saw from their father's face that he was serious, they slunk off° between the piles of scrap iron, tires, and spare parts to the most distant part of the ruins. There they continued their games, safe from his wrath.

5   Amna, hanging out the washing, paused and raised her head above the line stretched between a bar in the window of the room and the roof of an old truck. "You scared away the children," she called out at her husband in protest. "That blasted radio and its news!"

6   Dahroug, without anger, ignored her. He took a last puff from the cigarette butt he held between his fingers. "It's war, then!" he said.

7   Salama realized the words were directed at him, so he raised his head from the tire he had been fixing. With eyes gleaming out of a face surrounded by a thick black beard that reached down his neck, the man stared back, then said scornfully, "Yes, they finally believed it."

8   While Dahroug's head was turned toward the radio, Salama seized the chance to steal a glance at the woman. His gaze lingered on her face that craned upward. . . . Then she turned her back on him, and Salama leaned over the wheel, thinking how terrible was war in the heat of August. How terrible the heat!

9   Dahroug turned toward him. "For a long time they've been predicting it will bring the world to ruin. But what's it to us?"

10   "We're far away," answered the bearded man, smiling. "Let them devour one another."

11   Dahroug crossed his legs as he sat on an upturned can and cast° a dreamy look far afield. "We heard fantastic things about the last war," he said.

12   "The fact is you're old," said Amna, laughing.

13   Dahroug gave a laugh through his blackened teeth, saying scornfully, "all you care about is your stomach."

14   Salama, who though no longer young was a good ten years younger than his companion, said, "Yes, we certainly heard some fantastic things."

15   "Look at al-Asyouti for instance, who was he? Before the war he was nothing but a porter.°"

16   The children, having forgotten the threats, returned and brought with them their rowdiness.° Mahmoud, a boy of seven and the eldest, was running about with the young girls trailing after him. His father glanced at him admiringly and called out, "Mahmoud, my boy, take courage—war's broken out."

17   In the late afternoon Dahroug and Salama sat together on a piece of sacking outside the fence around the ruins. Before them stretched the desert right up to the foot of the Muqattam Hills, the sands extinguished under their shadow. A faded yellowness, the remnants° of choked breaths of high summer, was diffused into the limpid° sky. Feeble rays from the inclining sun were quickly scaling the mountain summit, though the desert was puffing out a refreshing breeze with the approach of the evening.

18   Dahroug began counting piasters,° while Salama, his head resting against the fence, gazed distractedly toward the horizon, Amna brought tea, and the children, barefoot and half-naked, ran to the wasteland. Dahroug sipped a little of the hot tea.

19   "My heart tells me, Salama, that the work's going to really take off."

20   "May your heart be right, Abu Mahmoud."

21   "I wish I could rely on you."

22   "I'm your friend and indebted to you for your generous kindness, but I can't leave the ruins."

23   Dahroug thought for a while, then asked, "Does anyone in the big city know you behind the beard?"

24   "They know the very djinn° themselves."

25   "And will you spend your life in the ruins?"

26   "Better than the hangman's noose, Abu Mahmoud."

27   Dahroug laughed loud and said, "I have to laugh whenever I remember the story of your escape from between two guards."

28   "The best way of escaping is when it's not expected."

29   Amna was standing facing the wasteland, her shawl drawn back over her jet black hair. "And the man got bumped off without any blood money."

30   "He was a murderer, the son of a murderer," said Salama angrily. "He was so old I was afraid death would get to him before I did. My family went on demanding that I take revenge."

31   Dahroug guffawed loudly. "And you made your escape when the papers were on their way to the Mufti to endorse the death sentence."

32   Salama tugged at his arm in gratitude.° "And I found myself desperate and said, 'I've got no one but Dahroug, my childhood friend,' and you gave me shelter, you noblest of men."

33   "We're men of honor, Salama."

34   "In any case the storehouse here is in need of a man—and I'm that man."

35   Their conversation was interrupted by the appearance of a funeral procession on the horizon. It was coming from where the buildings stood and it continued toward the road opposite the western fence of the ruins that led to the Khafeer cemetery. The coffin, shrouded with a white silk covering, came into view.

36   "A young girl," muttered Amna. "How sad!"

37   "This place is beautiful and safe," said Salama. "The only thing wrong with it is it's on the road to the cemetery."

38   "Isn't it the road we all take?" said Dahroug, laughing.

39   The wasteland had remained substantially unchanged since war was declared. It was a playground for the sun from its rising to its setting, a place for passage for coffins, and encampment for silence. The sirens were sounded in exercise for imaginary air raids. The old battered radio achieved the height of importance when it allowed Dahroug to calculate the shells exchanged between the Siegfried and Maginot Lines.

40   Whenever Salama's senses registered the tones of Amna's melodious voice, or a playful movement or glance, even if not intentional, he became aflame with a voracious° fire and at the same time with a merciless anger against himself.

41   "Things haven't changed," said Dahroug morosely. "Where's all we heard about the war?"

42   "Be patient. Don't you remember what your Jewish commission agent said?"

43   Dahroug looked towards the piles of iron with which, acting on the advice of his agent, he had filled up the place. "Let the days pass quickly."

44   "Let them pass quickly—and let them swallow up fifteen years."

45   "Fifteen years?"

46   "Then my sentence° becomes null and void.°"

47   "What a lifetime! By then we'll be on the brink° of a third war."

48   Salama began singing in a strange, hoarse voice, "Come tell me, Bahiyya." Then he called out, "Master Dahroug, none of my family will be left but the women."

49   He told himself that Amna, without knowing it—or perhaps knowing it—was turning his head and that he would be going through hell before death took him. The war did not concern him in the least, but in between musical intervals on the radio he heard the news of Holland and of Belgium being overrun, and of the fall of Paris. In front of his eyes there passed the successive columns of refugees, and the void was filled with sighs and tears. Then Italy declared war. "It's knocking at the gates," said Dahroug uneasily.

50   But Salama was indifferent.° "For us it's neither hear nor there."

51   "The good Lord will look after us," muttered Amna as her gaze followed the naked children playing around a barrel filled with water.

52   For the first time the siren sounded for a real air raid. Dahroug and his family awoke, as did Salama, bedded down in the truck. Amna was frightened for the children and said that the shelter was too far away.

53   "Stay in the room," said Dahroug. "They won't bomb the wasteland or the cemetery."

54   Salama raised his head toward the full moon which stared down at them, eternally calm. "I see nothing but crazy lights," he said.

   .

   .

   .

55   The raids plunged down at the city and destroys all that exists in it: it topples the law, the Mufti, the judge, the warden° and the hangman's noose. The innermost parts of the earth burst open, and it sweeps everything aside. Even noblemindedness has its breathing choked. From out of the debris° there rises a naked man and a woman with clothes ripped apart; the wardens have been killed.

56   Night after night the raids followed in close succession, raids that were either as silent as the wasteland or interspersed with anti-aircraft fire. Dahroug would go to Salama in the truck to look up at the sky and talk.

57   "The raids aren't as we heard."

58   "The Italians aren't like the Germans."

59   Dahroug laughed and clamped his hand on Salama's beard. "You're cheating the angel of death by going on living."

60   "Yes, I should have been in the grave at least a year and a half ago."

61   "Is that why you don't fear death?"

62   "No, I've feared it ever since I sniffed the smell of it as they carried me off to the Mufti."

63   "Just imagine what you'd look like now!"

64   "I give thanks to God who has spared me that I might see the searchlights and the anti-aircraft guns."

65   A new energy pervaded° the ruins, then things advanced a pace in a manner undreamt of by Dahroug. Every day he would spend several hours away from the place. Later his business outside took up the whole day. Salama meanwhile worked diligently in the ruins as watchman and warehouseman. . . .

66   Before dawn the sirens wailed, and Dahroug and Salama went out to the wasteland beyond the fence as they had taken to doing of late. "The siren no longer frightens anyone," said Dahroug.

67   A short silence descended, roofed by searchlights, then again Dahroug spoke in a tone that was both serious and brotherly. "Salama, today's not like yesterday. A lot of new clients will be coming, and I'm frightened for you."

68   "Must I go away?" asked Salama dejectedly.°

69   "Yes, I'll smuggle you out to Palestine, and you'll work there for me. How do you feel about that?"

70   "Whatever you think best."

71   "Everything's planned and decreed, you son of a bitch."

72   Suddenly the earth shook with the convulsive reverberation of an explosion that paralyzed° heartbeats. Dahroug pulled nervously at Salama's arm. "What's that?"

73   Salama, his face pallid in the moonlight, answered, "A bomb. Hurry to the room."

74   Amna's screams rang out, and Dahroug called to her, "Stay where you are . . . stay where you are, Amna."

75   The bombing continued without interruption. The two men ran towards the ruins. The next instant Dahroug gave a scream, then fell forward to the ground.

76   "Master!" shouted Salama. He leaned over to help the man to his feet, but he could do nothing. Then, helpless, he found himself flung on top of him, his

forehead sinking into the sand. The earth collapsed around him and the desert rose up toward the sky. Something opaque blotted out the face of the moon.

77   "What's wrong with you, Dahroug?"

78   A voice called, then darkness swallowed up all sound and color. Salama wanted to say to his companion: "Forgive me—I am overcome with sleep."

79   But he uttered not a word.

VOCABULARY GLOSS

The definitions given below will help you understand Mahfouz's story. Words that are defined are glossed in the text. Numbers in the parentheses to the right of the word refer to the paragraph in which the word appears. Not all words that you do not understand are glossed. Guess the meanings of those words in the reading selection which you do not understand.

aperture (2) (n.)	opening
to slink off (4) (v.)	to move away secretly as if in fear
scornfully (7) (adv.)	full of anger and disgust
to linger (8) (v.)	to be slow in stopping something
to cast (11) (v.)	to throw
porter (15) (n.)	a person who carries baggage
rowdiness (16) (n.)	naughty, loud behavior
remnant (17) (n.)	leftover part
limpid (17) (adj.)	calm and untroubled
piaster (18) (n.)	money
djinn (24) (n.)	(variation of the word *jinn*) spirits that, according to Moslem belief, live on the earth
in gratitude (32) (p.p.)	with thanks
procession (35) (n.)	parade
coffin (35) (n.)	box where dead person is placed before burial
voracious (40) (adj.)	having a very large appetite
sentence (46) (n.)	a decision reached by a formal court which pertains to the punishment a prisoner receives
null and void (46) (adj.)	having no legal force
brink (47) (n.)	edge
indifferent (50) (adj.)	not caring; characterized by no special liking for or disliking of something
warden (55) (n.)	an official in charge of operating a prison
debris (55) (n.)	remains of something destroyed or broken
to pervade (65) (v.)	to go throughout every part
dejectedly (68) (adv.)	in a way which is sad or gloomy
to paralyze (72) (v.)	to make powerless

Comprehension Workout

EXERCISE 21

Fill in the blanks with "T" if the sentence is true and "F" is the sentence is false.

_____   **1.** Amna is Dahroug's wife.

_____ 2. Salama escaped from jail.

_____ 3. Salama murdered a person.

_____ 4. Mahmoud is Dahroug's father.

_____ 5. Amna is happy that Salama murdered someone.

_____ 6. Salama helps Dahroug run a warehouse.

_____ 7. The warehouse is in the middle of the city.

_____ 8. When the story begins, World War II is taking place.

_____ 9. Dahroug's family is unaffected by the war.

_____ 10. In the end of the story, Salama, Dahroug, and Amna probably die.

Listening

Listen again to the audiotaped stories about war.

WHILE YOU LISTEN

IT WORKS!
Learning Strategy:
Listening for a
Specific Purpose

As you listen to the audio-taped stories, try to determine their purpose. What do you think the authors hoped to accomplish by writing them? Focus on the sounds and sights of the battlefield. Ask yourself these questions:

- What specific adjectives does the writer use to describe the sights of the battlefield?
- What specific adjectives does the writer use to describe the sounds of the battlefield?
- How do the writers paint a bleak picture of the battlefield?

AFTER YOU LISTEN

React to the audiotaped stories in your journal. If you are having difficulty reacting to the essays, consider the following questions.

1. The focus of this lesson is impressions of war. What impressions do the writers of these stories make? For example, do they make war seem exciting or dreadful?
2. How do the writers organize their stories in such a way that their readers/listeners are able to visualize war? (For example, do they use dialog to make the characters in their stories come alive? Do they use vivid vocabulary words? Do their stories contain exciting plots?)
3. Would you like someone who you loved to fight on the battlefields described by these writers? Why or why not?

Grammar Explanation

RELATIVE CLAUSES

Explanation: In the next Quick Write activity, you will be asked to describe the sights and sounds of the battlefield. In writing this description, you will probably want to use relative clauses. Relative clauses tell the reader more about a noun. They modify the noun by describing or identifying it.

1. They follow nouns.

   The soldiers <u>who are married</u> dread war more than the soldiers <u>who are unmarried</u>.

2. They are introduced by the relative pronouns *who, which,* and *that.* Generally, though not always:

   who = for people

   which = for things

   that = for people and things

3. They can modify the object of a main clause. Notice in the examples below that object pronouns (but not subject pronouns) may be deleted.

	OBJECT PRONOUN	
The soldier shot the boy	*who*	I knew.
The soldier shot the boy I knew.		
He gave the reward to the soldier	*whom*	he respected.
He gave the reward to the soldier he respected.		

   (Notice that it is incorrect to state: "The soldier shot the boy who I know him." Also notice that *whom* is used in formal situations when the relative pronoun replaces a person which functions as the object of the sentence.)

4. A relative clause may modify the subject of the main clause. Subject pronouns may never be deleted.

	SUBJECT PRONOUN	
The soldier	*who/that*	shook with fear was unmarried.
The war	*that/which*	he fought brought freedom of speech.
The hill	*where*	the battle was fought was now empty.

5. Relative clauses can be restrictive or nonrestrictive.

RESTRICTIVE RELATIVE CLAUSES

- Restrictive relative clauses are necessary parts of the sentence. When the relative clause is deleted, either the sentence does not make sense or it is false.

  All parents <u>who abuse their children</u> should be put in jail. Notice that if you delete the restrictive relative clauses *who abuse their children* the resulting sentence (All parents should be put in jail) does not make sense.

- Restrictive clauses are not set off by commas.

NONRESTRICTIVE RELATIVE CLAUSES

- Nonrestrictive relative clauses are not a necessary part of the sentence. They provide additional information which is not needed to understand the sentence. They are not needed to identify the noun that they modify. When nonrestrictive relative clauses are deleted, the sentence still remains true. Notice in the example which follows that if you delete the nonrestrictive clause *which include guns, bombs, dynamite, and grenades,* the sentence still makes sense.

  All weapons, <u>which include guns, bombs, dynamite, and grenades,</u> should be abolished.

- Use commas to set off nonrestrictive relative clauses.
- The pronoun <u>that</u> cannot be used in nonrestrictive relative clauses.

  For further information about relative clauses, refer to your grammar workout books.

Grammar Practice: Relative Clauses

EXERCISE 22

Combine the two sentences in each group by using an appropriate relative clause.

1. Slowly, the soldier made his way across the battlefield.
   He carried the heavy equipment.

   _____

2. When twilight came, the soldiers gazed at the sky.
   The sky was suddenly lit up by anti-aircraft missiles.

   _____

3. The soldiers grew fearful.
   The soldiers could hear their own hearts pounding.

   _____

4. The battlefield was so quiet that no one heard the enemy advance.
   The soldiers waited to fight in the battlefield.

   _____

5. The soldiers tormented the enemy on the battlefield.
   The soldiers should be accused of war crimes.

   _____

6. The morning breeze cooled the soldiers' bodies.
   The morning breeze chilled their spirits.

   _____

7. The bombs sometimes seemed to explode unexpectedly.
   The bombs killed hundreds of soldiers.

   _____

8. The soldiers' faces displayed their fear.
   The soldiers' faces dripped with perspiration.

   _____

9. The hills looked difficult to climb.
   The enemy hid in the hills.

   _____

10. The unmarried soldier took his last breath of air.
    The unmarried soldier was dying.

    _____

Write two sentences of your own which contain relative clauses and which describe the sights, sounds, or smells of war.

11. _____

    _____

12. _____

    _____

Text Analysis: Restrictive and Nonrestrictive Clauses

EXERCISE 23

The following reading passages contain both restrictive and nonrestrictive clauses. In small groups of three to four students, find these clauses. Underline the clauses and discuss why they are restrictive or nonrestrictive. Report on your discussion to the class.

CARL VON OSSIETZKY

World War II made a powerful impression on Carl von Ossietzky who had fought for Germany in World War I. When Ossietzky was called from his desk job as a reporter to fight in this war, he was appalled by the slaughter he witnessed. He hated the sounds and sights of the battlefield. In his memories, he could hear the bombs drop, destroying buildings and killing innocent civilians. He could see nothing heroic about turning young men, who were at the peak of their lives, into piles of dead bodies. He decided to use his writing skill to begin his own peace campaign. He became the editor of *Die Weltbane,* which was a magazine read throughout Germany. In his writing, he tried to persuade the German people to remember the sights and sounds of World War I and to avoid another war. He pleaded with the Germans to give up their dreams of power over all other nations.

While Ossietzky was warning of the dangers of the battlefield, another man was promising to rebuild the German military. The German people were interested in this rising newcomer whose name was Adolf Hitler. However, Ossietzky realized that Hitler was an evil man who only desired power. Ossietzky attacked Hitler in his writing. In 1933, the Nazis threw Ossietzky in jail—along with 4,000 writers, lawyers, and others who had publicly criticized Hitler. Although Ossietzky remained in prison, in 1935 he was awarded the Nobel Peace Prize, which is awarded each year to the person who does the most to advance world peace. Ossietzky paid the ultimate price for his fight for peace and freedom of expression, death. In 1938, he died in a Nazi concentration camp.

Ossietzky did not live to see the results of his sacrifices for peace. Nevertheless, the courage of this German writer, whose name is barely known in most of the world, has led observers to call him the "hero who painted vivid pictures of the horrors of war."

Poems

Explanation: Poets often use language in interesting, descriptive ways. The two poems on pages 98-99 will help you build up the vocabulary you need to describe the sights and sounds of the battlefield.

IT WORKS!
Learning Strategy:
Visualizing

About the Poem

John McCrae describes the sights of a World War I battlefield in his famous poem, "In Flanders Fields."

WHILE YOU READ

Read this poem silently. Pay particular attention to the vivid imagery created by the poet.

In Flanders Fields

In Flanders Fields the poppies blow
    Between the crosses, row on row
That mark our place; and in the sky
    The larks, still bravely singing, fly
Scarce heard amid the guns below.
    We are the dead. Short days ago
    We lived, felt dawn, saw sunset glow,
Loved and were loved, and now we lie
    In Flanders Fields.
    Take up our quarrel with the foe:
    To you from failing hands we throw
The torch; be yours to hold it high.
    If ye break faith with us who die
    We shall not sleep, though poppies grow
In Flanders Fields.

John McCrae

AFTER YOU READ

As a class, listen to your teacher read this poem. Discuss the meaning of the poem as well as any words that you do not know. Find a partner. Practice reading the poem to one another.

About the Poem

J. A. Armstrong wrote this poem as a response to John McCrae's poem. Notice the forceful vocabulary words he uses to describe war.

A Reply to "In Flanders Fields"

In Flanders Fields the cannons boom,°
  And fitful° flashes light the gloom;
  While up above, like eagles, fly
  The fierce destroyers of the sky;°
  With stains° the earth wherein you lie
  Is redder than the poppy bloom,
    In Flanders Fields.
Sleep on, ye brave! The shrieking° shell,°
  The quaking° trench,° the startling° yell,
  The fury° of the battle hell
  Shall wake you not, for all is well;
  Sleep peacefully, for all is well.
  Your flaming torch° aloft we bear;°
  With burning heart and oath° we swear
  To keep the faith, to fight it through,
  To crush° the foe,° or sleep with you,
    In Flanders Fields.

J. A. Armstrong

VOCABULARY

The definitions given below will help you understand Armstrong's poem. Not all words that you do not understand are glossed. You will need to guess the meanings of those words in the poem which you do not understand.

to boom (v.)	to make a loud noise
fitful (adj.)	restless
destroyers of the sky (n.)	war planes
stain (n.)	a spot which is left from blood
shrieking (adj.)	the quality of a loud, high-pitched cry
shell (n.)	ammunition
quaking (adj.)	moving
trench (n.)	a long hole dug out of dirt used for protection during war
startling (adj.)	surprising
fury (n.)	extreme anger
torch (n.)	fire used to provide light
to bear (v.)	to carry
oath (n.)	promise
to crush (v.)	to destroy
foe (n.)	enemy

AFTER YOU READ

Discuss the poem as a class. Then, find a partner. Practice reading the poem to one another. After you have each practiced reading the poem, make a list with your partner of all the descriptive adjectives Armstrong uses to describe war.

Quick Write

WRITING A PERSONAL LETTER

This strategy is useful whenever you are having difficulty getting started writing.

Imagine that you are a soldier waiting for battle. What would you like to say to your husband, wife, or children? Write a letter of one or two paragraphs describing the sights and sounds of the battlefield and explaining your feelings.

BEFORE YOU WRITE

Consider this strategy:

LEARNING STRATEGY

Understanding and Using Emotions: Sharing your feelings about a particular writing task helps lower your anxiety and makes it easier to get started.

Team up with a classmate. Ask your classmate how she or he feels about the writing task. Ask her or him what difficulties she or he might encounter and how she or he intends to overcome these difficulties. Then, share your feelings about the assignment.

WRITE

You are now ready to write your letter.

AFTER YOU WRITE

Consider this strategy:

LEARNING STRATEGY

Managing Your Learning: Rewriting what you have already written helps you gain confidence and proficiency.

Rewrite as many times as you like. Don't be afraid to rewrite any of your writing—even Quick Writes. Write, rewrite, and rewrite again! Generally, it takes about three "rewrites" before you achieve a polished piece of writing. If you feel additional rewrites would strengthen your writing further, by all means make the rewrites.

EDIT YOUR WRITING

Correct your grammar mistakes. Consider this strategy:

LEARNING STRATEGY

Managing Your Learning: When you identify problem areas to work on, you can focus on them and improve them.

Analyze the types of grammar mistakes you made. Try to identify very specific problem areas (such as subject/verb agreement or parallel structures). Then, devise ways to improve in these areas. For example, you might want to seek books with exercises for correcting your problems or ask your teacher and friends for advice.

Punctuation Explanation

COLONS

Explanation: In the next writing task, you will be asked to write a comparison of two kinds of soldiers. Colons are sometimes helpful in making comparisons, especially when you are writing about a number of characteristics. Consider the examples below:

> The married soldiers had three traits in common: fear, anxiety, and caution.

> Unmarried soldiers had a different set of traits: recklessness, bravery, and carelessness.

A colon (:) is often used to introduce lists or series of items. The part of the sentence which follows the colon gives details about what appears in the sentence before the colon. When the word in front of the series is a verb or a preposition, do not use a colon. If the word in front of the colon is a noun, do use a colon.

EXAMPLE: **Colon Used:** They fought in three wars: World War II, the Korean War, and the Vietnam War.

Colon Not Used: He fought in World War II, the Korean War, and the Vietnam War.

Colon Not Used: The three wars in which he fought are World War II, the Korean War, and the Vietnam War.

Punctuation Practice: Colons

EXERCISE 24

Add colons and commas where appropriate. Note that some sentences need no colon.

1. Weapons can be divided up into several groups bombs missiles and bullets.
2. To fight a war you need tanks, guns, and ammunition.
3. Four major wars include the War in Kuwait the War in Yugoslavia the Vietnam War and the Korean War.
4. Soldiers have several major characteristics courage persistence and strength.
5. When people are afraid, they may do several things run away fight or cry.
6. To participate in a nonviolent demonstration you need some signs comfortable clothing and food.
7. There are several areas in the world which have experienced frequent war Indo–China Eastern Europe and the Middle East.
8. There are several reasons to fight desire for more territory religious conflicts and lust of power.
9. A reporter needs the following writing tools paper pencils and a computer.
10. The six republics of Yugoslavia which sometimes fought each other are Slovenia Croatia Serbia Bosnia–Herzegovina, Montenegro and Macedonia.

Write two of your own sentences that use colons.

11. _____

_____

12. _____

_____

Gaining Writing Competence

COMPARING AND CONTRASTING

Explanation: In the next writing activity, you will be asked to write an essay in which you compare and contrast the feelings of an unmarried soldier with that of a married one. The following guidelines will help you.

GUIDELINES FOR COMPARING AND CONTRASTING

When you write about the similarities of two objects, people, or ideas, you are making a comparison. When you write about their differences, you are making a contrast. Although you can organize a comparison-contrast essay in several different ways, there are two major ones: the block style and the point-by-point style.

BLOCK STYLE

The topics may be presented one at a time, as in this paragraph.

Married and unmarried men faced war differently. The married men were nervous and fearful. They were not anxious to go into combat. In contrast, the unmarried men were calm and fearless. They were eager to fight the enemy.

Notice that in this paragraph, the characteristics of one group are contrasted with the characteristics of another.

THE POINT-BY-POINT STYLE

The paragraph may also be presented in the point-by-point style, as in this paragraph:

Married and unmarried men faced war differently. The married soldiers were more nervous than the unmarried ones. They were also more fearful than the unmarried ones. Not surprisingly, the married soldiers were less anxious to go into combat than the unmarried ones.

Notice that in this paragraph, two types of people are contrasted first in terms of one point and then in terms of another.

Useful Expressions for Contrast Writing

TRANSITION WORDS

Contrasts	Examples
on the other hand	On the one hand, the married soldiers were cautious; <u>on the other hand</u>, the unmarried ones were not.
in contrast	Married soldiers were cautious. <u>In contrast</u>, unmarried ones were careless.
whereas	<u>Whereas</u> married soldiers were cautious, unmarried soldiers were careless.
but	Married soldiers were cautious, <u>but</u> unmarried soldiers were not.
however	Married soldiers were cautious; <u>however</u>, unmarried soldiers were not.

Contrasts	Examples
1. X and Y differ.	Married and unmarried soldiers differ.
2. There are many differences between X and Y.	There are many differences between married and unmarried soldiers.
3. X and Y are very different.	Married and unmarried soldiers are very different.

4. X and Y have many different	Married and unmarried soldiers have many characteristics different characteristics. traits
5. X and Y are <u>different</u>. dissimilar.	Married and unmarried soldiers are dissimilar.
6. X differs from Y.	Married soldiers differ from unmarried ones.
7. X s more/less/-er than Y.	Married soldiers are more fearful than unmarried ones.
8. <u>One</u> <u>difference</u> <u>is</u>. . . One concerns. . . Yet another	One difference concerns attitudes. Another difference concerns motivation. Yet another difference concerns experience.

Writing Task

WRITING AN ESSAY

Write a one page essay in which you compare and contrast the feelings of an unmarried soldier who is going into combat with the feelings of a married soldier who is going into combat. Your audience is the class. Your purpose is to inform Americans who have never fought in war about the horrors of the battlefield. (For more information concerning comparison-contrast writing, refer to pages 67–69.)

Use this strategy before you write your first-draft of a piece of writing.

BEFORE YOU WRITE

Consider this strategy:

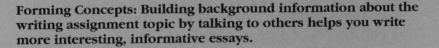

LEARNING STRATEGY

Forming Concepts: Building background information about the writing assignment topic by talking to others helps you write more interesting, informative essays.

To gain background knowledge, talk to people about issues that are related to the writing topic and record your findings in a notebook. Whether you talk to others in your first or second language, you will gain important background information that you can use in your writing.

Consider this strategy:

LEARNING STRATEGY

Managing Your Learning: When you visualize your audience, it helps you shape your writing to the audience's needs and interests.

Imagine that you are writing your paragraph for a group of American college students who have never been in a war before. These questions will help you visualize your audience:

AUDIENCE PROFILE QUESTIONS

1. What are some of the characteristics of the audience?
2. What are their interests?
3. How much background information about war does your audience need to understand your paragraph?
4. What's the best way to engage this audience's interest?

WRITE

Write your essay. As you write, visualize your audience reading over your shoulder.

REVISE YOUR ESSAY

Read your essay to yourself. Use the Revision Checklist below to revise your essay.

REVISION CHECKLIST

1. Check the essay to make sure that you have included a strong thesis statement.
2. Check to make sure that you wrote as much about the unmarried soldiers as you did about the married ones. If you described specific characteristics of unmarried soldiers, did you also describe these same characteristics when discussing the married ones?
3. Did you provide enough descriptive information for your audience to understand what you are stating? (Remember, your audience has never experienced war.)
4. Look for spots in the essay that could be stated more vividly. Is there a more lively way of stating your thoughts?
5. Are there words, phrases, or entire sentences which need to be deleted or expanded?

EDIT YOUR ESSAY

Consider this strategy:

Threads

From 1982 to 1986, sales of G.I. Joe toys rose 177%.

Hasbro, Inc.

LEARNING STRATEGY

Managing Your Learning: Paying attention to only a few features of English at a time helps you edit your written work more effectively.

Edit your essay carefully. Pay particular attention to the use of relative clauses, subject/verb agreement, and punctuation.

Quick Write

REPORTING SURVEY DATA

Thus far, you have examined feelings towards war in two ways: by writing an informal letter and by comparing the feelings of two kinds of soldiers. It is time to reconsider your classmates' feelings about war. Write a one paragraph summary of the data which you collected from the survey questionnaire on page 84. Your purpose is to describe your classmates' feelings about war. Imagine that you are writing this summary for a group of American students.

As a class, review the survey data on the chalkboard. Analyze the data by your classmates' native language backgrounds. In other words, tally the responses to the survey items by the different native languages your classmates speak. In this way, you will be able to determine whether students from diverse cultures think differently or similarly about war.

Discuss the findings. Do all the students in the class feel the same about war? Do students who have experienced war feel differently about it than students who have not experienced it?

Optional Quick Write

Use the survey with Americans outside of your ESL class. Find out how they feel about war. Then, write a one page description of your findings. Your purpose is to inform. You are writing this description for your classmates.

Using a Language Learning Log

1. Vocabulary:
   Write down as many new words from the lesson as you can remember.

   _____

   _____

   _____

   _____

   _____

IT WORKS!
Learning Strategy:
Keeping Track of
Your Progress

2. Grammar:
   Note examples of any grammatical structures from the lesson learned or reviewed. Write a brief explanation of the grammar points that they illustrate.

   _____

   _____

   _____

   _____

   _____

3. Punctuation:
Write down any new punctuation rules that you learned.

_____

_____

_____

_____

_____

4. Gaining Writing Competence:
List any new composition techniques that you learned. (Such techniques might include those for making your writing cohesive; writing interesting introductions, bodies, and conclusions; and composing different types of writing effectively.)

_____

_____

_____

_____

_____

5. Learning Strategies:
Briefly describe any new learning strategies that you have applied in your writing.

_____

_____

_____

_____

_____

6. Areas that Need More Work:
Note here in brief form any areas that you are still trying to improve. Try to be as specific as possible.

_____

_____

_____

_____

_____

IT WORKS!
Learning Strategy:
Making Action Plans

Quick Write

LANGUAGE LEARNING OBJECTIVES

What are three of your most important language learning objectives? Write one paragraph in which you describe these objectives and your plan to accomplish them. Your objectives should be as specific as possible. Your plan might include learning a specific number of vocabulary words each week, talking to native English speakers to develop fluency, visiting your teachers in their office to review specific aspects of your writing, or studying your grammar textbook to learn more about avoiding sentence fragments.

SUMMARY OF LESSON 1: IMPRESSIONS OF WAR

In this lesson, you have examined feelings about war. You have written an informal personal letter expressing feelings, a paragraph contrasting two types of soldiers, and a summary report of survey data. In the next lesson, you will consider the causes and effects of war as well as ways to prevent it.

QUICK REFERENCE TO STRATEGIES

Understanding and Using Emotions: Sharing Your Feelings (p. 100)

Managing Your Learning: Writing, Rewriting, and Rewriting Again (p. 100)

Managing Your Learning: Identifying Problem Areas (p. 101)

Forming Concepts: Talking to Others (p. 104)

Managing Your Learning: Visualizing the Audience (p. 104)

Managing Your Learning: Narrowing Your Focus (p. 105)

LESSON 2: REASONS FOR WAR

Overview

In the previous lesson, you examined some of the sights and sounds of war. The focus of this lesson is reasons for war. Is war innate or is it learned? Why does war develop? How can we prevent war? Is war glorified in some cultures more than it is in others? These are just a few of the questions raised in this lesson. In answering these questions, you will write a definition for the word *war* as well as an essay concerning the reasons war develops.

About the Reading

In this essay, Adrian Burley summarizes the work of the famous biologist, Huxley, who questions whether war is inevitable and whether war results from basic human desires.

BEFORE YOU READ

Before reading Burley's essay, it is useful to explore your own opinions of the essay topic. These questions will help you:

1. Do you think that war is inevitable?
2. How can nations avoid war?
3. Is the instinct to fight universal? In other words, do all humans have this instinct or do people from some cultures have the instinct while those of other cultures do not?

109

WHILE YOU READ

Look for the general ideas in this essay. Later you will be asked to complete an outline. Do not stop to try to understand every word. As you read, guess the meanings of new words from the context in which they occur. If you cannot guess the meanings, use the gloss at the end of the chapter. Do not take the time to use a dictionary. That would slow you down so much that you would lose track of the general ideas.

IS WAR NECESSARY?

Adrian Burley

1   Huxley, a well-known biologist, did not believe that war is innate. In his famous essay, "Is war inevitable?" he argued that war does not result from a war instinct.° Rather, he argued that war is a result of the human being's desire to fight. I too believe that war does not have to happen, it is not necessary.

2   Huxley argued that war is not innate; in other words, people are not born with a war instinct. For Huxley, people are merely born with an impulse° that makes them want to fight. This impulse makes war possible, but not inevitable. In order for war to occur, the impulse to fight must be developed. To cultivate this impulse, people must be properly motivated.

3   Huxley further argued that various psychological variables develop the motivation to fight. For Huxley, these variables include: patriotism, love of glory, self-interest, fear, dislike of what is different, the feeling of superiority, the sense of shame, and the belief in one's ideas and those of one's group.

4   Propaganda° and patriotic campaigns help to motivate people to fight. This was the case in World War II (when the Nazis exterminated the Jews) as well as

in the American Revolution (when the American colonists fought against the British). Huxley suggested that propaganda is especially necessary in anti-militarist° countries like the United States, which has always mistrusted° a permanent army; or Britain, where the soldier in peace time has almost always been looked at with disapproval.

5   There are two conditions which Huxley suggested permit the development of the motivation to fight. The first condition is that human beings are organized into separate groups such as tribes or kingdoms, empires or nations. The second condition is that there is serious competition between these groups. This competition could be for land or natural resources. Humans can reduce the possibility of war either by reducing nationalism (in other words, by encouraging people to live together peacefully under one world government) or by reducing the competition between groups (for example, by promoting wealth for all people).

6   One of the factors that increases the likelihood of war is nationalism. However, people do not need to destroy nations to eliminate war. They must only ensure that all nations are subordinated° to world sovereignty.° National governments must somehow come to support a single world government, just as local and regional governments support national ones.

7   However, even with a single world government, wars still might occur. Huxley suggested that to lessen the risk of war, people must reduce the competition between groups. This means creating a world in which there is enough food, space, and resources to satisfy the needs of all people. Throughout the world, the wealth must be spread evenly. If wealth is spread too unequally, the poorer regions may become jealous of the wealthier regions and want to fight to gain their goods. Today, the United States should not merely develop her own economic well-being and not help the poorer nations. In addition to the jealousies to which this undoubtedly causes, it is likely to lead to an imbalance° in the world's economic structure, which will one day crash, bringing down rich and poor countries alike in its fall.

8   Although the causes of war may be reduced by developing a world government and creating a world in which goods are plentiful and equally shared, the human being's basic urge to fight is still innate. To prevent this urge from developing into war, people must find what William James (a 19th century American philosopher) called "a moral equivalent of war"°—an outlet° for the urge to fight, an outlet for frustration, hate and aggression. In other words, people must develop activities which substitute for war, while at the same time, satisfying their own basic urge to fight. They can satisfy this urge by engaging in constructive° activities which do not harm anyone. To create such activities, people need to find out what kind of activities are most suitable and satisfying for what people. In addition, they need to make others realize that these activities are not only worthwhile, but also highly satisfying.

9   To sum up Huxley's theory very briefly, Huxley denies emphatically that a human war instinct exists. However, he does argue that all humans are born with an impulse to fight, which can develop into war as long as conditions encourage or permit it. Fortunately, for Huxley, people can change the conditions so as to prevent the human's impulse to fight from expressing itself in war. To eliminate war, Huxley argued, people need a world government, a general high level of productivity, and activities which provide a moral equivalent of war.

Threads

War has. . .become a luxury which only the small nations can afford.

Hannah Arendt
1906–1975

VOCABULARY GLOSS

The definitions given will help you understand this essay. Underlined words in the essay are glossed. Numbers in the parentheses to the right of the word refer to the paragraph in which the word appears. Not all words that you do not understand are glossed. You will need to guess the meanings of those words in the reading selection which you do not understand.

instinct (1) (n.)	a natural or inherent tendency which cannot be changed
impulse (2) (n.)	a sudden, spontaneous act
propaganda (4) (n.)	the spreading of ideas, information, or rumor for the purpose of helping or hurting a cause
anti-militarist (4) (adj.)	against war
mistrust (4) (n.)	a lack of confidence
sovereignty (6) (n.)	supreme power
subordinate (6) (v.)	to place in a lower rank
imbalance (7) (n.)	lack of balance
moral equivalent (8) (n.)	an ethical substitute
outlet (8) (n.)	a means of satisfying an impulse
constructive (8) (adj.)	promoting improvement

LEARNING STRATEGY

Forming Concepts: Reading widely increases your exposure to English and improves your English vocabulary and grammar.

Comprehension Workout

Find a classmate with whom you have not previously worked. With this classmate, complete the outline below. Reread Burley's essay if necessary.

NOTES ON "IS WAR NECESSARY?"

Ways to Motivate People to Engage in Warfare

1. _propaganda_____

2. _____

Conditions which Encourage People to Fight

1. _organization of separate groups_

2. _____

Ways to Minimize the Risk of War

1. _provide food, space and natural_
   resources for all people

2. _establish a world government_

3. _____

Answer the following questions individually in writing.

1. What are several conditions which lead to war?

2. Do you think that some cultures promote these conditions and others discourage them? Why?

3. The author appears to distinguish the term *instinct* from *impulse* or *drive*. Why? Consider the meanings of these three words:

   instinct: natural or inherent aptitude or capacity; largely inheritable; cannot be changed; doe snot involve reason

   impulse: the act of doing something suddenly and spontaneously without thinking; can be changed, learned

   drive: strong desire; can be changed; learned

4. Can you think of any appropriate moral alternatives to war? Would any sports or leisure activities be suitable substitutes?

5. Huxley summarizes his entire essay in the last paragraph. Reread this last paragraph carefully. Then attempt to restate it in your own words.

Grammar Review

COUNT AND NONCOUNT NOUNS

Explanation: In the next writing assignment, you will need to use count and noncount nouns correctly. ESL students at the University of California frequently misused the ones given below. The list on the left-hand side contains nouns which are noncount in most situations. The list on the right-hand side contains nouns which are count in most situations. All of these nouns relate to the theme of war.

NONCOUNT	COUNT
abuse	battle
aggression	battlefield
combat	civilian
evil	conflict
destruction	hand grenade
glory	hand gun
hate	missile
injustice	nuclear weapon
justice	suicide
mental violence	tank
nationalism	victim
police	war
propaganda	
sorrow	
suffering	
torture	
violence	
warfare	

(For a review of count and noncount nouns, see pages 14–17.)

Grammar Practice: Count and Noncount Nouns

EXERCISE 27

Fill in the blanks with the correct form of the verb. Remember, noncount nouns are used with the third person singular verb (he/she/it verb form as in *The war begins soon.*)

1. Propaganda _____ (encourage) the development of war sentiment.

2. Extreme nationalism sometimes _____ (lead) to war.

3. Hand grenades _____ (be) a type of crude weapon.

4. Thousands of innocent victims _____ (die) in wars each year.

5. Mental abuse _____ (be) sometimes more painful than physical abuse.

6. Hand guns _____ (be) legal in the United States.

7. A long battle _____ (take) years to win.

8. Untold suffering _____ (result) from violence.

9. Wife beating _____ (constitute) a serious problem in some countries.

10. Civilians sometimes _____ (avoid) the police.

Editing Practice: Count and Noncount Nouns

EXERCISE 28

The sample student paragraph below contains *six* errors related to the use of count and noncount nouns. Make the necessary corrections. Note that when you correct the noun forms, you may also need to correct verbs as well as the adjective modifiers.

STUDENT WRITING SAMPLE:
PHYSICAL VIOLENCE

One type of physical violences is police brutalities. This type of abuse occurs when law officers refuse to follow the laws and needlessly beat innocent civilians because they feel powerful when they inflict pain. The victims of police brutalities endure many sufferings. As a result of police brutalities, violences increase, hatreds grow, and victims suffer.—*S.T.*

Quick Write

WRITING DEFINITIONS

Write a one paragraph definition of two of the following words and expressions: *physical violence, mental abuse, international bitterness, world sovereignty, police brutality,* and *war sentiment.* Write these definitions for peer readers. Your purpose is to inform.

BEFORE YOU WRITE

Study these guidelines.

GUIDELINES FOR WRITING A DEFINITION

A good definition always provides more information than that which is found in the dictionary. You can write a good definition of the expression *war sentiment* by explaining what war sentiment is, what the characteristics of war sentiment are, who fosters war sentiment, and what war sentiment does.

How should I begin?

QUESTIONS TO ASK WHEN WRITING A DEFINITION

IT WORKS!
Learning Strategy:
Getting Help

What is X?

What are the characteristics of X?

Who uses X?

Where does X come from?

What is X similar to or different from?

(If you need further information concerning how to write a definition, refer to pages 17–19.)

Consider this strategy:

LEARNING STRATEGY

Personalizing: Find out what your audience expects you to write by directly questioning them.

Ask a classmate what type of information he or she expects you to include in your definition.

WRITE

Write your definitions. While you write, ask someone to help you by requesting that the person provide you with useful expressions that you can't think of, a better way of saying something, or more information.

AFTER YOU WRITE

Consider this strategy:

LEARNING STRATEGY

Understanding and Using Emotions: Discussing how to give and receive constructive feedback allows everyone to feel good about it.

Find a partner. Share how you feel about error correction. Explain what types of error correction marks best for you and how you want your mistakes corrected [a check (✓) in the margin? a rewrite of a portion of your essay? grammar mistakes highlighted with a pen?].

Ask the same classmate who just worked with you to help you edit your definition.

Gaining Writing Competence

DEVELOPING INTRODUCTIONS

Explanation: In the next writing activity, you will write an essay about the causes of war. The information below will help you write an effective introduction.

INTRODUCTIONS

A well-developed introduction makes your essay interesting to read. Introductions arouse the reader's attention, motivate the reader to read more, and unify your essay. Sometimes they lead up to the main idea. The following examples illustrate how writers use effective introductory techniques. Note that all the techniques below lead to the thesis statement, "World War III must never take place."

TECHNIQUES FOR WRITING EFFECTIVE INTRODUCTIONS

1. *Ask a question.*

   There is much discussion today about the possibility of a third world war. What would happen if such a war broke out today? How would it affect the earth and the people who live on the earth? Would people be prepared to handle the devastating consequences of a third world war? Most people are unprepared to meet the challenges of the next world war. World War III must never take place.

2. *Present an interesting idea, a startling fact, or a surprising statistic.*

   Four million Jews were killed in World War II. Today, we have more powerful weapons than we had in World War II. These weapons are capable of destroying whole nations. World War III must never take place.

3. *Develop background or historical perspective.*

   Since our creation, we have been engaged in warfare. In ancient times, we fought territorial and religious wars. In the Middle Ages, we fought for land, for money, and for power. Today, we fight among ourselves for a variety of reasons. However, wars must not be fought in the future. World War III must never take place.

4. *Use a quotation which illustrates or makes a statement about the subject.*

   Abraham Lincoln once said, "War can only result in the destruction of the human species." If we believe this statement, then, we must believe that war is wrong. World War III must never take place.

5. *Narrate an interesting, funny, sad, or unusual incident.*

   Stacy Trang, from Vietnam, was the only surviving daughter of a family of ten children. She survived because of the efforts of several American soldiers who brought her safely out of Vietnam during the Vietnam War. Her mother was killed by soldiers. Her father died in prison; and her siblings died of starvation. Stacy is just one of millions who suffered the consequences of the war. War is destructive. World War III must never take place.

6. *Appeal to the reader for some action or change.*

   War is evil and needless. You can help prevent it by taking specific actions. World War III must never take place.

7. *Illustrate the importance of the topic.*

   If World War III takes place, the earth will be completely destroyed. The lives of millions of soldiers and civilians will be lost. World War III must never take place.

Text Analysis: Introductions

EXERCISE 29

In small groups, analyze the introduction of the following essays from this unit. Answer the questions below.

1. Which of the above techniques do the authors use in their introductions?

Simpson ("Tianenmen Square")

_____

_____

Burley ("Is War Inevitable?")

_____

_____

2. How do the authors tie the introduction to the conclusion?

Simpson ("Tianenmen Square")

_____

_____

Burley ("Is War Inevitable?")

_____

_____

3. What make these introductions effective?

Simpson ("Tianenmen Square")

_____

_____

Burley ("Is War Inevitable?")

_____

_____

EXERCISE 30

In a small group of four to five students, decide which of the essays in this lesson has the best introduction and which has the worst one. Report on your decisions to the class.

Best Introduction: _____

Worst Introduction: _____

Gaining Writing Competence

USING EXAMPLES

Explanation: In the next writing task, you will write an analysis of physical violence. Using effective examples will help you write a clear analysis.

EXAMPLES

Examples add information which helps clarify your writing. Read the sentence below. War is terrible. What does the word *terrible* mean? Is the writer talking about death, the destruction of buildings, or something else? When writers provide examples to connect specific information to general statements, it makes their writing more comprehensible and detailed.

> **EXAMPLE** War is terrible. For example, it results in untold suffering, leads nations into poverty, and destroys property.

Gaining Writing Practice: Using Examples

EXERCISE 31

Add examples to the sentences below. Use words such as *for example* and *for instance* to connect the examples to the general statements. Follow the example below.

> **EXAMPLE** The battlefield was quiet.
>
> The battlefield was quiet. For instance, the noise from the guns had ceased, the planes were not roaring above, and the soldiers sat still waiting for the battle to begin.

1. War results from many causes.

    _____

2. There are ways to prevent war.

    _____

3. Environmental conditions help develop a war sentiment.

    _____

4. The soldiers fought for many reasons.

    _____

5. Television glorifies war.

    _____

6. The war negatively affected the nation.

_____

7. War kills many innocent civilians.

_____

8. Wars change history.

_____

9. War can be justified in some situations.

_____

10. War is destructive.

_____

Editing Practice: Using Examples

EXERCISE 32

The second paragraph below might be revised so that examples are added to clarify the writer's ideas. Rewrite the second paragraph, adding examples to clarify.

STUDENT WRITING SAMPLE
IS WAR NECESSARY?

If war is necessary, it is a necessary evil. Its evilness is sometimes concealed for a time by its glamour and excitement; but when war is seen in its reality, there is very little glory about it. At its best, it is a hideous calamity.

Think of the loss of lives caused by war. War generally sweeps away the strongest and best men of a country, and it leaves the aged, the weak and the unfit to carry on. Think of the sorrow and suffering war causes to those whom it does not kill. Think, too, of the destruction of property. Think also of the total destruction of nations. Finally, think of the international hatred and bitterness that remain as seeds of future wars.—*L.H.*

Threads

Nuclear weapons are stationed in 27 of the 50 U.S. states.

*Nuclear Battlefields:
Global Links in the Arms Race*
William M. Arkin and
Richard W. Fieldhouse

Writing Task

WRITING AN ANALYSIS

Write a three- to five-paragraph essay in which you analyze the various causes of physical violence. You may write about war in general, a specific war, or a different type of physical violence other than war. Your essay is for a group of American college students who is interested in your particular viewpoint.

BEFORE YOU WRITE

Consider the following strategy:

Forming Concepts: Analyzing your readers—their personal biases, knowledge about the topic, and interests—helps you shape your writing to their particular needs.

Try to figure out the characteristics of the audience who will read your writing. What are the readers of your writing like? What are their personal biases? For example, are they liberals or conservatives? Are they _hawks_ (that is, do they support war) or _doves_ (in other words, are they opposed to war)? What do they need or want to learn? Basic information about your readers concerns age, gender, ethnic identity, income level, occupation and professional status, educational level, and political affiliation.

Make lists of what you think your readers know and don't know about your topic and what you think the readers expect to find out. Use the topics below.

HERE'S WHAT I THINK MY READERS KNOW

_____

_____

_____

_____

HERE'S WHAT I THINK MY READERS DON'T KNOW

_____

_____

_____

_____

HERE'S WHAT I THINK MY READERS EXPECT TO FIND OUT

_____

_____

_____

_____

Threads

A 1991 poll in the U.S. found that 47% of respondents said they have a gun in their house.

Gallup Poll (1991)

Use this strategy in the prewriting stage of the composing process.

Managing Your Learning: Being aware of the purpose (reason and content) of your writing helps you write more effectively.

Write the purpose of your essay below.

_____

_____

_____

_____

_____

If you lack information about this writing assignment, read widely, both in English and in your native language.

WRITE

You are now ready to write.

AFTER YOU WRITE

Reread what you have written. Before you share it with a classmate, make any changes that you like.

After you have rewritten your paper, read it to a classmate. Ask your classmate to complete the Peer Revising Form below.

PEER REVISING FORM

1. What parts did you particularly enjoy?
2. What parts provided you with interesting new information?
3. Did the introduction engage the reader's attention? How could the introduction be improved?
4. What is the thesis?
5. What details and/or examples support the thesis?
6. What additional details and/or examples are needed?
7. What parts should be clarified?
8. How are the conclusion and introduction related? How could they be related?

Consider this strategy:

Imagine that you are an American college student. Read your essay to yourself from the point of view of that student. Before revising your essay, use the Revision Checklist.

REVISION CHECKLIST

1. Take a close look at the introduction. Does your essay need a new introduction in light of the changes that you have made? Does your introduction make the reader want to read the rest of your essay?
2. Examine your thesis statement. Is it stated clearly? Revise it if necessary.
3. In this essay, you discussed reasons for war or the effects of war. Are the reasons or effects discussed in a logical order?
4. Check to make sure that your thesis is supported with enough details and examples. How could examples be used more effectively?
5. Look for spots in your essay which do not seem to meet the readers' needs.
6. Reconsider the conclusion. Should the essay end where it does or should you write a bit more?

Revise your essay. Concentrate on improving the organization and content.

EDIT

Correct your grammar mistakes. Focus particularly on correcting errors involving count and noncount nouns.

IT WORKS!
Learning Strategy:
Keeping Track of
Your Progress

Using a Language Learning Log

1. Vocabulary:
   Write down as many new words from the lesson as you can remember.

   _____

   _____

   _____

2. Grammar:
   Note examples of any grammatical structures from the lesson learned or reviewed. Write a brief explanation of the grammar points that they illustrate.

   _____

   _____

   _____

3. Punctuation:
   Write down any new punctuation rules that you learned.

   _____

   _____

   _____

4. Gaining Writing Competence:
List any new composition techniques that you learned. (Such techniques might include those for writing interesting introductions, bodies, and conclusions or for composing different types of writing effectively.)

_____

_____

_____

5. Learning Strategies:
Briefly describe any new learning strategies that you have applied in your writing.

_____

_____

_____

6. Areas that Need More Work:
Note here in brief form any areas that you are still trying to improve. Try to be as specific as possible.

_____

_____

_____

_____

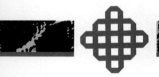

SUMMARY OF LESSON 2: REASONS FOR WAR

In this lesson, you have examined the causes of war. You have written definitions as well as an analysis. In the next lesson, you will examine one particular reason for physical violence: injustice.

QUICK REFERENCE TO LEARNING STRATEGIES

Forming Concepts: Reading Widely (p. 112)

Personalizing: Questioning Your Audience (p. 116)

Understanding and Using Emotions: Discussing How to Give and Receive Constructive Feedback (p. 116)

Forming Concepts: Analyzing the Readers (p. 121)

Managing Your Learning: Analyzing the Purpose (p. 121)

Understanding and Using Emotions: Believing in the Purpose of Your Writing (p. 122)

Personalizing: Putting Yourself in the Reader's Shoes (p. 122)

Overview

In what specific situations is violence justified? How do Americans feel about the justification of violence? Do people in other cultures feel the same way? These are just a few of the questions which you will consider in this lesson. The lesson is designed to give you additional experience writing stories and reports. Information obtained in this lesson will help you complete the essay assignment given on page 143.

About the Reading

The story below was written by a famous reporter, John Simpson. It was written at the time that Chinese university students and civilians were protesting against Communism. These Chinese people believed that their government was an unjust one since it placed many restrictions on their lifestyle which they did not like. After you read the story, you will retell the most important events. More specifically, you will reconstruct John Simpson's experience as he set out for Tianenmen Square.

AS YOU READ

As you read "Tianenmen Square," try to understand the big picture; do not try to read and understand all the details. Concentrate on what the reporter sees and feels as he finds himself in the midst of a massacre. To understand the main idea, read the story quickly. Remember what you learned so far in Chapters 1 and 2: one or two quick reads will help you understand the main point of the story more quickly than slow, careful reading. As you read, try to answer these questions:

1. What were the students protesting?
2. Did the students who John Simpson describes have the right to protest against injustice?
3. Did they have the right to try to kill the Chinese soldiers who attempted to take them out of Tianenmen Square?
4. Did the resulting physical violence help them achieve justice?

TIANENMEN SQUARE

John Simpson

1   It was humid and airless, and the streets around our hotel were empty. We had set out for Tianenmen Square: a big, conspicuous European television team reporter, producer, cameraman, sound-recordist, translator, lighting man, complete with equipment. A cyclist rode past, shouting and pointing. What it meant we couldn't tell. Then we came upon a line of soldiers. Some of them had bleeding faces; one cradled a broken arm. They were walking slowly, limping. There had been a battle somewhere, but we couldn't tell where.

2   When we reached Chagan Avenue, the main east-west thoroughfare, it was as full of people as in the days of the great demonstrations—a human river. We followed the flow of it to the Gate of Heavenly Peace, under the bland, moonlike portrait of Chairman Mao. There were hundreds of small groups, each concentrated around someone who was haranguing° or lecturing the others, using the familiar, heavy public gestures of the Chinese. Other groups had formed around radios turned to foreign stations. People were moving from group to group, pushing in, crushing around a speaker, arguing, moving on, passing along any new information.

3   For the most part these were not students. They were from the factories, and the red cloths tied around their heads made them look aggressive, even piratical.° Trucks started arriving from the edge of the city, full of more young workers, waving the banners of their factories, singing, chanting, looking forward to trouble.

4   People were shouting: There was a battle going on between the tanks and the crowd, somewhere to the east of the city center. Details differed, and I had trouble finding out what was being said: I watched the animated faces, everyone pushing closer to each new source of information, pulling at each other's sleeves or shoulders. Tanks and armored personnel carriers,° they were saying, were heading towards the Square. They were coming from two directions, east and west. The crowds that gathered couldn't stop them.

5   "It's a different army. It's not the Thirty-eighth!" The man who said this was screaming it, grabbing at our translator, holding on to him, trying to make him understand the significance of it. "It is not the Thirty-eighth!" It had been the Thirty-eighth Army that had tried to recapture the city twice before. The soldiers had been unarmed; the commander, the father of a student in the Square, had ordered that operations be carried out peacefully.

6   We pushed our way towards the Square where, despite the rumors and the panic, we saw something very different: several thousand people standing in silence, motionless, listening to a large loudspeaker, bolted° to a street lamp:

Go home and save your life. You will fail. You are not behaving in the correct Chinese manner. This is not the West. It is China. You should behave like a good Chinese. Go home and save your life. Go home and save your life.

7   The voice was expressionless, like that of a hypnotist. I looked at the silent, serious faces, illuminated by the orange light of the street lamps, studying the loudspeaker. Even the small children, brought there with the rest of the family, stared intently. The order was repeated again and again. It was a voice the people of China had been listening to for forty years, and continued listening to even now. But now no one did what the hypnotist said. No one moved.

8   And then, suddenly, everything changed: the loudspeaker's spell was broken by shouts that the army was coming. There was the sound of a violent scraping, and across the avenue I saw people pulling at the railings that ran along the roadway and dragging them across the pavement to build a barricade.° Everyone moved quickly, a crowd suddenly animated, its actions fast and decisive,° sometimes brutal. They blocked off Changan Avenue and the Square itself, and we began filming, flooding the sweating enthusiasts with our camera-light. People danced around us, showing off their weaponry: knives, crude spears, bricks. A boy rushed up to our camera and opened his shabby green jacket like a black marketeer° to reveal a row of Coca-Cola bottles strapped to his waist, filled with petrol and plugged with rags. He laughed, and mimed° the action of pulling out each bottle and throwing it. I asked him his age. He was sixteen. Why was he against the government? He couldn't answer. He gripped another of his Molotov cocktails,° laughing all the time.

9   That the army was coming was no longer rumor but fact and our translator heard that it would move in at one o'clock. It was half-past midnight. In the distance, above the noise of the crowd, I thought I could hear the sound of guns. I wanted to find a vantage point from which we could film, without being spotted by the army. But the tension that was bonding members of the crowd together did not have the same effect on the members of our small team. It was hot and noisy. We argued. We started shouting, and I headed off on my own.

10   I pushed through the crowds, immediately feeling better for being on my own. There were very few foreign journalists left in the Square by now, and I felt especially conspicuous.° But I also felt good. People grabbed my hand, thanking me for being with them. I gave them a V for Victory sign and was applauded by everyone around me. It was hard to define the mood. There was still a spirit of celebration, that they were out on the streets, challenging the government, but the spirit was also giving way to a terrible foreboding.° There was something else. Something I hadn't seen before: a reckless ferocity° of purpose.

11   I crossed back into the main part of Tianenmen Square, the village of student tents. There were sticks and cardboard and broken glass underfoot. The smells were familiar and strong—wood-smoke, urine, and heavy disinfectant.° A couple clung to each other, her head on his shoulder. I passed in front of them, but they didn't raise their eyes. A student asked me to sign his T-shirt, a craze from earlier days. He had thick glasses and a bad complexion,° and he spoke English. "It will be dangerous tonight," he said. "We are all very afraid here."

12   I finished signing his shirt, at the back below the collar. He grabbed my hand and shook it excitedly. His grip was bony and greasy. I asked him what he thought would happen.

13   "We will all die."

14   He straightened up and shook my hand again, and slipped between the tents.

15   The camp was dark. There were a few students left; most of them had gathered in the center of the Square, around the Monument to the People's Heroes. I could hear their speeches and the occasional burst of singing—the Internationale,[1] as always. Here, though, it was quiet. This was where the students had chosen to build their statue of the Goddess of Democracy, with her sightless eyes, her torch held in both hands. The symbol of all our aspirations,° one of the student leaders called her: the fruit of our struggle. To me, she looked very fragile.

16   The speeches and the songs continued in the distance. Then suddenly they stopped. There was a violent squealing° sound—the familiar sound of an armored personnel carrier. I heard screaming, and behind me, in the Avenue, everyone started running. When I finally spotted the vehicle, I could see that it was making its way with speed down the side of the Square. It seemed uncertain of its direction—one moment driving straight for the Square, and then stopping, turning, stopping again, as if looking for a way to escape. There was a sudden angry roar, and I know it was because the vehicle had crushed someone under its tracks. It then turned in my direction—it was pointed at me—and I felt a different kind of panic. The action was starting and I was separated from my colleagues;° it is a rule of my job to stay with camera crew in times of danger.

17   The vehicle carried on, swaying back and forth. It must have knocked down six or seven people. By now it was on fire, having been hit repeatedly by Molotov cocktails. Somehow, though, it escaped and headed off to the west.

18   Then a second armored personnel carrier came along Changan Avenue, alone and unsupported like the first. This time everyone turned and ran hard towards the vehicle, knowing that they, with their numbers and their petrol bombs, had the power to knock it out. They screamed with anger and hate as the vehicle swung randomly in different directions, threatening to knock people down as it made its way through the Square. The Molotov cocktails above our heads, spinning over and over, exploding on the thin shell of armor that protected the men inside. Still the vehicle carried on, zigzagging, crossing the Avenue, trying to find a way through the barricade. A pause, and it charged, head-on, straight into a block of concrete—and then stuck, its engine whirring wildly. A terrible shout of triumph came from the crowd; primitive and dark, its prey° finally caught. The smell of petrol and sweat was in the air, primitive and dark, intoxicating and violent. Everyone around me was pushing and shoving to get to the vehicle. At first I resisted; then, close behind it, I saw the light of a camera, just where the crowd was starting to swarm. There were only three cameramen still filming in the entire Square, and I knew that my colleague was the only one crazy enough to be that close. Now I was the one fighting, struggling to get through the crowd, pulling people back, pushing them out of my path, swearing, a big brutal English man stronger than any of them. I tore one man's shirt and punched another in the back. All around me the men seemed to be yelling at the sky, their faces lit up; the vehicle had caught fire. A man—his chest bare—climbed up the side of the vehicle and stood on top of it, his arms raised in victory, the noise of the mob° around him. They knew they had the vehicle's crew trapped inside. Someone started beating at the armored glass with an iron bar.

19   I reached the cameraman and pulled hard at his arm to get his attention. He scarcely noticed me, in the middle of the noise and the violence, and carried on filming. He and his sound recordist and the Chinese lighting men were a few feet from the vehicle close enough to be killed if it exploded or if the soldiers came out shooting. But I couldn't make them step back, and so we stayed there, the four of us, the heat beating against our faces as people continued to pour petrol on the bonnet° and roof and smashed at the doors and the armored glass. What was it like inside? I imagined the soldiers half-crazed with the noise and the heat and the fear of being burned alive.

20   The screaming around me rose even louder: the handle of the door at the rear of the vehicle had turned a little, and the door began to open. A soldier pushed the barrel of a gun out, but it was grabbed from his hands, and then everyone started grabbing his arms, pulling and wrenching° until finally he came free, and then he was gone: I saw the arms of the mob, raised above their heads as they fought to get their blows in. He was dead within seconds, and his body was dragged away in triumph. A second soldier showed his head through the door and was then immediately pulled out by his hair and ears and the skin on his face. This soldier I could see: his eyes were rolling, and his mouth was open, and he was covered with blood where the skin had been ripped off. Only his eyes remained—white and clear—but then someone was trying to get them as well, and someone else began beating his skull until the skull came apart, and there was blood all over the ground, and his brains, and still they kept on beating and beating what was left. Then the horrible sight passed away, and the ground was wet where he had been.

21   There was a third soldier inside. I could see his face in the light of the flames, and some of the crowd could too. They pulled him out, screaming, wild at having missed killing the other soldiers. It was his blood they wanted, I was certain, it was to feel the blood running over their hands. Their mouths were open and panting, like dogs, and their eyes were expressionless. They were shouting, the Chinese lighting man told me afterwards, that the soldier they were about to kill wasn't human, that he was just a thing, an object, which had to be destroyed. And all the time the noise and the heat and the stench of oil burning on hot metal beat at us, overwhelming° our senses, deadening° them.

22   Just as the third soldier was lifted out of the vehicle, almost fainting, a bus rushed towards us stopping, with great skill, so that its rear door opened just beside the group with the soldier. The students had heard what was happening, and a group had raced the bus over to save whomever they could. The mob did not want to give up its prize. The students tried to drag the soldier on board, and the crowd held on to him, pulling him back. By some mischance° the bus door started closing and it seemed that he must be killed.

23   I had seen people die in front of me before. But I had never seen three people die, one after the other, in this way. Once again the members of the crowd closed around the soldier, their arms raised over their heads to beat him to death. The bus and the safety it promised were so close. It seemed to me then that I couldn't look on any longer, a passive observer, watching another man's skin torn away or his head broken open, and do nothing. I saw the soldier's face, expressing only horror and pain as he sank under the blows of the people around him, and I started to move forward. The ferocity of the crowd had entered me, but I felt it was the crowd that was the animal, that it wasn't properly human. The soldier had sunk down to the ground, and a man was trying to break his skull with a half-brick, bringing it down with full force. I screamed obscenities° at the man—stupid obscenities, as no one except my colleagues could have understood them—and threw myself at him, catching him with his arm up, ready for another blow. He looked at me blankly, and his thin arm went limp in my grasp. I stopped shouting. He relaxed his grip on the brick, and I threw it under the bus. It felt wet. A little room had been created around the soldier, and the student who had tried to rescue him before could now get to him. The rest of the mob hadn't given up, but the students were able to pull the soldier away and get him on to the bus by the other door. He was safe.

24   The vehicle burned for a long time, its driver and the man beside him burning with it. The flames lit up the Square and reflected on the face of the Monument where the students had taken their stand. The crowd in Changan Avenue had been satisfied. The loudspeakers had stopped telling people to save their lives. There was silence.

The students sang the Internationale. It would be for the last time, and it sounded weak and faint in the vastness° of the Square. Many were crying. No doubt some students joined in the attacks on the army, but those in the Square kept to their principle of nonviolence. Although the army suffered the first casualties, it was the students who would be the martyrs° that night.

26   My colleagues and I wanted to save our pictures in case we were arrested, and I told the others that we should go back to the Beijing Hotel and come out again later. I now feel guilty about the decision; it was wrong. We ought to have stayed in the Square, even though the other camera crews had already left and it might have cost us our lives. Someone should have been there when the massacre° took place, filming what happened, showing the courage of the students as they were surrounded by tanks and the army advancing, firing as it went.

27   Instead, we took up our position on the fourteenth floor of the Beijing Hotel. From there, everything seemed gray and distant. We saw most of what happened, but we were separated from the fear and the noise and the stench° of it. We saw the troops pouring out of the Gate of Heavenly Peace, bayonets° fixed, shooting first into the air and then straight ahead of them. They looked like robots, with their rounded dark helmets. We filmed them charging across and clearing the northern end of the Square, where I had signed the student's T-shirt. We filmed the tanks as they drove over the tents where some of the students had taken refuge,° among them, perhaps, the young couple I had seen sitting silently, their arms around each other. Dozens of people seemed to have died in that way, and those who saw it said they could hear the screams of the people inside the tents over the noise of the tanks. We filmed as the lights in the Square were switched off at 4:00 A.M. They were switched on again forty minutes later, when the troops and the tanks moved towards the Monument itself, shooting first in the air and then, again, directly at the students themselves, so that the steps of the Monument and the heroic reliefs° which decorated it were smashed by bullets.

28   Once or twice, we were ourselves shot at, and during the night the security police sent men to our room to arrest us: but I shouted at them in English, and they went away, uncertain of the extent of their powers. Below us, people still gathered in the avenue, shouting their defiance° at the troops who were massed at the farther end. Every now and then the crack of a rifle would bring down another demonstrator, and the body would be rescued by a trishaw° driver or the crew of an ambulance. Below us, the best and noblest political protest since Czechoslovakia in 1969² was being crushed as we watched. I knelt on the balcony, beside the cameraman and a Chinese women, one of the student leaders.

29   She had taken refuge in our room because we were foreigners. I shouted at her to go back inside, but she refused, turning her head from me so that I wouldn't see that she was crying, her hands clenched° tight enough to hurt, intent on watching the rape of her country and the movement she and her friends had built up in the course of twenty-two days. I had seen the river of protest running along Changan Avenue in that time; I had seen a million people in the streets, demanding a way of life that was better than rule by corruption and secret police. I recalled the lines of the T'ang dynasty poet Li Po that if you cut water with a sword you merely made it run faster. But the river of change had been damned, and below me, in the Avenue where it had run, people were dying. Beside me, the cameraman spotted something and started filming. Down in the Square, in the early light, the soldiers were busy unrolling something and lifting it up. Soon a great curtain of black cloth covered the entrance to Tianenmen Square. What was happening there was hidden from us.

¹Communist anthem or song of praise.
²The famous Prague spring.

VOCABULARY GLOSS

The definitions given below will help you understand this story. Numbers in the parenthesis to the right of the word refer to the paragraph in which the word appears. Not all words that you do not understand are glossed. Guess the meanings of those words in Simpson's story which you do not understand.

to harangue (2) (v.)	to make claims that are unjustified or excessive (too many)
piratical (3) (adj.)	resembling a pirate or thief
armored personnel carriers (4) (n.)	transportation used to carry army officials—protected by a defensive covering of metal, used in combat
bolted (6) (adj.)	fastened
barricade (8) (n.)	barrier or obstacle used to prevent army from advancing
decisive (8) (adj.)	determined, firm
black marketer (8) (n.)	a person who buys and sells illegal products
to mime (8) (v.)	to gesture (use hand and body movements) without words
Molotov cocktail (8) (n.)	a crude hand grenade (weapon) made of a bottle filled with gasoline which ignites (lights and blows up) when thrown
conspicuous (10) (adj.)	attracting attention
foreboding (10) (n.)	prediction, especially of misfortune
ferocity (10) (n.)	the quality of being deeply felt
disinfectant (11) (n.)	a product which cleans and kills harmful bacteria
complexion (11) (n.)	the appearance of the skin on the face
aspiration (15) (n.)	a strong desire to achieve something great
squealing (16) (n.)	the sound of a loud, shrill (high-pitched) noise
colleague (16) (n.)	associate in a field
prey (18) (n.)	a victim, one that is helpless or unable to prevent attack
mob (18) (n.)	a crowd of people
bonnet (19) (n.)	automobile hood (*British English*)
to wrench (20) (v.)	to pull violently, hurting the body
to overwhelm (21) (v.)	to overcome or crush
to deaden (21) (v.)	to become dead
mischance (22) (n.)	a misfortune
obscenity (23) (n.)	a disgusting, offensive word
vastness (25) (n.)	huge space
martyr (25) (n.)	a person who voluntarily dies because of personal beliefs
massacre (26) (n.)	the act of killing a large number of people cruelly
stench (27) (n.)	a strong, bad odor
bayonet (27) (n.)	a weapon with a steel blade used in hand-to-hand combat
to take refuge (27) (v.)	to flee for protection or to escape danger
relief (27) (n.)	sculpture or forms showing figures
defiance (28) (n.)	the act of challenging
trishaw (28) (n.)	a type of carriage pulled by humans
to clench (29) (v.)	to hold firmly

Comprehension Workout

COOPERATIVE LEARNING: ROUND ROBIN

Reconstruct the story that you just read.

BEFORE YOU BEGIN

Consider this strategy:

LEARNING STRATEGY

Remembering New Material: Reconstructing a story helps you remember and synthesize the entire story and then express it in your own words.

This ancient strategy has been successfully used throughout Asia and the Middle East for thousands of years.

EXERCISE 33

Divide into small groups of about four students. Circulate a piece of paper. The first student writes one sentence which attempts to answer the question below. Then, he or she hands the paper to the next student who writes another sentence which attempts to answer the question. Each student passes the paper to the next until the answer is complete. Do not be concerned with grammatical errors. Concentrate on answering the question. If someone in the group makes a mistake, keep going. You have twenty minutes to complete this assignment.

Question: What happened to John Simpson the night of June 4, 1989? Begin by describing the events which affected the author that night.

Listening

Listen again to the audiotaped story about war.

WHILE YOU LISTEN

As you listen to the audiotaped story, focus on the notion of injustice. Ask yourself these questions:

1. In what specific circumstances is war fair?
2. Is the war described in this story fair? If not, why? Were innocent victims hurt?
3. In what specific ways, if any, does the writer describe injustice?

AFTER YOU LISTEN

React to the audiotaped story in your journal. If you are having difficulty reacting to the stories, consider the following questions.

1. The focus of this lesson is violence and injustice. Do you think war is ever fair? If yes, when? Do you think the writer of this story would agree with you?
2. How does the writer use language in such a way that the readers/listeners are able to feel the injustice of war?
3. Do people from some cultures suffer more from war than people from other cultures? Explain your answer. Do you think the writer of the audiotaped war story would agree with you?

Gaining Writing Competence

ENDING A STORY

One of the reasons the story on pages 126–130 is so effective is because Simpson is able to end it in an interesting way. Note that the ending of the story coincides with the Communists' efforts to end the Tianenmen Square protest and end the world's understanding of the event. In the writing task which follows, you will be asked to write a short story about war. The following guidelines are intended to help you end your story effectively.

GUIDELINES FOR WRITING AN EFFECTIVE ENDING

An effective ending may:

1. lead to the thesis of the story for the first time
2. emphasize the thesis or the main points of the story
3. draw a conclusion about the story
4. state an opinion about the story
5. ask a question provoking thought about the story

WHAT TO AVOID WHEN WRITING AN ENDING

1. *Denying the importance of your story.* Avoid stating: "This story is not really important" or "This story really isn't true" or "And then I woke up and found out the whole story was just a dream."
2. *Stating the obvious.* When you state the obvious, you tell readers what they already know. Here is an example of stating the obvious: "By the way, in case you missed the meaning of the entire story which I summarized above, this is what the story meant. . . ." This type of ending prevents readers from drawing their own conclusions about the ending.
3. *Leaving the reader unsatisfied.* Sometimes authors fail to add an ending which ties the story together. This leaves the readers feeling unsatisfied.

Text Analysis: Endings

EXERCISE 34

Individually, analyze John Simpson's story, "Tianenmen Square." Determine what type of conclusion he uses.

Gaining Writing Competence

USING DIALOGUE TO MAKE A STORY COME ALIVE

Explanation: In the writing task which follows, you will write a story. To make the people in your story come alive, it will be helpful to use dialogue.

PUNCTUATION RULES FOR USING DIALOGUE

The following rules will help you use dialogue properly.

1. Use quotation marks (" ") at the beginning and the end of the words spoken by the person you are quoting. The name of the person and a verb (such as *said*) are outside of the quotation marks.

   EXAMPLES: John said, "Leave me here."

   "Save yourself while you have time," John said.

2. Commas, periods, and question marks are put inside the quotation marks.

   EXAMPLES: "Why are you leaving me here to suffer?" John asked.

3. In writing the words of more than one speaker, new quotation marks and a new paragraph are used each time the speaker changes.

   EXAMPLES: "Duck!" Henri shouted.
   "No need to," I yelled back.

Punctuation Practice: Using Quotation Marks

EXERCISE 35

Add quotations to the sentences below where needed.

Just as the moon came up, I saw my friend lying on the battlefield. "Joe, Joe, I called. Are you all right?

No. I've been wounded he yelled out to me. Can you help me out of here. I'm stuck in this ditch and I can't move. My body aches all over.

For a long period I just sat there. I couldn't decide what to do. Should I risk my life trying to help my friend out of his precarious situation, or should I ignore his call? Our batallion had left us long ago, and I alone could help my friend.

Again, Joe called to me. This time, without thinking, I yelled back, I'll get you out of there. Then, I ran as I had never run before. I was convinced that at any moment I would step on a mine and my life would be over.

What took you so long? Joe asked when I reached him. I never answered his question.

Writing Task

WRITING A STORY

Write a one page story about war. Your story should have an introduction, a body, and a conclusion. It should be written for your classmates from a personal point of view. Your purpose is to entertain.

BEFORE YOU WRITE

Answer the prewriting questions below.

PREWRITING QUESTIONS

Who are the main characters in your story?

What happens to these characters?

Where does your story take place?

What interesting event or events take place?

What happens at the end of your story?

Does your story give a personal opinion about war or evaluate it?

Consider the following strategy:

LEARNING STRATEGY

Managing Your Learning: If you are having difficulty getting started, divide your writing assignment into several components and work on one component at a time.

Break up the Writing Task into several sections. Perhaps you could write one section on the main characters, another on the events which happen, and another on your own opinions of the story. When you are finished writing these sections, try putting the entire essay together. You've already done a lot of the work so this writing task should be easy now.

AFTER YOU WRITE

Reread your story. The Revision Checklist will help you consider changes that you would like to make to the organization and content of your story. As you review this checklist, take notes. You will use these notes in revising your story.

REVISION CHECKLIST

1. Consider ways of expanding your story. Add any information which is needed to make your story clearer.
2. Check to see that you have used effective transitions. Watch out for too many sentences beginning with "So," "And," or "And then." Replace these transitions with better ones.
3. If your story seems too dense or boring, try adding more dialogue to paint a vivid picture of the story for the readers. Dialogue can be used effectively to help your story come alive.
4. Consider the plot. Is there a tension between the characters in the story? Good stories often describe a tension or conflict. If your story has no such tension or conflict in it, consider revising it so that it contains one.
5. Take a long look at the ending. Does your story end effectively? If it doesn't, try writing an entirely different ending.

REVISE YOUR STORY

Refer back to your notes as you revise your story.

AFTER YOU HAVE REVISED YOUR STORY

Find a partner. Read each other your stories. Then, fill out the Peer Revising Form below for both stories.

PEER REVISING FORM

1. What is the main point of this story?

_____

_____

2. Is the introduction interesting?

_____

_____

3. Who are the main characters?

_____

_____

4. What happens to them?

_____

_____

5. Does your classmate use dialogue effectively to make the characters in the story come alive?

_____

_____

6. Is the conclusion effective? How could it be made more interesting?

_____

_____

7. Which part of this story is your favorite?

_____

_____

8. What one piece of advice could you give your classmate which would improve his/her story?

_____

_____

REVISE YOUR STORY AGAIN

Make whatever changes to the organization and content that you like.

EDIT YOUR STORY

Edit your story carefully.

AFTER YOU HAVE FINISHED EDITING YOUR STORY

Consider this strategy:

LEARNING STRATEGY

Understanding and Using Emotions: When you take time to consider the positive aspects of your writing, it encourages you to keep writing.

Take out a yellow marking pen and mark all the areas in the story which you just wrote that you like. Don't be modest. Reflect on your writing. How did you do? What did you like about your writing?

Grammar Explanation

PARALLEL STRUCTURES

Explanation: In the next writing activity, you will write about the survey on page 84. Knowing how to use parallelism effectively will help you.

With a partner, discuss the rules for using parallel structures given below. When you have finished, complete the exercise on page 139. Discuss well! You will be graded on your own ability to form parallel structures and your partner's ability.

PARALLELISM

Use parallel constructions to add unity to your writing and emphasize certain points. Within sentences, they add grammatical balance.

SINGLE WORDS

Notice in the examples below that noun phases in a series are connected with the word *and* and are made up of the identical parts of speech. In the first sentence, the words are nouns, and in the second sentence, the words are verbs.

1. The speeches and the song continued in the distance.
2. Terrified, the reporter ran and screamed.

PHRASES

Notice that in these examples, the phrases are made up of the same parts of speech. The first sentence contains gerunds followed by prepositional phrases, and the second sentence contains infinitives followed by prepositional phrases.

1. I saw people pulling at the railing and jumping on the pavement.
2. The reporter was ready to leave Tianenmen Square and to return to the United States.

CLAUSES

Notice in the examples that the underlined clauses which make up the parallel structure are identical. The first sentence contains two "if" clauses, while the second sentence contains two relative clauses.

1. He and his sound recordist and the Chinese lighting men were a few feet from the vehicle, close enough to be killed if it exploded or if the soldiers came out shooting.
2. I knew that he would throw the brick, and that he would crush the soldier's skull.

Grammar Practice: Parallel Structure

EXERCISE 36

Underline the parallel structures in the following sentences taken from the reading in this lesson. Explain why they are parallel structures in the space provided. Follow the example given below.

EXAMPLE   **EXPLANATION**

All is fair in <u>love</u> and <u>war</u>.   Both <u>love</u> and <u>war</u> are nouns.

1. The man who said this was screaming it, clutching at our translator, holding on to him, trying to make him understand the significance of it.

   _____

2. The speeches and the songs continued in the distance.

   _____

3. It seemed uncertain of its direction—one moment driving straight for the Square, and then stopping, turning , stopping again, as if looking for a way to escape.

   _____

4. It was hot and noisy.

   _____

5. I imagined the soldiers half-crazed with the noise and the heat and the fear of being burned alive.

   _____

6. Somehow, though, the vehicle escaped and headed off to the west.

   _____

Cooperative Learning Quiz: Just for Fun

EXERCISE 37

The sentences on page 140 fail to use parallel structures appropriately. Write an accurate revision of each of the sentences using correct parallel structures. Do not be concerned if your revision changes words in the original sentence. Follow the example below. When you are finished, you will receive a score for your own work and your partner's work. You will also receive a combined score.

EXAMPLE: Some people hate war and for other people war is their love.

REVISION: Some people hate war and other people love it.

1. The teacher asked the children not to engage in physical violence and for them to stay seated.

   _____

2. Tomoko preferred staying home and to study rather than to watch a war movie.

   _____

3. The soldiers fought the battle in the meadow overlooking the river and watching the mountain.

   _____

4. The factor produces new weapons and it can make tanks.

   _____

5. They ate many foods on the battlefield—canned beans, dried fruits, and they ate hot dogs.

   _____

6. A battlefield is a place to make friends and for watching them die.

   _____

7. Marta believes that women should be allowed to fight in wars and that they should protect their country.

   _____

8. Mike is interested in avoiding the army, work, and he does not want to go to college.

   _____

9. The army is the place to foster friendships, to develop an understanding of values and beliefs, and for meeting others with similar interests.

   _____

10. It is everyone's responsibility to consider carefully those actions which might lead to international warfare, those ways to prevent war, and to avoid conflict.

    _____

HOW WELL DID YOU DO?

Your score: _____
Your partner's score: _____
Your combined score: _____

LEARNING STRATEGY

Remembering New Material: Practicing grammar structures in your writing helps you learn them.

Grammar Practice

PARALLEL STRUCTURES

Seek opportunities to use the parallel structures that you studied on page 138. Simply studying a grammar explanation once or twice is not enough to learn it. Try using specific grammatical structures in your writing. For example, try using parallel structures in your final essay assignment (refer to page 143) as well in the Quick Write activity below.

LEARNING STRATEGY

Remembering New Material: Discussing grammar rules with a classmate helps you remember these rules.

Quick Write

REPORTING SURVEY DATA

Simpson, the author of "Tianenmen Square," seems to think that the Chinese students were unjustified in committing acts of violence. (Recall his description of his own efforts to prevent the students from killing a soldier.) However, he also seems opposed to the violence committed by the Chinese soldiers who massacred the students in Tianenmen Square. Unlike Simpson, many people believe that violence is a reasonable response to injustice. Do your classmates believe that physical violence is an effective response? Write a brief one or two paragraph report in which you summarize two or three major findings from your class survey. The survey questionnaire is on page 84. You may write about how the class in general responded or how students from different cultural backgrounds responded. Your purpose is to inform and your readers are your classmates.

BEFORE YOU WRITE

As a class, review the results of the survey. After you have done this, analyze the results by culture on the blackboard. Do students from some cultures feel differently about war than students from other cultures? Discuss possible reasons for the results. You are just about to write. Before doing so, consider the strategy below:

LEARNING STRATEGY

Understanding and Using Emotions: Prior to writing, you need to calm down to lower your anxiety to write more effectively.

Try taking a deep breath or listening to soft music. This will lower your anxiety. (If you need to get psyched up, listen to more lively music!)

AFTER YOU WRITE

Form small groups. Discuss your reports with the students in your group.

Using a Language Learning Log

IT WORKS!
Learning Strategy:
Keeping Track of
Your Progress

1. Vocabulary:
   Write down as many new words from the lesson as you can remember.

   _____

   _____

2. Grammar:
   Note examples of any grammatical structures from the lesson learned or reviewed. Write a brief explanation of the grammar points that they illustrate.

   _____

   _____

3. Punctuation:
   Write down any new punctuation rules that you learned.

   _____

   _____

4. Techniques for Gaining Writing Competence:
   List any new composition techniques that you learned. (Such techniques might include those for writing interesting introductions, bodies, and conclusions or for composing different types of writing effectively.)

   _____

   _____

5. Learning Strategies:
   Briefly describe any new learning strategies that you have applied in your writing.

   _____

   _____

6. Areas that Need More Work:
   Note here in brief form any areas that you are still trying to improve. Try to be as specific as possible.

   _____

   _____

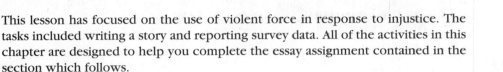

SUMMARY OF LESSON 3:
FORCE IN RESPONSE TO INJUSTICE

This lesson has focused on the use of violent force in response to injustice. The tasks included writing a story and reporting survey data. All of the activities in this chapter are designed to help you complete the essay assignment contained in the section which follows.

QUICK REFERENCE TO LEARNING STRATEGIES

Remembering New Material: Reconstructing a Story (p. 132)

Managing Your Learning: Starting a Writing Task by Breaking It Up into Parts (p. 135)

Understanding and Using Emotions: Considering the Positive Aspects of Your
    Writing (p. 137)

Remembering New Material: Using Practicing Grammar Rules (p. 140)

Understanding and Using Emotions: Lowering Your Anxiety before Writing (p. 141)

WRITING ASSIGNMENT FOR CHAPTER 2

Description of Writing Assignment

Although this unit focused on wars, battles, and violent protests, there are many other types of physical violence. These include rape, wife-beating, child abuse, gang-related fighting, and drug wars. Describe one specific type of physical violence. Argue that it is important to prevent the type of violence which you have described and suggest several steps your readers can take to stop it.

You are writing this essay for your instructor and classmates. Your purpose is to convince them to fight against the particular type of physical violence which you discuss.

PREWRITING ACTIVITIES

BRAINSTORMING

In this activity, you will be asked to make three lists pertaining to physical violence. You will have five minutes to make each list. Your teacher will tell you when your time begins and ends. In small groups, take five minutes to write a list of different types of physical violence. Then, individually, choose one type of physical violence.

1. Take five minutes to write a second list of ways to prevent this type of violence.
2. Take another five minutes to write a third list of events which happen when this type of violence is not stopped.

Discuss your lists with two classmates. Then, take ten minutes to revise your lists.

143

FAST WRITING

When you have finished revising your list, choose one type of physical violence to write about. At the top of your paper write, "How to Prevent _____." Complete the blank with the type of violence that you have chosen. Then, write for ten minutes in response to the question that you have just written. (For more information about fast writing, refer to pages 75-76.)

LOOPING

1. Review your free writing. Underline those parts which you found most interesting and would like to write about more. Choose one of these parts and do a second free writing (your first loop) for about ten minutes.
2. Underline those parts of your free writing (this time, your first loop) that you found interesting and would like to develop further. Then choose one of these and write on it for about ten minutes. This is your "second loop." Continue writing until you think you have gathered enough ideas to write the first draft of your essay. Refer to your free writing and loops when you write your first draft.

REVISING ACTIVITIES

Choose someone in the class whom you have never worked with before as your partner in this peer editing session. Read each other's essays. Then complete the Peer Revising Form for both essays. Keep in mind that you are responding to the content and organization, not the grammar and mechanics.

PEER REVISING FORM

1. What is your favorite art of this essay?
2. Does the introduction interest you? If so, what do you like about it?
3. Underline the thesis statement. What do you expect this essay to be about.?
4. Write the purpose of each paragraph.
5. Circle the words and expressions which link paragraphs.
6. Are there parts of the essay which lack sufficient information or detail? What should be added to support the thesis better?
7. Is the conclusion effective? Why?
8. What words does the writer use effectively?

After you have finished commenting on each other's papers, consider your classmate's comments. Make any revisions you think would improve your essay. If you need to add supporting details to your writing, you might want to do some library research.

EDITING ACTIVITIES

Once you have finished the final revision of your essay, it is time to edit it. Editing means correcting your mistakes.

1. Read your paper aloud to yourself. First, try to correct *anything that doesn't sound right*. If you are unsure of a specific grammar structure, check a grammar reference handbook, or try to restate what you have written in a simpler way. If you are unsure of the spelling of a word, look it up.

2. Reread your essay again. Make sure that you have used parallel structures correctly.

3. Reread your essay a third time. This time, focus on one specific aspect of English with which you are having difficulty. (This might be count and noncount nouns, pronoun reference, modal auxiliaries, relative clauses, etc.) Correct your errors.

SHARE YOUR WRITING

In small groups, choose those writings which best illustrate what you have learned in this chapter. Then share them with the rest of the class and your teacher.

Power and the Environment

Nature hates all sudden changes.

Nature is conquered by obeying her.

Nature will have her course.

INTRODUCTION

This chapter focuses on the following question: Given the fact that we have the power to change the environment, how should we use this power? The question is a particularly thorny one, especially in cases in which we are faced with choices between immediate human needs (for example, the need for firewood in Africa) and long-term environmental needs (for example, the need to prevent deforestation). Some of the questions which you will consider in this unit include:

- How can we improve the environment while, simultaneously, improving the development of the world economy?
- How can we satisfy our immediate needs for goods without polluting our environment?
- How do different cultures regard the environment?

Your main task in this unit is to contribute to a set of class essays on environmental issues. The essay assignment for this unit is described on pages 206-207. All the readings and activities are designed to help you write this essay by providing you with appropriate ideas and language.

Needs Analysis and Goal Setting

Before you start, find out about your own learning needs, preferences, and goals.

SELF-EVALUATION OF LEARNING ACTIVITIES

First, check (✓) the boxes below which apply to you.

ACTIVITY	I LIKE	IT'S OKAY	I DON'T LIKE
Reading poems	___	___	___
Reading essays	___	___	___
Writing a journal	___	___	___
Doing grammar exercises	___	___	___
Doing punctuation exercises	___	___	___
Participating in discussions	___	___	___
Writing stories	___	___	___
Writing summaries	___	___	___
Writing essays	___	___	___

148

Next, find out about your learning goals. Complete the Self-Diagnosis of Writing Goals below. Number your learning objectives for this chapter from 1 to 10—with 1 as your most important goal and 10 as your least important goal. When you set goals, you gain power over your own learning process.

SELF-DIAGNOSIS OF WRITING GOALS

My goals are:

_____ to get my ideas together before I write an essay

_____ to organize my essay appropriately

_____ to improve my vocabulary

_____ to improve my punctuation

_____ to write grammatically correct sentences

_____ to write a persuasive essay

_____ to write a story

_____ to write a definition

_____ to write a summary

_____ to write an essay in which I compare and contrast

Cooperative Learning

NUMBERED HEADS TOGETHER

Divide up into teams of four. Number off within groups (1, 2, 3, or 4). Your team will have five minutes to discuss each question below and to come up with an answer. Make sure that everyone on your team can answer the questions. Your teacher will call a number from one to four. Only students with that number can raise their hands if they have the answer.

Question 1: What are five types of pollution?

Question 2: What are ten actions which responsible individuals can take to reduce pollution?

Question 3: Does the notion of protecting the environment vary across cultures? That is, do some cultures place greater emphasis on the importance of protecting the environment than other cultures? Why?

Question 4: What are three negative consequences of wide-scale pollution for the global environment?

Survey On The Environment

Find out what your classmates are doing about pollution. Some may be doing a lot to prevent it, while others may be doing very little. Do not judge your classmates negatively. There are many reasons for people's actions and the negative effects of pollution are only now being recognized. Complete the survey below. Fill in the blanks with "T" if the statement is "true" and "F" if the statement is false. If there are words which you do not understand, ask your instructor to explain them.

RECYCLING (NOT TURNING THINGS INTO GARBAGE)

_____ **1.** I recycle paper of all kinds—cereal boxes, note paper, bags, newspaper, and so on.

_____ **2.** I use both sides of a piece of paper whenever possible.

_____ **3.** I recycle bottles and jars.

_____ **4.** When I'm at the supermarket and I buy something small, I tell the clerk that I do not need a bag.

_____ **5.** I bring my own bags to the supermarket.

_____ **6.** I ask for paper bags when I am at the supermarket.

_____ **7.** I recycle aluminum cans.

_____ **8.** I frequently look for those clothes in my closet which I do not want any longer and I give them away to others who can use them.

_____ **9.** I try to buy greeting cards which are made out of recycled paper.

_____ **10.** I save paper bags.

_____ **11.** I reuse aluminum foil by washing it off, letting it dry, and putting it away.

_____ **12.** I practice precycling. Precycling means that I buy products at the store which come in packages that can be recycled.

SAVING ENERGY

_____ **13.** I use products that don't use batteries, such as solar calculators which run on light.

_____ **14.** I turn off electrical appliances when I am not using them.

_____ **15.** I turn out lights when I am not using them and no one else is in the room.

_____ **16.** If it's not too far, I walk or ride my bike instead of taking the car or going by bus.

REDUCING THE OZONE HOLE

_____ **17.** I avoid buying Styrofoam products such as picnic plates, cups, and egg cartons. Since plastic foam is usually made with CFC's which make the ozone hole bigger.

_____ **18.** I avoid using aerosol spray cans that contain gases call CFC's.

_____ **19.** To keep the air clean, I grow plants in my place of residence.

SAVING WATER

_____ **20.** When I brush my teeth, I just wet my brush, then turn off the water and turn it on again when I need to rinse my brush off. (I do this to save up to nine gallons of water each time I brush my teeth.)

_____ **21.** I keep bottles of water in the refrigerator so that I do not have to let the faucet run when I want a cold glass of water.

_____ **22.** I take showers instead of baths.

_____ **23.** When I do take a bath, I plug the tub before I let the water run so that I do not waste water.

_____ **24.** Instead of wasting water by pouring water I do not want down the sink, I pour it on a thirsty plant.

_____ **25.** I put small rocks in my toilet tank to take up space so that there will be less room in the tank and my toilet will use less water.

_____ **26.** When I water my garden or grass, I water only in the morning or in the evening when it is less likely that the water will dry up in the heat.

_____ **27.** I make sure that my sprinklers water only the lawn and not the sidewalk or driveway.

REDUCING LITTER

_____ **28.** I throw garbage in trash cans, not on the ground.

_____ **29.** When I see trash on the ground, I take time to throw it away.

Analyze the survey data with the entire class. How many students answer "true" and how many students answer "false" for each item? Tally the responses of each item on the chalkboard. Discuss the data as a class. When you are finished, keep the data on hand. You will be referring to it throughout this chapter.

Manufactured gases called CFCs, which come from air conditioners, refrigerators, plastic foam containers, and some spray cans, can pollute our air.

LESSON 1: PERSPECTIVES OF POLLUTION

Overview

This lesson will explore various views of pollution. You will write a story about your own experience with pollution as well as a report about your classmates' experiences with it.

About the Reading

In the reading selection below, people from diverse fields argue that pollution helps as well as hurts us.

BEFORE YOU READ

Before reading, answer these questions:

1. In your own opinion, is pollution good or bad? Why?
2. What are several types of pollution?
3. Why do we have these types of pollution?

Perspectives of Pollution: Excerpts From Interviews About Pollution

POLLUTION IS BAD

Mark Meyer, a scientist at the University of California, thinks pollution will destroy our planet.

"Each day, 250,000 people are added to the world's population, up to 140 species of living creatures are doomed° to extinction, nearly 140,000 new cars, trucks and buses join the 500 million already on the road, forests covering an area more than one-third the size of Los Angeles are destroyed, and more than 12,000 barrels of crude oil are spilled into the world's oceans. Mother Earth has recuperative° powers. However, the scientist in me knows that the pollution is too much for the Earth to recover from."

POLLUTION IS NECESSARY FOR ECONOMIC GROWTH

Mary Guerra, a successful business woman from Stanford, California, argues that pollution is necessary for economic growth.

"Why do people pollute? Pollution is necessary for economic growth. Americans may complain about the smog, but they do not want to pay some $5.00 for a gallon of gasoline just to help Mother Earth. Third World countries may believe in preventing deforestation,° but they need to feed their hungry people. They must earn enough money to repay enormous foreign debts. Industrialists° everywhere insist that environmental rules make it impossible for them to compete in a free but cruel market. Governmental policies drive businessmen crazy and strangle° business. Consumers are greedy and cry out for products—products which lead to pollution, but also lead to economic growth. Our standard of living, one of the highest in the world, requires the consumption° of manufactured products in ever-increasing amounts. This is capitalism."

OUR SURVIVAL DEPENDS ON POLLUTION

Dan Holmes, a Boston businessman, believes that it is impossible to eliminate pollution.

"Today we pollute so much that total elimination° of pollution would require drastic measures. Every power plant would have to shut down. Industries would have to close. We would have to leave all our cars in the garage. Every bus and truck and airplane would have to stop running. There would be no way to bring food to the cities. There would be no heat and no light. Under these conditions, our population would die in a short time. Our survival° depends on pollution."

TECHNOLOGY MUST BE DEVELOPED WHICH WILL REDUCE POLLUTION AND STIMULATE THE ECONOMY

Janet Abramson, a San Francisco attorney, believes the development of new technologies can stimulate economic development while simultaneously eliminating pollution.

"New technologies are needed to promote economic growth. The development of electric cars, solar energy, and alternative food and water sources will improve our economy and reduce the pollution."

THE POLLUTION PROBLEM IS NOT SERIOUS

Henry Jordans, an economist, believes that pollution is a problem which can be eliminated in the coming years

"As an economist, I analyze trends in terms of savings, investment, and growth. There is little reason to worry about natural constraints° on our ability to increase the world economy. Indicators° of economic growth as well as those measuring the earth's environmental health could not be higher. Constraints on economic expansion must be discouraged. Pollution can be controlled through new technologies."

THE WORLD IS ON THE BRINK° OF A DISASTER

Karen Thorton, a biologist, believes that continuing the single-minded pursuit of economic growth will eventually lead to the destruction of the world economy as well as the planet.

Threads

In 1985, British scientists discovered a hole in the ozone layer over Antarctica.

"We are on the brink of economic collapse.° We need to restructure the nations' economies so that progress can be sustained° at the same time that we limit economic growth. If not, we will use up all our natural resources and destroy our planet. On the environmental front, the situation could not be worse. Anyone who regularly reads scientific journals realizes that the world is quickly deteriorating:° forests are shrinking,° greenhouse gases are accumulating; plants and animal species are diminishing; pollution is threatening lives."

PEOPLE MUST DEVELOP GLOBAL RESPONSIBILITY

Vaclav Havel, former President of Czechoslovakia, argues that only changes in human values will improve the global environment.

"Certain changes of the human mentality are necessary in order to deepen the feeling of global responsibility. The renewal of global responsibility is not possible without a certain respect for a higher principle above my own personal existence."

VOCABULARY

to doom (v.)	to make certain the failure (of something)
recuperative (adj.)	characterized by the ability to repair itself or make itself better
deforestation (n.)	the burning or cutting down of forests
industrialist (n.)	one owning an industry; a manufacturer
to strangle (v.)	to kill by choking
consumption (n.)	the use of products to satisfy personal desires
elimination (n.)	getting rid of, removing
survival (n.)	the act of staying alive
constraint (n.)	the state of being restricted or limited
indicator (n.)	a sign
brink (n.)	edge
collapse (n.)	a breakdown
to sustain (v.)	to keep something going at the same rate
to deteriorate (v.)	to get worse; to fall apart
to shrink (v.)	to get smaller

Comprehension Workout

EXERCISE 38

Answer the questions below in small groups. Choose a group leader to make sure everyone contributes to the discussion and a reporter to summarize your discussion for the class. Follow the cooperative learning guidelines below.

1. What are some ways in which pollution contributes to the growth of the world economy?
2. Economists and biologists seem to have very different views of pollution. Why?
3. In what ways are Americans in the United States consumer-oriented?

consumer-oriented (adj.): characterized by buying many products.

4. Are people from some countries less consumer-oriented than people from the United States? Explain your answer.

COOPERATIVE LEARNING GUIDELINES

Assess your own contribution to the group. Circle the appropriate number.

	ALWAYS				NEVER
I contributed to the discussion.	5	4	3	2	1
I listened to others' opinions carefully.	5	4	3	2	1
I asked others to explain when I did not understand them.	5	4	3	2	1
I showed appreciation for others ideas.	5	4	3	2	1

Quick Write

WRITING A REACTION

After reading the quotations on pages 152–154, choose one that you reacted to very strongly. Write a one paragraph reaction to the quotation. Make sure that you express your agreement or disagreement as well as your personal opinion. You are the primary audience for this piece of writing. Your purpose is to explore your own feelings.

Listening

Listen to the audiotaped essays about the environment.

BEFORE YOU LISTEN

Consider this strategy:

LEARNING STRATEGY

Forming Concepts: Listening for the main ideas helps you enjoy English and understand more of it.

WHILE YOU LISTEN

As you listen, try to identify the main idea of each essay. Don't try to understand every word you hear. That makes listening a difficult task and prevents you from understanding the gist.

AFTER YOU LISTEN

React to the audiotaped essays in your journal. If you are having difficulty reacting to the essays, consider the following questions.

1. Focus on the content of the essays. Were there any parts of the essays which you particularly liked? Were there any parts of the essays which bothered you? Why?
2. Concentrate on the argumentation. Did the authors provide convincing evidence for their cases? Why or why not?
3. Now that you have listened to the audiotapes, answer the question raised in the introduction of this chapter: Given the fact that we have the power to alter the environment, how should we use this power? In answering this question, consider those cases in which we are faced with choices between immediate human needs (for example, the need for firewood in Africa) and long-term environmental needs (for example, the need to stop deforestation).

Gaining Writing Competence

WRITING EXTENDED DEFINITIONS

Explanation: In the previous reading selection, you examined various perspectives of pollution. It is difficult to discuss pollution without identifying specific types. This calls for defining terms. In the next writing activity, you will be asked to write extended definitions.

QUESTIONS FOR WRITING AN EXTENDED DEFINITION

When you write an extended definition, you need to include more information about the term than is in the dictionary. These questions are helpful.

1. What is X?
2. Who is associated with X?
3. Where can you find X?
4. What is the historical background of X?
5. How can X be prevented?
6. What are the problems associated with X?
7. What are the sounds and/or smells associated with X?
8. Does X have any positive attributes?
9. If X fell in love with someone, who would it be? What would their children be like?
10. What is your personal perspective of X?

(For more information about extended definitions, refer to page 19. For an excellent example of an extended definition, refer to Syfers's essay on pp. 52-53.)

Threads

Pollution is nothing but the resources we are not harvesting. We allow them to disperse because we've been ignorant of their value.

R. Buckminster Fuller
(1895–1983)

Quick Write

WRITING EXTENDED DEFINITIONS

Read the definitions below. Some of the words which you may not understand are glossed in the margin. These words are underlined in the definitions below. When you have finished reading, select three of these terms and write extended definitions of them. Each definition should be two or three paragraphs in length. It should include a concise definition of the term (based on the definitions below or your own more detailed definition) and your own perspective of the term. Your audience for these definitions is the general public. Your purpose is to inform.

TERMS AND DEFINITIONS

Acid Rain. This problem occurs when sulfur and nitrogen compounds in the air react with water vapor and fall back to earth. It pollutes drinking water as well as the oceans and seas. In addition, it results in the poisoning and extinction of fish, aquatic° life, plants, and insects.

Air Pollution. Air pollution means dirty or poisonous air. It is caused by the overuse of fossil fuel energy (such as gas and oil). Too many cars, buses, and trucks can clog° the highways and choke cities with pollution. Air pollution can damage trees, plants, and crops and lead to breathing difficulties.

Deforestation. Deforestation is the cutting or burning down of forest areas. As many as 100 plant and animal species become extinct each week as a result of deforestation. Burning trees also results in large amounts of carbon dioxide entering the atmosphere.

Extinction. Extinction is the elimination° of an entire animal or plant species. At present rates, 40,000 species per year will become victims of extinction by the year 2000. A plant or animal species becomes extinct at the rate of at least one species per hour.

Ecology. Ecology is the discipline which examines the condition of air, water, plants, animals, and soil as well as the general health of the planet. This scientific field explores the interrelationship of living things and their surroundings, and seeks solutions to the earth's problems.

Groundwater. Groundwater is water which fills the cracks and pores in rocks and sediment beneath the earth's surface. Ninety percent of the world's drinkable water comes from under the ground. It is easy to pollute this substance by spilling toxins into the ground.

The Greenhouse Effect. A greenhouse traps the sun's rays so that flowers can grow even when it is snowing outside. A greenhouse effect occurs when the heat around the earth is trapped by gas so that the heat cannot leave the surface of the earth. Carbon dioxide, an invisible gas, is responsible for the greenhouse effect. Gas acts much like the glass of a greenhouse. Billions of tons of this gas are added to the earth's atmosphere each year. The gas is released when trees are burned down and when fossil fuels are burned. When heated by the sun, carbon dioxide contributes to the greenhouse effect. The greenhouse effect could ruin the habitats of many animals, disrupt worldwide weather patterns, and cause global temperatures to rise. This in turn could cause many seaports to flood and make it too hot to grow some crops.

Oil Spills. The problem is accidentally caused by the seepage° of oil from oil tankers or off-shore drilling rigs° into oceans and seas. It harms fish, aquatic birds, mammals, and other sea creatures. Marine wildlife can be damaged for several generations.

Overgrazing. Overgrazing is the practice of feeding livestock (cattle, sheep, and goats) in too small an area. It results in the destruction of vegetation as well as the erosion° of valuable soil.

Ozone. Ozone is a pale blue, odorless° gas. When the gas forms at ground level, it is harmful to humans. When the gas forms in the upper atmosphere, it protects people from harmful solar radiation.

The Ozone Hole. When the stratospheric layer of ozone becomes thin, it creates a hole which allows harmful rays of the sun to reach earth. Some aerosol sprays and industrial waste are making a hole in the ozone layer which protects people from cancer-causing solar radiation.

Poaching. Poaching is the illegal practice of collecting rare or endangered animals or plants. Efficient weapons have led to the increase of this illegal practice. Concern about the practice has resulted in protective laws.

Rain Forests. Rain forests are large areas of trees which have heavy rainfall. They support more than half of the earth's plant and animal population. They are being cut down at a rate of at least 1,000 acres per hour. Destruction of rain forests can affect the weather and air around the entire planet. Covering 2,400,000 square miles, the Amazon basin is the world's largest rain forest.

Toxins. Toxins come in gaseous, liquid, or solid forms. They are poisonous substances which are found in many pesticides. They are also found in many everyday products which we use around the house. These include cleansers, paints, and insect sprays. Toxins can leak into our underground water if not disposed of properly.

Water Pollution. This term refers to dirty water. Although the Earth is made up of 70% water, only 3% of that percentage is drinkable. Dumping wastes into lakes, rivers, and streams is one of the causes of this problem. Untreated wastes from sewage systems is another source of the problem. If uncontrolled, the problem could eliminate all the planet's sources of drinkable water.

VOCABULARY

aquatic (adj.)	growing or living in the water
to clog (v.)	to prevent operation (of something)
elimination (n.)	removal, destruction
seepage (n.)	the process of passing slowly through (something)
drilling rig (n.)	equipment used to obtain oil
erosion (n.)	the process of slowly destroying (dirt)
odorless (adj.)	characterized by having no smell

Additional Reading

ABOUT THE READING

Paul R. Ehrlich, Jr., a famous scientist, whose work focuses on population biology, describes his own perspective of overpopulation, a problem which contributes to pollution. His experience in Delhi, India, increased his own awareness of the severe difficulties which result from overpopulation. The excerpt below comes from his well-known volume, *The Population Bomb*.

WHILE YOU READ

Consider these questions:

1. Who is writing the description?
2. Where is the author?
3. Who is he with?
4. Why does he feel uncomfortable?
5. What is he afraid of?

Consider this strategy:

LEARNING STRATEGY

Forming Concepts: Analyzing the writing of published authors gives you ideas for improving your writing.

Take notes when you are reading the story below. Jot down any interesting words or writing techniques that Ehrlich uses as well as any interesting information that you might later want to include in your own writing. Pay particular attention to the effective ways Ehrlich uses language.

THE POPULATION BOMB (Excerpt)

Paul R. Ehrlich, Jr.

I have understood the population explosion intellectually for a long time. I came to understand it emotionally one stinking hot night in Delhi a couple of years ago. My wife and daughter and I were returning to our hotel in an ancient taxi. The seats were hopping with fleas. The only functional gear° was third. As we crawled through the city, we entered a crowded slum° area. The temperature was well over 100, and the air was a haze of dust and smoke. The streets seemed alive with people. People eating, people washing, people sleeping. People visiting, arguing, and screaming. People thrusting° their hands through the taxi window begging. People defecating and urinating. People clinging to buses. People, people, people, people, people. As we moved slowly through the mob,

hand horn squawking, the dust, noise, heat, and cooking fires gave the scene a hellish aspect. Would we ever get to our hotel? All three of us were, frankly, frightened. It seemed that anything could happen—but of course nothing did. Old India hands will laugh at our reaction. We were just some over-privileged tourists, unaccustomed to the sights and sounds of India. Perhaps, but since that night I've known the "feel" of overpopulation.

Source: *The Population Bomb*, Revised Edition, Paul R. Ehrlich, Jr. Copyright 1968, 1971. Reprinted by permission of Ballantine Books, a Division of Random House, Inc.

VOCABULARY

gear (n.)	a mechanism on the car
slum (n.)	a poor housing area
to thrust (v.)	to push with force

Comprehension Workout

Considering the author's purpose and use of descriptive language helps you understand descriptive writing. In the next Quick Write activity, you will be asked to describe an overcrowded city. One way to improve your description is by carefully analyzing published ones. Analyze the reading above. The questions below are designed to guide your analysis.

1. What is Ehrlich's purpose?
2. How does Ehrlich make the reader see a vivid picture of the devastating effects of overcrowding?
3. What specific evidence does Ehrlich give you which supports his belief that Delhi is overcrowded?
4. In what interesting way does Ehrlich use repetition to convince the reader that Delhi is overcrowded?
5. How does Ehrlich help the reader visualize the "ancient taxi"?

Quick Write

WRITING DESCRIPTIONS

Write a one paragraph description of an overcrowded city. Your purpose is to convey your own perspective of overpopulation. The readers are your classmates.

BEFORE YOU WRITE

Consider this strategy:

Use your imagination to go to a specific overcrowded city. Go on a specific day. Feel the weather, hear the sounds of the city, smell the odors coming from the doorways, and see the various sights. Answer these questions:

1. How do you feel about being in the city? How is your mood affected? Is it a pleasant or unpleasant experience?
2. Imagine that you have spent an entire year living in the city. Now how do you feel?
3. If someone said, "This city reminds me of _____," how would he or she complete the sentence?
4. Imagine that you are describing the city to a blind friend. What words would you use to describe it? Since your friend is blind, you might want to emphasize the sounds and smells rather than the sights.
5. If your city were an animal, what kind would it be?

WRITE

You are now ready to write. You will probably enjoy your experience more if you use this writing activity to experiment a bit. Don't worry about writing a perfect paper.

Grammar Explanation

PRONOUN REFERENCE

Explanation: In the next writing activity, you will write a story about pollution. The following information will help you.

PRONOUNS

Pronouns allow you to avoid repetition. The table on the following page lists the various forms of personal pronouns.

Personal Pronouns

SUBJECT PRONOUNS	OBJECT PRONOUNS	POSSESSIVE ADJECTIVES	POSSESSIVE PRONOUNS	REFLEXIVE PRONOUNS
I	me	my	mine	myself
we	us	our	ours	ourselves
you (sing.)	you	your	yours	yourself
you (plural)	you	your	yours	yourselves
he	him	his	his	himself
she	her	her	hers	herself
it	it	its	—	itself
they	them	their	theirs	themselves
one	one	one's	—	oneself

1. The word that a pronoun refers to is called its *referent*.

REFERENT		PRONOUN	
The boy	put	his	bottle in the recycle bin.

Make sure that the pronoun agrees with its referent in number and in gender. A singular pronoun is used to refer to a singular noun.

Singular: The man is putting bottles into his garbage can.

Singular: The woman is putting bottles into her garbage can.

A plural pronoun is used to refer to a plural noun.

Plural: The children are putting bottles into their garbage can.

Plural: The garbage cans are full. Empty them.

2. Subject/verb agreement is determined by the noun referent.

	SINGULAR NOUN REFERENT	SINGULAR VERB FORM	
We each have	a garbage can.	*Mine* is	red.

	PLURAL NOUN REFERENT	PLURAL VERB FORM	
We each have	two garbage cans.	*Mine* are	red.

3. Ambiguous reference errors occur when the pronoun could refer to two possible referents.

To keep the wheels of industry turning, manufacturers produce consumer goods in endless quantities, and in the process <u>they</u> exhaust <u>their</u> natural resources.

The pronouns <u>they</u> and <u>their</u> are ambiguous in this sentence. Does <u>they</u> refer to the manufacturers or the consumer goods? Does <u>their</u> refer to the manufacturers' or someone else's natural resources?

4. A pronoun refers to a particular referent, not to a word that is implied but not present in the text.

Incorrect: "Wear <u>them</u> once and throw <u>them</u> away" will soon be a popular slogan of the fashion conscious.

Correct: Soon we will wear clothes made out of paper. "Wear <u>them</u> once and throw <u>them</u> away " will soon be a popular slogan of the fashion conscious."

<u>Them</u> in the correct sentence refers to <u>clothes</u>. In spoken English, <u>they</u> is used to refer to persons who have not been specifically identified. Do not use it in this way in written English. Use pronouns only when the referents are clearly specified.

Incorrect: <u>They</u> are guilty of polluting. (Who? Citizens? Factory owners?)
Correct: The owners of the factory are guilty of polluting.

5. Pronouns should not be used immediately after their referents. "The garbage <u>it</u> is on the floor" should be "The garbage is on the floor."

6. Pronoun object forms are always used after prepositions.

John gave the book to <u>me</u>.
She sat on <u>it</u>.
He wrote with <u>it</u>.
She stared at <u>me</u>.

7. These indefinite pronouns require a singular verb:

anyone	no one
anybody	nobody
everyone	someone
everybody	somebody
	something

<u>No one</u> <u>knows</u> how to eliminate smog completely. <u>Everyone</u> here <u>works</u> to reduce pollution.

Studying a grammar explanation once is not enough to learn it. Review the Grammar Explanation on pronoun reference alone. Then, ten minutes later, try reviewing it with a friend. Study the explanation again the next day, then two days later, and so on. Your goal is to overlearn the explanation so that you can more easily apply it to improve your writing.

Grammar Practice: Pronoun Reference

EXERCISE 39

Fill in the blanks with the appropriate pronouns.

Each year our factories produce more and more cars. These cars create pollution. (a) _____ require gas to run. Many suggest, therefore, that cars are directly responsible for smog. Smog comes in all forms. We see (b) _____, smell (c) _____, taste (d) _____, and drink (e) _____. Unfortunately, (f) _____ live and breathe smog, and (g) _____ is beginning to destroy our very society. However, factories cannot stop producing cars, because workers need jobs, and our society demands cars. Our standard of living requires a large number of cars. What do we do with cars when (h) _____ are worn out? Instead of repairing a car, it is always cheaper to buy a new one. This means getting rid of the old, even though most of (i) _____ parts still work. Many cars are disposed of in junkyards which are already full of rusting cars. (j) _____ are also abandoned. Each year, over 150,000 are abandoned in the United States. Can we eliminate cars altogether? Probably not. Total elimination would require drastic changes in lifestyles. Industries would have to close. We would have to leave (k) _____ cars at home and walk to (l) _____ jobs.

Grammar Explanation

VERB FORMS

Explanation: The information below will help you improve your verb forms when you write a story in the next writing activity.

AVOIDING VERB FORM ERRORS

One common mistake you are probably making in your writing concerns verb forms. Perhaps you know the correct verb tense to use, but simply use verb forms incorrectly. If this is the case, it is probably because you are focused only on what you are writing, rather than the way you are forming words. Look at the following verb forms:

Verb Forms

SIMPLE	-S	-ING	PAST	PARTICIPLE
walk	walks	walking	walked	walked
sleep	sleeps	sleeping	slept	slept
eat	eats	eating	ate	eaten

Avoid verb form errors of the following types:

1. Deleting the **-ed** ending

   EXAMPLE Business people are less <u>concern</u> about the problem of pollution
   than ecologists because they believe that there are economic
   solutions to this problem.

   This student forgot to write the **-ed** ending on the word <u>concerned</u>.

2. Deleting the **-s** ending

   EXAMPLE He <u>pollute</u> year after year. The student who wrote this sentence
   forgot to write the -s ending on the word <u>pollutes</u>.

3. Adding an **-s** ending which is ungrammatical

   EXAMPLE You can <u>prevents</u> pollution. When this student added an -s ending
   to the word <u>prevent</u>, her sentence became ungrammatical.

Editing Practice: Verb Forms

EXERCISE 40

The following passage printed here contains *six* verb form errors. Correct
them. If you have difficulty correcting the errors, consult your grammar workout
book.

LIVING IN TOXIC WASTE

Mr. and Mrs. Robertson were happy when
they first moved to Midbrae. However, they
quickly became disturbed by their new
surroundings. They lived close to a large
company. They suspect that the company was
dumping toxic waste into a nearby river and
worried that something in the waste was attacking
their own immune° systems.

Soon after they moved to Midbrae, the
Robertsons figure out the source of the
contamination. For 29 years the Midbrae Company
have manufactured parts of nuclear bombs. In the
process, the company dumped the radioactive

material into Midbrae river. The owners of the Midbrae Company were aware of the damage to the community which they caused. They have admit that they have litter the countryside with mercury and uranium. Although the company try to create a major clean-up effort years ago, it was too late to help people of Midbrae who have lived in Midbrae for generations.

VOCABULARY

immune (adj.)   characterized by the ability to prevent diseases

Writing Task

WRITING A STORY

Write a one page story about your own experience with pollution. Assume that the reader does not know anything about the experience. You will have to imagine some of the questions the reader might want to have answered. You are writing for the general public. Your purpose is to convey your own perspective of pollution in a story format.

BEFORE YOU WRITE

Spend a few minutes with a partner discussing some of your experiences with different types of pollution. Think of experiences which readers might find particularly interesting. Next, write a list of the types of information your readers would like to know. This list might include:

- background information/the context of the experience
- a description of the characters involved
- a list of events which took place
- the effects these events had on the characters/situation
- a description of what was remarkable/interesting/noteworthy about the experience
- the writer's reactions to, or feelings about, the experience

Listen to the audiotaped stories written by ESL students. Read the sample story below.

SAMPLE STORY WRITTEN BY AN ESL STUDENT

On the bottom of the Mississippi River lived a family of fish. These fresh water fish had lived there for thousands of years. One group of fish, that called themselves the fish's had four family members: Papa Fish, Mama Fish, Nick Fish (the son) and Salina Fish (the daughter).

This family lived a peaceful life. The water was their home and they lived as their ancestors did. Papa Fish was big and strong with great fins. He swam up and down the river with great strength. His wife, Mama Fish, and their children swam close behind him.

One day, as the family swam down the river, they discovered that many fish were dying. They didn't know what was happening. Since Salina Fish was having a difficult time swimming through the thick, greyish water, they decided it was best to head back home. When they returned, Salina was feeling sick. "Help, Mama," Salina cried. "I feel so feverish." Papa and Mama couldn't help her. They didn't know what was wrong. In a few days, Salina's condition had grown much worse. Papa went to ask others for help. They tried to help, but there was nothing they could do. Salina died a few weeks later. Papa, Mama and Nick grieved her loss. One of Papa's friends told him that the reason the water in the lower part of the river was polluted was because humans had constructed a factory down the stream and were dumping large quantities of garbage from the factory into the river. Another friend told Papa that he had seen humans beginning construction on a new factory on the upper river.

As the years passed, there came no resolution to the problem of water pollution. The factory on the upper river was completed, and humans began to dump more poisonous liquids into the Mississippi. Within a few weeks, all the diverse types of fish that lived in that section of the Mississippi were completely wiped out. Fish's family died too.

Humans have the power to stop such needless death, but they also have the power to continue it to satisfy their own selfish desires. Had it not been for humans, Fish's family would still be swimming happily in the Mississippi.—*J.D.*

Consider this strategy:

LEARNING STRATEGY

Forming Concepts: Picturing the experience in your mind helps you write about it.

Think about who you are in the story, what you are doing, and what is going on around you. Your picture need not reflect reality. Now consider these questions:

1. Will you leave out important information until the end of your story to surprise your reader?
2. Will you provide relevant background information for the reader before you describe the events which took place?
3. Will you first describe the events which took place in your story and only later explain these events?
4. Will you write your story chronologically, describing each event sequentially?
5. Will you begin your story by describing the final event which took place and then explain the series of events which led up to this event?

WHILE YOU ARE WRITING

Consider this strategy:

LEARNING STRATEGY

Overcoming Limitations: Changing your words when you are having a difficult time writing something will help you write more fluently.

If you cannot express yourself in the way you want, try writing something different that means almost the same thing, or making your ideas simpler.

WRITE

You are now ready to write. Find a quiet place where you can write without being interrupted.

EDIT YOUR WRITING

Use the ending checklist below to edit your story.

EDITING CHECKLIST

_____ **1.** I have used pronouns correctly.

_____ **2.** I have used subject/verb agreement correctly.

_____ **3.** I have used the -s ending on verbs correctly.

_____ **4.** I have used the -ed ending on verbs correctly.

AFTER YOU WRITE

Reflect on your writing. Consider your personal goals. What had you hoped to learn when you began this class? What did this writing task teach you?

Quick Write

REPORTING SURVEY DATA

Report on the results of the survey on page 150–151 in a one page report. In writing this report, try to summarize at least two major findings. You may want to address the two questions raised earlier:

1. Which pollution-preventing measures do all students in the class take?
2. Which pollution-preventing measures do few students take?

The report is for your classmates, your instructor, and yourself. The purpose of the report is to inform. Earlier, you completed a survey pertaining to your own efforts to prevent pollution. As a class, review the survey results on the chalkboard. What does every student in the class do to prevent pollution?

Which pollution-preventing actions do few students take? Discuss the results in small groups. Try to explain them.

WRITE

Put pen to paper (or hands to keyboard) and write your report.

Using A Language Learning Log

1. Vocabulary:

Write down as many new words from the lesson as you can remember.

_____

_____

_____

_____

_____

_____

IT WORKS!
Learning Strategy:
Keeping Track of
Your Progress

2. Grammar:

Note examples of any grammatical structures from the lesson learned or reviewed. Write a brief explanation of the grammar points that they illustrate.

_____

_____

_____

_____

_____

_____

3. Punctuation:

Briefly describe any punctuation rules that you learned.

_____

_____

_____

_____

_____

_____

4. Techniques for Gaining Writing Competence:

List any new techniques for gaining writing competence that you learned. (Such techniques might include those for making your writing cohesive, those for writing interesting introductions and conclusions, and those for composing different types of writing such as letters and essays.)

_____

_____

_____

_____

_____

_____

5. Learning Strategies:

Describe briefly any new learning strategies that you learned.

_____

_____

_____

_____

_____

_____

IT WORKS!
Learning Strategy:
Making Action Plans

6. Areas that Need More Work:

Note here any areas that you are still trying to improve. Try to be as specific as possible.

_____

_____

_____

_____

_____

_____

How many learning objectives have you been able to accomplish? (Refer to page 169; also, consider the strategy in the margin.)

Quick Write

DESCRIBING AN ACTION PLAN

Write a two paragraph description of your most important language learning objectives and your plan for accomplishing these objectives.

SUMMARY OF LESSON 1: PERSPECTIVES OF POLLUTION

This lesson has given you a general overview of the various types of pollution which endanger the earth. You investigated your own experiences with pollution through narratives. In the next lesson, you will learn what people are doing to fight pollution.

QUICK REFERENCE TO LEARNING STRATEGIES

Forming Concepts: Listening for the Main Ideas (p. 155)

Forming Concepts: Analyzing the Writing of Published Authors (p. 159)

Forming Concepts: Visualizing (p. 161)

Remembering New Material: Reviewing Your Knowledge (p. 163)

Forming Concepts: Picturing the Experience in Your Mind (p. 167)

Overcoming Limitations: Changing Your Words (p. 168)

LESSON 2:
EFFORTS TO CONTROL POLLUTION

Overview

In the previous lesson, you identified some of the types of pollution affecting our earth. In this lesson, you will learn about some major efforts to reduce pollution.

About the Reading

Greenpeace is an international organization that fights against pollution of all types. This organization now has 3.3 million members in 20 different countries. It published the advertisement below in several newspapers.

WHILE YOU READ

First, read the advertisement quickly to get its main ideas. You do not have to read every word. Don't worry about the vocabulary words that you do not know. Either skip over them quickly, or try to guess their meanings from the context in which they occur. As you read the story, answer these questions:

1. What are the major goals of Greenpeace?
2. Which objectives has Greenpeace accomplished?
3. Who would be interested in reading this advertisement?
4. What is the purpose of this advertisement?
5. What persuasive point is made?
6. Which language features help influence your reactions as readers to the text?

GREENPEACE ADVERTISEMENT

Against all odds, Greenpeace has brought pollution to the attention of caring people. Terrible abuses to the environment often carried out in remote places or far out to sea have been headlined on television and in the press.

Greenpeace began with a protest voyage into a nuclear test zone. The test was disrupted. Today, the site at Amchitka in the Aleutian Islands is a bird sanctuary.

Then Greenpeace sent its tiny inflatable boats to protect the whales. They took up position between the harpoons and the fleeing whales. Today, commercial whaling is banned.

On the ice floes of Newfoundland, Greenpeace volunteers placed their bodies between the seal hunters and the helpless seal pups. The hunt has since been called off.

In the North Atlantic, Greenpeace drove its inflatables underneath falling barrels of radioactive waste. Now nuclear waste dumping at sea has been stopped.

In the North Sea, Greenpeace swimmers turned back dump ships carrying chemical wastes. New laws to protect the North Sea have been promised.

Peaceful direct action by Greenpeace has used the power of public opinion to force changes in the law to protect wildlife and to stop the pollution of the natural world.

The Greenpeace vessel, Rainbow Warrior.

Comprehension Workout

Find a partner. With your partner, make up three or four of your own comprehension questions based on the main points of the reading. Prepare an oral presentation of the information needed to answer the questions. When you feel ready to share the information, it is time to combine groups. Join another pair of students to form a group of four. Answer each others' questions.

Gaining Writing Competence

TEXT ANALYSIS

In analyzing the Greenpeace advertisement, reconsider some of the questions previously raised.

- Who would be interested in reading this advertisement?
- What is the purpose of this advertisement?
- What persuasive point is made?
- Which language features help to influence your reactions as readers to the text?

The form below is designed to help you complete the analysis.

TEXT	ADVERTISEMENT
AUDIENCE	_____
PURPOSE	_____
PERSUASIVE POINT	_____
	_____
	_____
LANGUAGE FEATURES	_____

Compare the analysis you made to the one made by a group of students at the University of California.

TEXT	ADVERTISEMENT
Audience	People who are aware of need for protection of the environment but who are not very strongly committed
Purpose	To draw more attention to human race's destruction of the planet
	To persuade more people to join Greenpeace campaign
Persuasive point	Greenpeace is successful
Language features	<u>negative words</u>: terrible, abuses, remote, helpless, waste, dump
	<u>positive words</u>: caring, peaceful, sanctuary, protect, peaceful direct action

Source: Adapted from Ronald White and Valerie Arnt 1990. Process Writing. London: Longman, p. 64.

Gaining Writing Competence

WRITING INFORMAL LETTERS

Explanation: In the next writing activity, you will write an informal letter. Here is some information that will help you.

INFORMAL LETTERS

In nearly all cultures, special expressions are used in informal letters. Letters are begun and ended in conventional ways. See the example below.

Because personal letters are informal, you do not have to begin with "Dear" and end with "Sincerely." Also, many people end their letters with "Love." This often indicates a close, trusting relationship, not a desire for a romance.

> May 15, 1993
>
> Dear Fred,
>   Just a note to let you know that I too am fighting against the mayor's desire to build high-rise apartments on the beach. I've got a lot to tell you about my efforts.
>   Talk to you this Friday.
>
> Sincerely,
>
> *Judy*

Quick Write

WRITING AN INFORMAL LETTER

Write a one to two paragraph response to the letter below. You are writing to a stranger. Your purpose is to advise and console.

Dear Ada Advice Columnist,

    I am sick and tired of noise pollution. All day long my neighbor, Bill, blasts his radio. His taste in music is terrible. Not only are the melodies atonal, but the words are obscene. Bill's raucous music prevents me from concentrating on my studies. I've repeatedly asked Bill to be more considerate, but he never pays any attention to my requests. He just nods his head and says, "Sure, I'll turn my radio lower." For a few hours, he keeps the volume turned low, but by the end of the day, he forgets all about my request.
    Help! What should I do?

—Going Crazy

WRITE

In responding to this letter, consider the case to be argued. How can Ada help "Going Crazy" persuade Bill that lowering the volume of his radio will benefit everyone? What types of positive words can she use?

Grammar Explanation

COHESIVE DEVICES

Explanation: Cohesive devices are very important in written language. They are words and phrases that the writer uses to increase the readers' comprehension. They are essential in writing persuasively. In the next writing activity, you will write a persuasive essay. The information given below will help you.

COHESIVE DEVICES

Cohesive devices help writers encourage the reader to refer back to previous text. They include:

reference pronouns (he, she, his, hers, etc.)

demonstrative pronouns (those, this, that, etc.)

demonstrative adjectives (this house, that dog, etc.)

repetition of key words or phrases

synonyms

articles (the, a)

transitional words (first, second, third, moreover, therefore)

Grammar Practice: Cohesive Devices

EXERCISE 43

Greenpeace also published the advertisement below. However, the paragraphs in this advertisement are out of order. In small groups, use the underlined cues to sequence the passages correctly. Notice that the underlined cohesive devices (pronoun and time references) help you put the reading back into chronological order. Number the passages in the order that they should appear. Then, check the reading on the following page to make sure that you have the correct order.

PLANET EARTH IS 4,600 MILLION YEARS OLD (GREENPEACE ADVERTISEMENT)

Number: _____
Nothing is known about <u>the first seven years of this person's life</u>, and while only little information exists about the middle span, we do know that <u>only at the age of 42</u> did the earth begin to flower.

Number: _____
During <u>those sixty seconds</u> of biological time, Modern Man has made a garbage dump of Paradise.

Number: _____
He has multiplied his numbers, caused the extinction of 500 species of animals, ransacked the planet for fuels, and now stands like a naughty child gloating over his control of earth.

Number: _____
We can liken the Earth to a person of <u>46 years of age</u>.

Number: _____
Dinosaurs and the great reptiles did not appear until <u>one year ago</u>, when the planet was <u>45</u>. Mammals arrived <u>only eight months ago</u>; <u>in the middle of last week</u> man-like apes evolved into ape-like men, and <u>on the weekend</u> the last ice age enveloped the earth.

Number: _____
Modern man has been around for four hours. <u>During the last hour</u>, Man discovered agriculture. The industrial revolution began <u>a minute ago</u>.

Here is the original version.

PLANET EARTH IS 4,600 MILLION YEARS OLD (GREENPEACE ADVERTISEMENT)

We can liken the Earth to a person of 46 years of age.

Nothing is known about the first seven years of this person's life, and while only little information exists about the middle span, we do know that only at the age of 42 did the earth begin to flower.

Dinosaurs and the great reptiles did not appear until one year ago, when the planet was 45. Mammals arrived only eight months ago; in the middle of last week man-like apes evolved into ape-like men, and on the weekend the last ice age enveloped the Earth.

Modern man has been around for four hours. During the last hour, Man discovered agriculture. The industrial revolution began a minute ago.

During those sixty seconds of biological time, Modern Man has made a garbage dump of Paradise.

He has multiplied his numbers, caused the extinction of 500 species of animals, ransacked the planet for fuels, and now stands like a naughty child gloating over his control of earth.

Cooperative Learning

PARAPHRASE PASSPORT

Consider this strategy:

LEARNING STRATEGY

Remembering New Material: Paraphrasing what you have read helps you remember key words and phrases.

Form pairs. One student begins by making a comment about the reading passage above. The other student paraphrases his or her partner's comment and then makes his or her own comment about the reading passage.

EXAMPLE

Student 1:
Comment   I didn't know that mankind is responsible for the extinction of 500 kinds of animals.

Student 2:
Paraphrase You are saying that man has caused the extinction of 500 animals species.
Comment   I suppose that information is accurate. Even today many animal species are endangered.

Grammar Review

COUNT AND NONCOUNT NOUNS FOR ABSTRACT IDEAS

Explanation: In Chapters 1 and 2, you learned how to use count and noncount nouns. Familiarizing yourself with the specific count and noncount nouns related to the environment will help you complete the writing task which follows.

COUNT AND NONCOUNT NOUNS

Count nouns describe something that we can count. They have both singular and plural forms.

SINGULAR FORM	PLURAL FORM
a polluted <u>river</u>	five polluted <u>rivers</u>
a beautiful <u>rain forest</u>	five beautiful <u>rain forests</u>
a serious <u>oil spill</u>	three serious <u>oil spills</u>

Noncount nouns describe something that we cannot count in a specific context in English.

EXAMPLES

pollution	<u>Pollution</u> is a serious problem.
garbage	There is too much <u>garbage</u> on the streets.
smog	<u>Smog</u> can hurt your eyes.

Some noncount nouns which are frequently used in most contexts include:

NONCOUNT NOUNS

climate	nature
contamination	overgrazing
deforestation	overpopulation
elimination	ozone
energy	pollution
extinction	population
garbage	recycling
global warming	smog
groundwater	waste

For additional information about count and noncount nouns, refer to pages 14–15.

Gaining Writing Competence

WRITING A PERSUASIVE ESSAY

Explanation: In the next writing task, you will be asked to write a persuasive essay. The following guidelines will help you complete this task.

GUIDELINES FOR WRITING A PERSUASIVE ESSAY

1. Believe in the position which you are taking. Never take a position that you do not believe in.
2. Know your audience. Develop a strategy for selling the audience your position. Emotional appeals will probably fail with academic audiences. That audience is likely to appreciate strong, logical arguments in favor of your position. You may not get the audience to change its position on an issue, but, if successful, you can get the audience to see the position that you present through your eyes. Avoid using sentences such as "Here's what you should do to prevent the damage you are doing to the earth." Instead, try: "Here are the reasons and experiences that have led me to believe pollution should be decreased, and these are the specific steps I am taking in my effort to decrease it." Whenever possible, talk to people who hold positions which are different from your own. Listen to their ideas carefully. Find out why their opinions differ from your own. To write a successful persuasive essay, you need to see the world through the eyes of your opponent.
3. Find good arguments to support your position. Whenever possible, provide evidence for your position. Evidence might come from statistics, personal experience, or research.
4. Identify possible counterarguments and answer them.

EXPRESSIONS TO AVOID WHEN WRITING A PERSUASIVE ESSAY

Take out those small words which qualify the way you feel about a position: *a bit, a little, sort of, kind of, rather, quite, too, very, in a sense,* and many others. These weaken your persuasiveness. Don't say that pollution is "somewhat of a problem" or "sort of damaging." Persuasive writing sounds more confident than that. Don't say that "the smog may have somewhat led to your mother's lung disease." It either did or it didn't. Remember: Every qualifier you use takes away the reader's confidence in your authority. In Zinsser's words, "Don't be kind of bold. Be bold."*

---

*William Zinsser. 1990. *On Writing Well.* Fourth Edition. New York: Harper Perennial, A Division of Harper Collins.

Writing Task

WRITING A PERSUASIVE ESSAY

Write a persuasive essay of about 250 words. Select a topic about the environment which has personal meaning to you. Consider the topic carefully. Write down possible topics. Talk to others about your possible topics in your first or second language. Do some research on these topics. Choose a topic that you are genuinely interested in. You may want to write about one of the following subjects.

acid rain

climate

ecosystem

endangered species

energy

global warming

greenhouse effect

natural resources

pollution

rain forest

recycling

Identify your own purpose for writing this essay and the audience who will read your essay. Use the library to develop your writing by providing relevant facts and details.

BEFORE YOU WRITE

Consider this strategy:

LEARNING STRATEGY

Understanding and Using Emotions: Having the right tools will encourage you to write because it is always more fun to write with tools that you like.

Gather everything you need for the writing task. If you are using pen and paper, try buying a new pen with a fine tip, several colors of ink, or erasable ink. Purchase your favorite kind of lined writing paper (recycled, of course!). If you are using a computer, make sure that you have enough paper and that the computer and printer are working well. Answer the questions on page 181.

PREWRITING QUESTIONS

1. What is your topic?
2. Why did you choose this topic?
3. Why should people be aware of your topic?
4. Can understanding your topic help improve the environment? If yes, how? If no, why not?
5. Does the topic have significance for the future? If yes, in what way?

Identify a purpose. Ask yourself what you want to write about related to your topic. What is your intention? What particular point of view do you want others to accept as a result of reading your essay?

Identify the readers of your essay. Write a list of their characteristics.

Working individually, list all the words, phrases, and ideas that relate to your topic. Then, look through the lists of words, phrases, and ideas that you have made. Are there any connections?

Brainstorm. Working with a partner, describe all your ideas and thoughts about your topic. Do not judge ideas or attempt to organize them at this point. The main objective is to generate as many ideas as you can about a particular topic.

By now you have gained a broad view of your topic. It is time to narrow it. Take ten minutes to write about the most interesting aspect of your topic.

Collect information about your topic. You may want to use a library and check out books, magazines, tapes, or films. You may want to use your personal observations, or interview or survey data. Make sure that when you obtain research from published materials that you credit material carefully and avoid plagiarism.

Consider this strategy:

> **Threads**
>
> U.S. factories are allowed by law to produce four times the amount of air pollution than a German factory.
>
> Curtis Moore, McLean, VA

LEARNING STRATEGY

Forming Concepts: Gathering information from friends provides you with valuable material that you can include in your essay.

Talk to your friends in either your native language or in English. Find out what they know about your topic. Analyze the information that you have obtained. Ask yourself, who? what? where? why? and how? Ask yourself if any of the information your friends gave you is now dated.

WRITE

Write your first draft. Do not worry about your grammar at this stage. Just write. Try to get all your ideas on paper.

REVISE YOUR PAPER

Revision is an important part of writing. It consists of revising your essay for organization and content. The checklist on page 182 can guide your revision.

REVISION CHECKLIST

1. What was my purpose for writing? Did I satisfy it?
2. Did I shape my writing to the interests of my audience?
3. Does my introduction capture the attention of my readers?
4. Did I develop my ideas logically in the body of my writing?
5. Did I write a conclusion?
6. Did I stick to my topic, or did I include unnecessary information?
7. Have I presented strong arguments to the reader?
8. Have I supported my main ideas with specific details and examples?
9. Are my facts accurate?
10. Is my essay cohesive? In other words, are the ideas connected appropriately?
11. What part of my essay can I still improve?
12. What do I like best about this essay?

LEARNING STRATEGY

Forming Concepts: Providing constructive feedback to one another is especially valuable in the revising stage of the composition process.

REWRITE

In the next activity, you will be sharing your writing with your classmates. You may, at this point, want to make some changes in your essay. Make any changes that you like. Remember that a persuasive essay contains good arguments for your position. You might also want to consider counterarguments which refute your position.

Help one another by providing constructive feedback on each other's writing. Try to be as helpful as possible. Find a partner. Read each other's essays. Then, complete the Peer Review Form below and discuss each other's essays.

PEER REVIEW FORM	YES	NO
1. Can you understand the author's purpose?	___	___
2. Does the writing appeal to a specific audience?	___	___
3. Does the opening capture your attention?	___	___
4. Are the ideas developed logically?	___	___
5. Are the ideas presented clearly?	___	___
6. Are the main ideas presented with sufficient detail?	___	___
7. Are good arguments for the author's purpose given?	___	___
8. Is the essay cohesive?	___	___
9. Is the conclusion effective?	___	___

10. Did the author convince you that his/her position is the best one?   _____ _____

11. What was your position on this topic before you read the essay?

_____

_____

12. What changes were produced in your position? (An honest answer will be most helpful.)

_____

_____

_____

REVISE YOUR ESSAY

Use your teacher's feedback as well as your classmates' when you revise your essay.

EDIT YOUR ESSAY

Use the Editing Checklist below to correct your grammar mistakes.

EDITING CHECKLIST	YES	NO
1. Are verb tenses correct?	_____	_____
2. Do subjects and verbs agree with one another in number?	_____	_____
3. Are pronouns used correctly?	_____	_____
4. Are parallel structures used correctly?	_____	_____
5. Is the spelling correct?	_____	_____
6. Is the punctuation correct?	_____	_____

Using a Language Learning Log

Threads

More than 117 countries participated in the U.N. Conference on Environment & Development (The Earth Summit) in Rio de Janiero, Brazil on June 3-14, 1992.

1. Vocabulary:

Write down as many new words from the lesson as you can remember.

_____

_____

_____

_____

2. **Grammar:**
Note examples of any grammatical structures from the lesson learned or reviewed. Write a brief explanation of the grammar points that they illustrate.

_____
_____
_____
_____

3. **Punctuation:**
Briefly describe any punctuation rules that you learned.

_____
_____
_____
_____

IT WORKS!
Learning Strategy:
Keeping Track of
Your Progress

4. **Techniques for Gaining Writing Competence:**
List any new techniques for gaining writing competence that you learned. (Such techniques might include those for making your writing cohesive, those for writing interesting introductions and conclusions, and those for composing different types of writing such as letters and essays.)

_____
_____
_____
_____

5. **Learning Strategies:**
Describe briefly any new learning strategies that you learned.

_____
_____
_____
_____

Threads

One billion tons of top-soil are lost in the U.S. every year.

Worldwatch Institute, Washington, D.C. (1991)

6. **Areas that Need More Work:**
Note here any areas that you are still trying to improve. Try to be as specific as possible.

_____
_____
_____
_____

How many learning objectives have you been able to accomplish? (Refer to page 149.)

This lesson examined efforts to control pollution. In so doing, you analyzed Greenpeace advertisements and wrote an informal letter as well as a persuasive essay. In the next lesson, you will return to the original theme of this unit: power. More specifically, you will consider environmental concerns related to power and injustice. In examining this issue you will return, once more, to questions raised in the introduction of this chapter: Given the fact that humankind has the power to alter the environment, how should we use this power? Who has the right to change the environment and for whose benefit?

QUICK REFERENCE TO LEARNING STRATEGIES

Remembering New Material: Paraphrasing What You Have Read (p. 177)

Understanding and Using Emotions: Having the Right Tools (p. 180)

Forming Concepts: Gathering Information From Friends (p. 181)

Forming Concepts: Providing Constructive Feedback (p. 182)

Overview

In this lesson, we return to the original theme of this textbook: power. You will examine whether all people have equal access to the earth's richness. In addition, you will study your own cultural beliefs about the earth and your own feelings about the environment and injustice.

About the Reading

Chief Seattle reportedly wrote "Brother Eagle, Sister Sky" when handing over Indian lands to the government of the United States. He believed that destroying nature destroys life itself. His words were not understood in their time. Now his words haunt us.*

WHILE YOU READ

As you read the following passage, answer these questions:
1. In what ways does Chief Seattle respect nature?
2. Is it possible to have power over the earth?
3. Can people really own the earth?
4. Did the Native Americans really lose their land to the government of the United States?

BROTHER EAGLE, SISTER SKY

In a time so long ago that nearly all traces of it are lost in the prairie dust, an ancient people were a part of the land that we love and call America. Living here for thousands of years, their children became the great civilizations of the Choctow and Cherokee, Navaho, Iroquois, and Sioux, among others. Then white settlers from Europe began a bloody war against the Indians. In the span of a single lifetime, these settlers claimed all the Indians' land for themselves, allowing Indians only small tracts of land to live on. When the last of the Indian wars were drawing to a close, it was reported that one of the bravest and most respected of the Northwest Nations, Chief Seattle, sat at a white man's table to sign a paper presented by the new Commissioner of Indian Affairs for the Territory. The government in Washington, D.C. wished to buy the lands of Chief Seattle's people. With a commanding presence and eyes that mirrored the great soul that lived within, the Chief rose to speak to the gathering in a resounding voice.

How can you buy the sky? Chief Seattle began.

Threads

We must take into account the impact the actions we take have on the next seven generations.

Iroquois proverb

*We now know that these words were not said by Chief Seattle. It appears that they were written by a white man who sympathized with the Indians to such an extent that he falsified Chief Seattle's words.

How can you buy the rain and the wind?

My mother told me, Every part of the earth is sacred to our
    people.
Every pine needle. Every sandy shore.
Every mist in the dark woods.
Every meadow and humming insect.
All are holy in the memory of our people.

My father said to me,
I know the sap that runs through the trees
as I know the blood that flows in my veins.
We are part of the earth and it is part of us.
The perfumed flowers are our sisters.

The bear, the deer, the great eagle, these are our brothers.

The rocky crests, the meadows, the ponies—all belong to the
    same family
    . . . .

The voice of my grandfather said to me,
The air is precious. It shares its spirit with all the life it supports.
    The wind that gave me my first breath also received my last
    sigh.
You must keep the land and air apart and sacred, as a place
    where one can go to taste the wind that is sweetened by the
    meadow flowers.

When the last Red Man and Woman have vanished with their
    wilderness, and their memory is only the shadow of a cloud
    moving across the prairie, will the shores and forest still be
    here?
Will there be any of the spirit of my people left?
My ancestors said to me, This we know:
The earth does not belong to us. We belong to the earth.

The voice of my grandmother said to me,
Teach your children what you have been taught.
The earth is our mother.
What befalls the earth befalls all the sons and daughters of the
    earth.

Hear my voice and the voice of my ancestors,
Chief Seattle said,
The destiny of your people is a mystery to us.
What will happen when the buffalo are all slaughtered?
The wild horses tamed?
What will happen when the secret corners of the forest are
    heavy with the scent of men?

A statue of Chief Seattle.

When the view of the ripe hills is blotted by talking wires?
    Where will the thicket be? Gone!
Where will the eagle be? Gone!
And what will happen when we say good-bye to the swift pony
    and the hunt?
It will be the end of living and the beginning of survival.

This we know: All things are connected like the blood that
    unites us.
We did not weave the web of life,
We are merely a strand of it.
Whatever we do to the web, we do to ourselves.

We love this earth as a newborn loves its mother's heartbeat.
If we sell you our land, care for it as we have cared for it.
Hold in your mind the memory of the land as it is when you
    receive it.
Preserve the land and the air and the rivers for your children's
    children and love it as we have loved it.

Comprehension Workout

EXERCISE 44

Fill in the blanks below with a "T" if the statement is true and an "F" if the statement is false.

_____ 1. Today, most aspects of American Indian civilization have been lost in the prairie dust.

_____ 2. Chief Seattle was a brave Indian who fought during the American Revolution.

_____ 3. In a span of 300 years, the Indians lost the majority of their land to Europeans.

_____ 4. After the Indians lost most of their land, they were only allowed to live on small tracts of land, often called Indian reservations.

_____ 5. Chief Seattle thought it was possible to own the land.

_____ 6. Chief Seattle was worried that the Europeans would tame all the wild horses and kill all the buffalo.

_____ 7. Chief Seattle feared that when all the Indians were forgotten, there would be no more forests.

_____ 8. Chief Seattle thought that telephone wires were ugly since they obstruct the view of beautiful hillsides.

_____ 9. Chief Seattle argued that the Europeans should mix the air with chemicals from the land.

Threads

Between 1980 and 1989, the level of smog in the U.S. decreased 14%.

E.P.A., March 1991

_____ **10.** According to Chief Seattle, all things on the earth are united.

_____ **11.** Chief Seattle advised the Europeans to take excellent care of the land, air, and water of the earth for future generations.

Listening

Listen again to the audiotaped essays about the environment.

WHILE YOU LISTEN

As you listen to the audiotaped essays, try to answer these questions:

• What is the purpose of each essay?
• Why do you think that the writers composed the essays?
• What were the writers trying to accomplish?

AFTER YOU LISTEN

React to the audiotaped essays in your journal. If you are having difficulty reacting to them, consider these questions.

1. The focus of this lesson is injustice and the environment. What insights about this topic have you gained from listening to the audiotaped essays?
2. What environmental problems face third world countries? Are these the same types of problems which face wealthier countries?
3. To what extent are individuals responsible for eliminating injustices associated with pollution?
4. Reconsider the question raised at the beginning this chapter: Given the fact that humankind has the power to alter the environment, how should we use this power? In answering this question, consider whether deforestation helps meet the needs for fuel and land to grow crops and whether it is worth the environmental problems it causes.

Gaining Writing Competence

INTRODUCTIONS

One way to improve your writing is by carefully analyzing reading passages. Analyze the reading passage on pages 186–188. The questions below are designed to guide your analysis.

• Why should the readers be interested in Chief Seattle's concern for the earth?
• Is the way in which Chief Seattle opens his speech interesting? How does Chief Seattle begin? Does he start with a quotation, a generalization, a question, or a story? How is the beginning of Chief Seattle's speech related to the rest of his speech?

- How is the ending of Chief Seattle's speech linked to the beginning of his speech? How is the ending of Chief Seattle's speech related to the rest of his speech?

Quick Write

WRITING A LETTER OF ADVICE

Imagine that Chief Seattle is still living. Write a short one or two paragraph letter to him. Offer him advice. You are writing this to an elderly native American chief. Your purpose is to advise and console.

BEFORE YOU WRITE

Consider this strategy:

LEARNING STRATEGY

Understanding and Using Emotions: Sharing your feelings about writing helps you lower your anxiety and get started on the task.

With a partner, share any feelings about writing-related anxiety you may have.

WRITE

Put pen to paper (or hands to keyboard, if you are using a computer) and write your letter.

AFTER YOU WRITE

When you are finished, exchange letters with a partner. Put a check (✓) in the margin next to those places in your partner's letter that you consider well written. Then, mark the places in your partner's letter which you consider inadequate, wrong, or unnecessary. Discuss each other's work. Suggest ways of improving the letters.

Additional Reading

ABOUT THE READING

Jonathan Kozol, a well-known educator and child advocate, believes that inequality prevents people from having equal access to the richness of the earth. He suggests that poor people in the United States suffer more from pollution than wealthy people. Evidence for his belief is contained in his recent volume, *Savage Inequalities: Children in America's Schools.*

BEFORE YOU READ

Consider this strategy:

LEARNING STRATEGY

Forming Concepts: Guessing the meaning of a new word from the context in which it occurs can help you increase your reading fluency.

WHILE YOU READ

The first time you read the excerpts from *Savage Inequalities,* read them quickly. Try to identify the main point Kozol is making. Later, you can reread the excerpts to find supporting information and to check on possible misunderstandings. You will need to read the excerpts quickly two or three times to understand the evidence Kozol provides for his position. If you are having difficulty with the vocabulary, try to guess the words from the context in which they occur. Avoid using a dictionary—it will prevent you from reading quickly and zeroing in on Kozol's main ideas. As you read these excerpts, focus on Kozol's notion of inequality and the environment.

SAVAGE INEQUALITIES (Excerpts)

Jonathan Kozol

"East of anywhere," writes a reporter for the St. Louis Post–Dispatch, "often refers to the wrong side of the city. But, for first-time visitors who suddenly find themselves on its strangely empty streets, East St. Louis might suggest another world." The city, which is 98 percent black, has no obstetric° services, no trash collection, and few jobs. Nearly a third of its families live on less than $7,500 a year; 75 percent of its population lives on welfare° of some form. The U.S. Department of Housing and Urban Development describes it as "the most distressed° small city in America."

2   Only three of the 13 buildings on Missouri Avenue, one of the city's major streets, are occupied. A 13-story office building, tallest in the city, has been boarded up. Outside, on the sidewalk, a pile of garbage fills a ten-foot wooden box.

3   The city, which by night and day is clouded by the smoke that comes out of smokestacks at the Pfizer and Monsanto chemical companies, has one of the highest rates of child lung disease in America. . . .

4   Since October 1987, when the city's garbage pickups° stopped, the backyards of residents have been employed as dumpsites.° In the spring of 1988 a policeman tells a visitor that 40 plastic containers of trash are waiting for removal from his mother's yard. Public health officials are concerned the garbage will attract flies and rodents° in the summer. The policeman speaks of "rats as big as puppies" in his mother's yard. They are known as "bull rats". . . .

5   Railroad tracks still used to transport dangerous chemicals run through the city. "Always present," says Post–Dispatch [the local newspaper], "is the threat of chemical spills°. . . . The noise of sirens° warning residents to leave their homes after a spill is common." The most recent spill, the paper says, "was at the Monsanto Company plant. . . . Nearly 300 gallons of phosphorous trichloride spilled out of a railroad tank. About 450 residents were taken to St. Mary's Hospital". . . .

6   Flooding is another problem East St. Louis faces. East St. Louis lacks the funds to prevent the flooding problems on its own, or to rebuild its sewer system,° which, according to local experts, is "irreparable."° The problem is all the worst because the chemical plants in East St. Louis and adjacent towns have for decades been putting toxins° into the sewer system.

7   The dangers of raw sewage,° which backs up repeatedly into the homes of residents in East St. Louis, were first noticed in the spring of 1989, at a public housing project,° Villa Griffin. Raw sewage can cause many serious diseases, including cholera and hepatitis. A St. Louis health official complains that children live with sewage in their backyards. "The development of working sewage systems made cities livable a hundred years ago," she notes. . . .

8   "It's a terrible way to live," says a mother at the Villa Griffins homes, as she is taking raw sewage out of her sink. Health officials warn of cholera—and, this time, of typhoid also. . . . By April the pool of sewage behind the Villa Griffin project has become a lake of sewage. Two million gallons of raw sewage lie outside the children's homes.

9   In May, another health emergency develops. Soil samples tested at housing areas in East St. Louis contained disturbing quantities of arsenic,° mercury, and lead—as well as steroids dumped in previous years by stock yards° in the area. Lead levels found in the soil around one family's home, according to lead-poison experts, measure "an astronomical° 10,000 parts per million." Five of the children in the building have been poisoned. Although children rarely die of poisoning by lead, health experts note, its effects tend to be harmful. By the time the poisoning becomes apparent in a child's sleep disorders, stomach pains, and hyperactive° behavior, says a health official, "it is too late to undo the permanent brain damage." The poison, she says, "is destroying the learning ability of kids whose abilities have already been destroyed by their environment". . . .

10   The Daughters of Charity,° whose works of kindness are well-known in the Third World, operate a mission at the Villa Griffin homes. On an afternoon in early spring of 1990, Sister Julia Huiskamp meets me on King Boulevard and drives me to the Griffin homes.

11   As we ride past blocks and blocks of skeletal° structures, some of which are still lived in, she slows the car repeatedly at railroad crossings. A seemingly endless railroad train rolls past us to the right. On the left: a blackened lot where garbage has been burning. Next to the burning garbage is a row of 12 white

Threads

For information about environmental matters world–wide, contact: United Nations Environment Program (UNEP), New York Liaison Office, 2 United Nations Plaza, Room 812, New York, NY 10017

cabins, burned by fire. Next: a lot that holds a mountain of auto tires and tin cans. More burnt houses. More trash fires. The train moves almost unnoticed across the flatness of the land.

12   Fifty years old, and wearing a blue suit, white blouse, and blue head-cover, Sister Julia points to the nicest house in sight. The sign on the front reads MOTEL. "It's a whorehouse,"° Sister Julia says.

13   The 99 units of the Villa Griffin homes—two-story structures, brick on the first floor, yellow wood above—form one edge of a park and playground that were filled with fecal matter° last year when sewage pipes exploded. The sewage is gone now and the grass is very green and looks inviting. When nine-year-old Serena and her seven-year-old brother take me for a walk, however, I discover that our shoes sink into what is still sewage. Sewage water still remains. . . .

14   As the children drift back to their homes for supper, Sister Julia stands outside with me and talks about the health concerns that trouble people in the neighborhood. In the setting sun, the voices of the children fill the evening air. Helped to grow by the sewage, a field of flowers is blooming. Standing here, you wouldn't think that anything was wrong. The street is calm. The poison in the soil can't be seen. The sewage is invisible and only makes the grass a little greener. Bikes thrown down by children lie outside their kitchen doors. It could be an ordinary twilight in a small suburban town.

15   Night comes and Sister Julia goes inside to telephone a cab. . . . The taxis will not come into East St. Louis.

VOCABULARY GLOSS

The definitions given below will help you understand Kozol's writing better. Numbers in the parenthesis to the right of the word refer to the paragraph in which the word appears. Not all words that you do not understand are glossed. You will need to guess the meanings of those words in the reading selection which you do not understand.

obstetric (1) (n.)	a branch of medicine which deals with birth
welfare (1) (n.)	aid in the form of money given to the poor
distressed (1) (adj.)	troubled
pickup (4) (n.)	the act of picking up
dumpsite (4) (n.)	a place where garbage is put
rodent (4) (n.)	a member of the species of small animals that have sharp teeth and include mice and rats
spill (5) (n.)	the act of falling out
siren (5) (n.)	a device used to produce a loud warning sound (used by ambulances)
sewer system (6) (n.)	a system used to remove human wastes from homes and businesses
irreparable (6) (adj.)	state of being unable to repair
toxin (6) (n.)	a poison
raw sewage (7) (n.)	dangerous waste which has not been treated to remove toxins

public housing project (7) (n.)	free housing for the poor
arsenic (9) (n.)	a poisonous ingredient that is used to make paints
stock yard (9) (n.)	a yard with pens to keep cattle and livestock
astronomical (9) (adj.)	enormously large
hyperactive (9) (adj.)	extremely active, often requiring medication
charity (10) (n.)	goodwill toward or love of humanity
skeletal (11) (adj.)	resembling the bones of a skeleton
whorehouse (12) (n.)	a place where prostitutes work
fecal matter (13) (n.)	solid body waste

Comprehension Workout

EXERCISE 45

Answer the following questions in small groups.

1. What are three environmental problems facing the people who live in East St. Louis?
2. What is Kozol's main point?
3. What evidence does he give which supports this point?
4. The author seems to think that the environmental problems facing the people of East St. Louis are unfair. Why? Do you agree with Kozol?
5. Do people in some areas of the United States suffer the negative affects of pollution to a greater extent than people in other areas of the United States? Why?
6. Do people from some countries suffer the negative affects of pollution to a greater extent that people from other countries? Why?

Gaining Writing Competence

WRITING A PERSUASIVE LETTER

Explanation: In the next writing task, you will be asked to write a persuasive letter. The information below will help you write this letter.

GUIDELINES FOR WRITING PERSUASIVELY

The purpose of persuasive writing is to get the reader to see the issue that you have chosen from your perspective. You do not need to "sell" the reader on all your ideas, but you do need to convince the reader that your perspective of an issue is a credible one which deserves careful consideration. The reader of persuasive writing expects:

- a clear presentation of the issue under discussion or the case to be argued (including background knowledge)
- a discussion of why the writer feels this issue to be worthy of concern

- a review of arguments/opinions connected with the issue other than the writer's own
- a clear understanding of the writer's own evaluation/opinion of the issue

There are several different ways to organize persuasive writing, depending on the points that you want to make. In planning your writing, consider how you prioritize aspects of your particular issue and how you present your arguments and counter arguments.

Gaining Writing Competence

WRITING A BUSINESS LETTER

Explanation: In the next writing activity you will write a business letter which persuades. To write such a letter, you need to know the appropriate format of formal letters. The information below will help you learn this format.

BUSINESS LETTERS

When you write a business letter, you are often writing to a stranger. Politeness and clarity are called for. Business letters take many forms; the form given below is customary.

BLOCK STYLE—FORMAL BUSINESS LETTER

Your Name
Your Street
Your City, State, Zip

Name and Title of Addressee
Company Name
Street
City, State, Zip

Dear Mr./Ms. (Name of Person):

[Paragraphs are not indented in the body. Do not skip lines (except between paragraphs.]

Sincerely, (or other close)

Your name

ENDINGS USED TO CLOSE BUSINESS LETTERS

Express yourself with directness and clarity. Take a stand with conviction. In some cultures, indirectness is admired in business letters to strangers. This is not the case in the United States where clarity and directness are highly valued.

FORMAL CLOSES

Very truly yours,

Very sincerely yours,

Very respectfully yours,

Respectfully yours,

Respectfully,

Note that for variation, "yours" can be placed at the beginning of the line instead of the end:

Yours very truly,

Yours very sincerely,

Yours very respectfully,

Yours respectfully,

LESS FORMAL AND MORE FREQUENTLY USED CLOSES

Sincerely,

Yours truly,

Sincerely yours,

A COMPARISON OF BUSINESS LETTERS AND PERSONAL LETTERS

1. Paragraphs in business letters generally are not indented; those in personal letters are.
2. Writers only skip lines between paragraphs when writing business letters; they may skip lines whenever they like when writing personal letters.
3. Business letters begin with the greeting, "Dear _____" which is always followed by a colon (as in "Dear Mr. Brown:"). In personal letters, the greeting is always followed by a comma.

Writing Task

WRITING A PERSUASIVE LETTER

Here is a list of some environmental groups. Write a one page persuasive letter to one. Describe the situation in East St. Louis, Illinois, and try to persuade the group to work to improve the environmental conditions of the town. Express your opinion firmly. You need not mail your letter.

The Natural Resources Defense Council
40 West 20th Street
New York, New York 10011

The Environmental Defense Fund
1616 P Street NW, Suite 150
Washington, DC 20036

Renew America
Suite 710, 1400 16th NW
Washington, DC 20036

Greenpeace
1436 U Street NW
Washington, DC 20009

BEFORE YOU WRITE

Consider your audience and the task. Your audience favors environmental improvements. You do not need to convince them that pollution is wrong. They are well convinced of the damages caused by pollution. On the other hand, you will need to provide the audience with some background information about the city of East St. Louis, since they may not know about the troubles of this particular city. After you write your appeal for the organization to help the city, describe the city in a paragraph. Try to provide concrete detail. Then, present good arguments in a logical order.

Consider the tone of the letter that you want to write. Find a partner with whom you have not worked, and discuss the two letters below. Try to determine why the first letter is ineffective and the second effective.

GETTING THE RIGHT TONE

Asking people to do things requires politeness and delicacy. You must make it clear why they are the ones who are appropriate to help you and why they should be interested in doing so. Your tone should be complimentary but not overly so. Say exactly what is needed and what the person's support can do to help your cause. You might want to begin with a note of appreciation.

1. *An Ineffective Letter*

To Whom This May Concern:

I recently read excerpts from Kozol's book, *Savage Inequalities,* and was angry when I found out about the pollution in the city of East St. Louis. It was especially upsetting to read about the children who must play in garbage, because I am a child advocate.

Why isn't your organization doing anything to help East St. Louis? Isn't your organization responsible for reducing pollution? I want you to attend to this matter immediately.

Yours Truly,

Gray Grumble

2. *A More Effective Letter*

To Whom This May Concern:

I have supported your organization for many years and respect the work it is doing. I am sure that you will want to be aware of the serious environmental problems facing East St. Louis, a small city in Illinois. Kozol's new book, *Savage Inequalities,* details these problems. The pollution in East St. Louis has increased so dramatically over the past years that the polluted drinking water and inadequate sewage systems have caused young children needless illnesses.

Perhaps your organization has not heard of East St. Louis because this city is so small, or perhaps Kozol's description of the city is erroneous. In any case, I would appreciate your investigating the environmental conditions of East St. Louis. If they are as bad as I suspect, I know your organization will want to publicize them. Bringing them to the attention of the entire nation will pressure our government to help the city reduce its pollution.

Thank you in advance for your support. I stand behind you.

Sincerely,

Peter Persuasive

Consider this strategy:

LEARNING STRATEGY

Forming Concepts: Imitating effective writing techniques can improve your own ability to compose effectively.

Reread Kozol's excerpts to imitate some of the techniques that Kozol uses when he describes the town of East St. Louis. Underline effective expressions. Take notes on any part of Kozol's writing that you think you might be able to use in your business letter. Complete the questions below.

PREWRITING QUESTIONNAIRE

1. Which organization are you going to write to?
2. What are you going to ask them to do?
3. If they do what you ask them, what effect will it have on East St. Louis?
4. Why should the organization want to help you?
5. What does the organization gain by helping you?

WRITE

Use your notes and responses to the above questions to write the letter.

AFTER YOU HAVE WRITTEN YOUR FIRST DRAFT

Help your classmates revise their letters. Read the following suggestions:

SUGGESTIONS FOR SUCCESSFUL PEER REVISION WORK

1. Help one another. Make sure that the situation is non-threatening by finding something in your classmates' writing to praise.
2. Interact with one another. Establish a collaborative relationship.
3. Respond to the writing as work in progress.
4. Reread all written comments that you give. Make sure that these comments make sense.
5. Don't monopolize the conversation. Allow the writer to make his/her own decisions about revisions.
6. End the peer revision session by encouraging the author.

Find a partner. Read and respond orally to each other's writing. The gambits below can help in your discussion. Each student should use two gambits from each of the categories below.

GAMBITS TO BE USED IN PEER REVISING SESSIONS

Category 1: Asking for Information

I'd like to know. . .

I'm interested in. . .

Would your tell me. . . ?

Do you know. . . ?

What is. . . ?

Could I ask. . . ?

GAMBITS TO BE USED IN PEER REVISING SESSIONS (Continued)

Category 2: Requesting Information

I don't understand. . .

Sorry, I didn't get the last part.

You've lost me.

I don't follow you.

What was that?

Category 3: Requesting Explanations

Can you explain why. . . ?

Please explain. . .

Do you mean to say. . . ?

I don't understand why. . .

Why is it that. . . ?

How come. . . ?

Category 4: Requesting Confirmation

So what you're saying is. . .

What you are really saying is. . .

In other words. . .

So you mean that. . .

Does this mean. . . ?

Another way to say that is. . .

Category 5: Requesting Restating

Please say that again.

Please restate that.

What?

Category 6: Making Suggestions

Why not. . . ?

Perhaps you could. . .

Have you thought about. . . ?

Here's an idea.

Let's. . .

Source: Adapted from Ronald White and Valerie Arndt. 1990. Process Writing. *London: Longman, pg. 94.*

Provide your partner with written feedback on his or her essay. Remember: reread all written comments that you give. Make sure that these comments make sense and are helpful.

REVISE YOUR LETTER

EDIT YOUR LETTER

Once you are satisfied with the content and organization of your letter,
correct your grammatical and mechanical (spelling and punctuation) errors. Try
reading your letter aloud to yourself several times.

Quick Write

WRITING AN ESSAY ON THE TOPIC OF YOUR OWN CHOOSING

In this writing activity, you will write on a topic of your own choosing
related to the environment. If you are having difficulty getting started, try one of
these topics:

Examine further the notion of inequality and the environment.

Discuss different cultural perspectives of the environment.

Explore your own view of the environment, as it is shaped by the society in
which you live.

Write a page or two about your topic. Your audience and purpose will
influence the way you write about it. Imagine that the general public will read
your essay. Your purpose is to inform.

Gaining Writing Competence

WRITING A REPORT ABOUT SURVEY DATA

Explanation: In the next writing activity, you will report on the survey data collected earlier. The information below will help you write an effective report.

REPORTS

Reports come in many formats, but generally they contain these parts: an introduction, a body, and a conclusion. When headings are used, they often follow this format:

I. Introduction
   A. Statement of purpose
   B. Rationale
   C. Description of the problem or situation

II. Body
   A. Description of the means used to examine the problem or situation
   B. Overview of the findings
   C. Analysis and discussion of findings

III. Conclusion

INTRODUCTION

An introduction gives the reason for your report and states a problem or question which is being examined. Introductions pertaining to the survey data in this chapter might begin:

> Many people voice concern over the increase of pollution. To find out what is being done to fight pollution, the following survey was conducted. . . .

THE BODY

The body includes a description of the methods you used to examine the problem, the findings, and the analysis.

Methods. When you describe your methods, you discuss the survey that you used and the students who completed the survey.

Findings. One way of discussing the major findings is by listing them or by putting them in a table and briefly discussing the table.

Analysis   Often in the Analysis of Findings section, each major finding is discussed in a separate paragraph. The analysis section might begin something like this:

> A majority of the students recycled newspapers and bottles. This may be because of the university's recycling program which makes it convenient to recycle paper and glass.

> In contrast, relatively few students recycled plastic. This is probably because there is no plastic recycling program at the university. It is possible to recycle plastic in Marysville since that town has just begun to recycle plastic, but it is very difficult to do so since Marysville is a two-hour drive from the university.

CONCLUSION

The conclusion is brief and clear. It simply restates the major findings (sometimes in a list format) or makes recommendations based on the findings. For the survey data you have collected, the conclusion might look like this:

> The survey data indicate that students recycle when it is easy to do so and fail to recycle when it is difficult. Based on the survey results, the following recommendations are proposed:

RECOMMENDATIONS

1. Establish a program to recycle plastic in the college dorms.
2. Place paper recycling bins around campus.
3. Do not go to markets which sell products in containers which cannot be recycled.

Writing Task

REPORTING SURVEY DATA

Describe several trends in the survey data which indicate similarities and differences in the ways in which students of different cultural backgrounds strive to prevent pollution. Explain the results. Use the format described above. Make sure that you divide your paper into three sections: an introduction, a body, and a conclusion. Use the headings and subheadings suggested earlier. Your report should be one or two pages. You are writing the report for your instructor and your classmates. Your purpose is to inform.

BEFORE YOU WRITE

Make an outline of your report. Make sure that you use complete, grammatical sentences in your outline. The format on page 104 may be helpful.

I. Introduction

    A. _This survey focuses on ways my classmates prevent pollution._ _____

II. Body

    A. Results

        1. Finding 1: _____

        2. Finding 2: _____

    B. Discussion of Results (Why your classmates responded as they did.)

        1. _____

        2. _____

        3. _____

III. Conclusion

AFTER YOU WRITE

Divide into small groups. Take turns reading your reports to the group. As your classmates read their reports, take notes pertaining to interesting trends in the data that your classmates noticed and that you overlooked.

REVISE YOUR REPORT

Use your notes to revise your report. Incorporate any interesting insights from your notes into your report.

EDIT YOUR REPORT

Read your report to a native English writer. Ask the native English writer to help you correct grammar mistakes. Study two of the mistakes that you made. Use a grammar reference book to find out what you can do to prevent making these types of mistakes in your writing.

IT WORKS!
Learning Strategy:
Keeping Track of
Your Progress

Using A Language Learning Log

1. Vocabulary:

Write down as many new words from the lesson as you can remember.

_____

_____

_____

_____

2. Grammar:

Note examples of any grammatical structures from the lesson learned or reviewed. Write a brief explanation of the grammar points that they illustrate.

_____

_____

_____

_____

3. Punctuation:

Briefly describe any punctuation rules that you learned.

_____

_____

_____

_____

4. Techniques for Gaining Writing Competence:

List any new techniques for gaining writing competence that you learned. (Such techniques might include those for writing interesting introductions and conclusions, or those for composing different types of writing such as letters and essays.)

_____

_____

_____

_____

5. Learning Strategies:

Describe briefly any new learning strategies that you learned.

_____

_____

_____

_____

6. Areas that Need More Work:

Note here any areas that you are still trying to improve. Try to be as specific as possible.

_____

_____

_____

_____

How many learning objectives have you been able to accomplish? (Refer to page 149.)

Threads

The average fine levied in 1991 on U.S. companies convicted of illegal pollution in white communities was six times higher than fines in minority communities.

National Law Journal,
New York City

SUMMARY OF LESSON 3: THE ENVIRONMENT AND INJUSTICE

In this lesson, you learned about the Native American's perspective of owning the land and the European American's failure to protect it. All the activities in the last three lessons are designed to provide you with the information and language skills needed to complete the writing assignments contained in the section which follows.

QUICK REFERENCE TO LEARNING STRATEGIES

Understanding and Using Emotions: Sharing Your Feelings About Your Writing (p. 190)

Forming Concepts: Guessing a New Word Meaning From the Context (p. 191)

Forming Concepts: Imitating Effective Writing Techniques (p. 198)

Managing Your Learning: Revise Your Writing Carefully (p. 201)

Understanding and Using Emotions: Choosing an Interesting Topic (p. 201)

WRITING ASSIGNMENT FOR CHAPTER 3

Description of Writing Assignment

Choose one aspect of pollution that you would like to write about. Identify a specific issue related to this aspect that you would like to discuss. In addition, identify an opinion that you would like to argue either for or against, or a case that you would like to present. Your essay should be from 250 to 500 words in length. The general public is your audience. Your purpose is to persuade the general public to see the issue that you are discussing.

PREWRITING ACTIVITIES

BRAINSTORMING

Brainstorming is a quick way to develop your ideas. It helps you narrow your topic and define the audience you will be writing for. In this brainstorming activity, you will be exploring your topic with a partner.

Find a partner. Take turns answering the following questions:

What are you going to be writing about?

How are you going to put that down on paper?

How did you go about choosing your topic?

What problems might you run into?

To help you organize your ideas, answer the questions below.

GETTING YOUR IDEAS TOGETHER

What is the case to be argued?

_____

_____

What is the opinion to be made?

_____

_____

Why should readers be concerned?

_____

_____

What action has been taken to date?

_____

_____

What is your own evaluation?

_____

_____

REVISING ACTIVITIES

After you have written your first draft, work with a partner. Read each other's drafts silently. Make notes of places in your partner's draft:

- that you particularly enjoyed
- that you particularly disliked or found unnecessary
- that you found unclear
- that you would like to know more about

Summarize your partner's text. You might begin, "The main idea in this paper is. . . ."

Return each other's papers. Discuss the summaries and the points which you have noted, beginning with the good points and going onto the things that need clarifying or improving. In the process, jointly try to improve what you have written.

EDITING ACTIVITIES

Edit your essay. Before turning in your final draft, reread and edit your essay.

EDITING GUIDELINES

1. Read once to correct punctuation and capitalization mistakes.
2. Read a second time to correct problems related to pronoun reference.
3. Read a third time to correct subject/verb agreement errors and verb form problems.
4. Read once more to make sure that you have made effective use of cohesive devices.

SHARING YOUR WRITING

In small groups, choose those writings which best illustrate what you have learned in this chapter. Then, share them with the rest of the class and your teacher.

Power through the Written Word

The pen is mightier than the sword.

The pen is the tongue of the hand.

Tailors and writers must mind the fashion.

4

In the previous units, you examined three different perspectives of power: personal power, power and physical force, and power and the environment. In this unit, you will investigate power through the written word. You will also learn what professional writers think about powerful writing, how advertisers use writing to persuade others, and how you can use writing to make a difference in the world around you. All of the activities which you complete in this chapter are designed to help you write the final essay, an essay which might affect others in powerful ways.

Needs Analysis and Goal Setting

SELF-EVALUATION OF LEARNING ACTIVITIES

Before you start this chapter, be aware of your own learning needs, preferences, and goals. First, check the boxes below which apply to you.

ACTIVITY	I LIKE	IT'S OKAY	I DON'T LIKE
Reading stories	____	____	____
Reading essays	____	____	____
Reacting to audiotapes in a journal	____	____	____
Doing grammar exercises	____	____	____
Doing group work	____	____	____
Collecting and analyzing survey data	____	____	____
Analyzing the organization of stories and essays	____	____	____
Writing definitions	____	____	____
Writing summaries	____	____	____
Writing letters	____	____	____
Writing stories	____	____	____
Writing persuasive essays	____	____	____
Writing essays in which you compare and contrast	____	____	____
Reporting survey data	____	____	____

Next, find out what your goals for this unit are. Complete the Self-Diagnosis of Writing Goals below. Number the goals below from 1 to 12—with 1 as your most important goal and 12 as your least important goal. When you set goals, you gain power over your own learning process.

SELF-DIAGNOSIS OF WRITING GOALS

My goals are:

_____ to write cohesive essays (ones which stick together)

_____ to write an interesting introduction

_____ to write an interesting ending

_____ to improve my grammar

_____ to improve my vocabulary

_____ to improve my punctuation

_____ to learn how to write a definition

_____ to learn how to write a summary

_____ to learn how to write a story

_____ to learn how to write a formal business letter

_____ to learn how to write a paragraph to compare and contrast

_____ to learn how to write a persuasive essay

Cooperative Learning

NUMBERED HEADS TOGETHER

Divide up into teams of four. Number off within the groups (one, two, three, or four). Your instructor will call out the number of a question. Put your heads together to make sure that everyone in your group knows the answer. After five minutes, your instructor will call out a number from one to four. Only students with that number can raise their hand if they have the answer.

Question 1: What are ten characteristics of good writing?

Question 2: What specific situations, if any, do ESL learners face when learning to write in English?

Question 3: What are five reasons that students procrastinate when it comes to writing?

Question 4: What are four different ways in which writing can be used to affect positive changes in the writer's life?

Question 5: Does the notion of good writing vary across cultures? In answering this question, you may want to consider whether some cultures value different aspects of writing to a greater extent than others.

Survey

How do your classmates feel about writing? Do they value writing more than they value speaking? Do they believe that writing is a discovery process which they can use to gain knowledge, or do they think writing is primarily intended to help readers discover meaning? Do they find that writing empowers them? Find out how your classmates feel. Later, you will be asked to write a brief report of the findings. Complete the survey below.

SURVEY: ATTITUDES TOWARDS WRITING

Rank the following characteristics in the order of most importance to you: 1 represents the most important characteristic of good writing, and 10 represents the least important characteristic of good writing.

_____ 1. Good writing contains a thesis statement.

_____ 2. Good writing is informative.

_____ 3. Good writing is entertaining.

_____ 4. Good writing is honest; it does not contain lies.

_____ 5. Good writing influences others.

_____ 6. Good writing calls for the reader to think a lot.

_____ 7. Good writing is easy to understand.

_____ 8. Good writing is grammatically correct.

_____ 9. Good writing is well organized; it contains a definite introduction, body, and conclusion.

_____ 10. Good writing is cohesive; the writing flows smoothly, since all the sentences and paragraphs are linked together.

Fill in the blanks with "T" if you believe the statement is true and with "F" if you believe the statement is false.

CHARACTERISTICS OF PERSUASIVE WRITING

_____ 1. The primary objective of persuasive writing is to get the reader to agree with you.

_____ 2. The primary objective of persuasive writing is to get the reader, even for a short while, to understand your point of view.

_____ 3. Effective persuasive writing is direct and to the point.

_____ 4. Effective persuasive writing is indirect.

_____ 5. Writers can affect positive changes in others' lives through their writing.

Fill in the blanks with "T" if you believe the statement is true and with "F" if you believe the statement is false.

THE WRITING PROCESS

_____ 1. Writing is a discovery process. Writers discover new meaning when they write.

_____ 2. Good writing is a time-consuming process.

_____ 3. Good writing is primarily a thinking process. The actual writing takes little time.

_____ 4. When writing, outlines are very helpful.

_____ 5. Writers should wait until they have completed their final drafts before they correct their grammatical mistakes.

_____ 6. Writers should revise their writing many times.

_____ 7. Only those who have a lot of knowledge should write serious academic essays.

_____ 8. It helps to talk about an essay assignment with friends before writing a first draft.

_____ 9. It is a good idea to use at least five different references about a single topic or subtopic when writing a research paper.

_____ 10. Before starting to write, it is a good idea to know the characteristics of the readers.

Fill in the blanks with "T" if you believe the statement is true and with "F" if you believe the statement is false.

ATTITUDES TOWARDS WRITING

_____ 1. I like to write in English.

_____ 2. I like to write in my mother tongue.

_____ 3. When I write in English, I generally feel nervous.

_____ 4. My past experiences writing in English have been helpful.

The following list contains factors which might help an ESL student learn to write in English more effectively. Rank the factors in the order of most importance to you: 1 = the most important factor, and 12 = the least important factor.

OPINIONS ABOUT LEARNING TO WRITE IN ENGLISH

_____ 1. studying grammar rules

_____ 2. talking to friends

> ### Threads
>
> **The best way to become acquainted with a subject is to write a book about it.**
>
> Benjamin Disraeli
> 1804–1881

_____ **3.** writing every day

_____ **4.** reading a lot

_____ **5.** analyzing the writing of published authors

_____ **6.** going to my ESL writing class regularly

_____ **7.** using a dictionary

_____ **8.** using a grammar reference book

_____ **9.** getting a native English-speaking friend to help me edit my writing

_____ **10.** paying a secretary to correct all my grammar mistakes

_____ **11.** keeping a list of the types of writing errors that I make

_____ **12.** getting feedback on my writing from my teacher

As a class, analyze the results on the chalkboard. Try to identify several major findings from your class survey. Then, discuss possible reasons for the results.

LESSON 1: PERSPECTIVES OF GOOD WRITING

Overview

In this lesson, you explore various perspectives of good writing. You examine the views of your classmates as well as the views of professional writers. In so doing, you write an extended definition, a description, and a summary.

About the Reading

The following suggestions, comments, and opinions of noted authors are intended to inspire and encourage you.

SUGGESTIONS, COMMENTS, AND OPINIONS OF NOTED AUTHORS

If you would be a writer, first be a reader. Only through the assimilation of ideas, thoughts, and philosophies can one begin to focus his own ideas, thoughts, and philosophies.
—Allan W. Eckert, *The Scarlet Mansion*

Read at least one book a day. Study the memoirs of authors who interest you.
—Arthur C. Clarke, *The Songs of the Distant Earth*

You must write what you want to write, staying as close as possible to what the truth is for you, as much of the time as possible.
—Judith Arcana, *Every Mother's Son*

One must develop his or her own voice—that's what we call style, the name of the writing game.
—Judith Crist, *Take Twenty-Two*

Books aren't written, they're rewritten. Including your own. It is one of the hardest things to accept, especially after the seventh rewrite hasn't quite done it.
—Michael Crichton, *Electronic Life*

Write more, write earlier, write often.
—Andrew Greeley, *Patience of a Saint*

Source: These quotes appeared in the feature "187 Tips from Best-selling Writers" in the September 1986 issue of *Writer's Digest*. They are reprinted by permission of *Writer's Digest*.

Comprehension Workout

EXERCISE 46

Find a partner. With your partner, discuss the answers to the questions below. Whenever possible, refer to the quotations. When you have finished, answer the questions individually in writing.

1. What is good writing?
2. Does the notion of good writing vary across cultures? For example, is it the case that good writing in one culture might be perceived as bad writing in a different culture.
3. What are the characteristics of good writers?
4. In what specific ways can writing empower individuals?

Additional Reading

ABOUT THE READING

Donald Hall's essay "A Clear and Simple Style" is concerned with style as it refers to writing. Hall, an experienced writer, believes that propaganda is basically bad style because it is dishonest. In his view, good style is simple, clear, and above all, honest.

WHILE YOU READ

As you read this essay, try to decide whether you believe that language is an expression of self and whether, to become a good writer, you must know yourself thoroughly and hold good values.

A CLEAR AND SIMPLE STYLE

Donald Hall

1   Ezra Pound, George Orwell, James Thurber, and Ernest Hemmingway don't have much in common: Ezra Pound was a great poet who became a fascist, George Orwell was a disillusioned left-wing satirist, James Thurber was a comic essayist and cartoonist, and Ernest Hemmingway was a great novelist. If anything, they could represent the diversity° of modern literature. Yet one thing unites them. They share a common idea of good writing style;° they value clarity and simplicity. . . .

2   Style is the manner° of a sentence, not its matter.° Yet the distinction between manner and matter is a slippery° one; manner affects matter. When *Time* used to tell us that President Truman *slouched°* into one room, while General Eisenhower *strode°* into another, the manner in which these two sentences were written affects our feelings. The hotel which *invites me to enjoy my favorite beverage at the Crown Room* is trying not to sound crass° ("Have a drink at the bar"). One linguist° in discussing style took Caesar's "I came—I saw—I conquered" and revised it into, "I arrived on the scene of the battle, I observed the situation, I won the victory." Here the matter is the same, but Caesar's disappears in the longer version. It is impossible to say that the matter is unaffected. Still, let us say that this kind of difference, in the two versions of Caesar, is what we mean by style. . . .

3   In the phrase "good writing" or "good style," the word "good" has usually meant "beautiful" or "proficient"—like a good Rembrandt or a good kind of soap. However, more accurately, it means honest, as opposed to fake. Bad writing happens when the writer lies to himself, or to others, or to both. It may be necessary to lie to yourself in order to lie to others; advertising men used the products they praise. Bad writing may be proficient: It may persuade us to buy a poor car or to vote for a fool, but it is bad because it is tricky, false in its enthusiasm, and falsely motivated. It appeals to a part of us that wants to trick itself. I am encouraged to tell myself that I am enjoying my favorite beverage when I am really only getting sloshed.° . . .

4   A writer of bad prose, in order to become a writer of good prose, must change his character. He does not have to become good in terms of traditional morality,° but he must become honest in the expression of himself, which means that he must know himself. There must be no gap between expression and meaning, between real and declared aims. For some of the people, some of the time, this means not telling deliberate° lies. For most people, it means learning when they are lying and when they are not. It means learning the real names of their feelings. It means not saying or thinking, "I didn't mean to hurt your feelings," when there really existed a desire to hurt. It means not saying "luncheon" or "home" (instead of the simpler words "lunch" and "house") for the purpose of appearing upper-class or well-educated. It means not using the passive construction to give opinions that one is unwilling to call one's own. It means not disguising° banal° thinking by polysyllabic° writing, or the lack of feeling by cliches° which give the false appearance of showing feeling.

5   The style is the writer, and the writer can change himself by changing his style. Writing style is the way you think and the way you understand what you feel. Frequently we feel for each other a mixture of strong love and strong hate; if we call it love, and disguise the hate to ourselves . . . , we are thinking and feeling badly. Style is ethics and psychology; clarity is a psychological sort of ethic,° since it involves not general moral laws but truth. The examination of style is a moral and psychological study. We examine our own style to try to understand ourselves. Editing our own writing, or going over in memory our own spoken words, or even inwardly° examining our thoughts, we can ask why we used the passive in this case, or cliches in that.

6   When the smoke of bad prose fills the air, something is always on fire somewhere. If the style is really the writer, the style becomes an instrument for discovering and changing the writer. Language is expression of self, but language is also the instrument by which to know that self.

VOCABULARY GLOSS

The definitions given below will help you understand this essay. Numbers in the parentheses to the right of the word refer to the paragraph in which the word appears. Not all words that you do not understand are glossed. Guess the meanings of those words in the reading selection which you do not understand.

diversity (1) (n.)	the condition of being different
style (1) (n.)	a way of expressing thought in writing
manner (2) (n.)	a way of expressing oneself or behaving
matter (2) (n.)	content
slippery (2) (adj.)	tricky and difficult
to slouch (2) (v.)	a manner of standing which is not straight
to stride (2) (v.)	a manner of walking characterized by long steps
crass (2) adj.)	gross; insensitive; not delicate
linguist (2) (n.)	a person who specializes in the study of language
sloshed (3) adj.)	the state of being drunk
morality (4) (n.)	ideals of right and wrong ways of behaving
deliberate (4) (adj.)	resulting from careful and thorough consideration
to disguise (4) (v.)	to give a false appearance
banal (4) (adj.)	lacking originality or creativity
polysyllabic (4) (adj.)	having many syllables
cliches (4) (n.)	an overused phrase or expression
ethic (5) (n.)	a principle or value related to good and bad behavior
inwardly (5) (adj.)	privately; to oneself

Comprehension Workout

EXERCISE 47

Find a partner. Summarize the main idea of the following passages in a single sentence. Make sure that you omit supporting details.

1. Ezra Pound, George Orwell, James Thurber, and Ernest Hemmingway don't have much in common: Ezra Pound was a great poet who became a fascist, George Orwell was a disillusioned left-wing satirist, James Thurber was a comic essayist and cartoonist, and Ernest Hemmingway a great novelist. If anything, they could represent the diversity of modern literature. Yet one thing unites them. They share a common idea of good prose style; they value clarity and simplicity.

_____

_____

2. The style is the writer, and the writer can change himself by changing his style. Prose style is the way you think and the way you understand what you feel.

_____

_____

3. If the style is really the writer, the style becomes an instrument for discovering and changing the writer. Language is expression of self, but language is also the instrument by which to know that self.

_____

_____

Grammar Explanation

USING COMPLETE SENTENCES

Explanation: In the next writing activity, you will be asked to write a summary. When writing a summary, make sure that you use complete sentences. The following information will help you.

AVOIDING SENTENCE FRAGMENTS

Avoid using sentence fragments. Sentence fragments are incomplete sentences which have been punctuated as complete sentences. They often begin with a capital letter and end with a period. Sentence fragments do not contain a subject and a predicate.

SUBJECT	PREDICATE
The writing	is effective

Although sentence fragments are sometimes used creatively by professional writers, they are not acceptable in academic writing.

1. Dependent clauses are not complete sentences. They must be preceded or followed by independent clauses (which can stand alone and have both a subject and a predicate). Dependent clauses begin with these words: *who, which, that, after, although, because, before, even if, in order that, once, since, though, unless, until, when, where,* and *while.*

   a. **Sentence Fragment**

   My writing was bad. <u>Before I came to the United States</u>.

   Complete Sentence

   My writing was bad before I came to the United States.

   b. **Sentence Fragment**

   I didn't have the vocabulary to write well. <u>Since I didn't have much English proficiency</u>.

Complete Sentence

I didn't have the vocabulary to write well since I didn't have much English proficiency.

2. Prepositional phrases cannot stand alone. These phrases are made of prepositions (such as *in, on,* and *at*) and their related words.

a. Sentence Fragment

The writer understood nothing. <u>About himself</u>.

Complete Sentence

The writer understood nothing about himself.

b. Sentence Fragment

Her pen rolled slowly. <u>Under her desk</u>.

Complete Sentence

Her pen rolled slowly under her desk.

Grammar Practice: Avoiding Sentence Fragments

EXERCISE 48

Correct each of the sentence fragments in the following passage by creating new sentences or by combining the fragments with other sentences.

**SOME DIFFERENCES BETWEEN
NORTH AMERICAN AND KOREAN WRITING**

North Americans expect writing to help them achieve power. They value using language creatively. To discover new ideas. Although they believe that the writing process is a messy, time-consuming one. They also believe. That finished pieces of writing should be cohesive and accurate.

In general, Korean writing is very different than English writing. Koreans expect writing to empower the readers, not the authors. For Koreans, writing is not a discovery process. The act of writing is not a time-consuming one. Thinking *is*. Koreans value thinking. About ideas for a long time—perhaps years—and then writing these ideas down in a single sitting. They creatively lead their readers to discover these ideas on their own. Thesis statements are unnecessary. In many types of Korean writing. By being indirect, Korean writers show respect for the readers' intellect.

Gaining Writing Competence

WRITING A SUMMARY

Explanation: In the next writing task, you will summarize Hall's essay. The following information will help you.

SUMMARIES

Good summaries are easy to understand.

Summaries are concise statements of the author's main ideas.

They do *not*:

1. include details which are not directly related to the topic;
2. discuss the writer's own opinion; or
3. repeat the author's ideas word-for-word.

They *do*:

1. restate the author's thesis statement;
2. summarize the support for this thesis;
3. rephrase the author's words; and
4. explain the author's purpose.

Summaries provide enough general background information about the writing for the readers to understand it.

Writing Task

WRITING A SUMMARY

Write a one paragraph summary of Hall's essay. Your purpose is to inform the general public of the main ideas Hall presents in his essay. Imagine that you are writing this summary for that part of the general public who is unfamiliar with Hall's work.

BEFORE YOU WRITE

With a partner, discuss the items in the box below. While you are discussing these items, each student should complete the box.

TEXT ANALYSIS OF HALL'S ESSAY
Name of Text: _____
Purpose: _____

Description of the Readers:
(General public? College students? Make an educated guess.)

Thesis:

_____

_____

Support for Thesis:

_____

_____

WRITE

While you write, refer back to the items you responded to in the Text Analysis assignment above.

REVISE YOUR WRITING

Read your summary. Make sure that it is easy to understand. The following questions are intended to guide your revisions.

REVISION CHECKLIST

1. Is my summary easy to understand?
2. Is Hall's thesis statement clearly written in my own words?
3. Did I get to Hall's thesis statement immediately?
4. Did I briefly summarize Hall's supporting evidence for his thesis?
5. Did I rephrase Hall's words?
6. Did I avoid giving a personal opinion?

EDIT YOUR SUMMARY

First, concentrate on verb tenses. When summarizing Hall's views, you will be using the present tense (as in "Hall *believes* ," "Hall *thinks*," "In Hall's opinion, writing *is*. . ."). Next, concentrate on agreement. Make sure that nouns and verbs agree in number. Make sure that pronouns agree in number and gender. Finally, make sure that your summary contains no sentence fragment errors. This checklist will be helpful:

EDITING CHECKLIST

_____ Nouns and verbs agree in number
_____ Pronouns agree in number and gender.
_____ There are no sentence fragments.

Gaining Writing Competence

USING FAMILIAR WORDS

Short, familiar words can be very effective. The following passage, entitled "Strength of a Single Syllable," is taken from the book, *The Miracle of Language*. It is composed entirely of single-syllable words.

> When you speak and write, no law says that you have to use big words. Short words are as good as long ones, and short, old words like *sun* and *grass* and *home* are best of all. A lot of small words, more than you might think, can meet your needs with a strength, grace, and charm that large words lack.
>
> Big words can make the way dark for those who hear what you say and read what you write. They add fat to your prose. Small words are the ones we seem to have known from birth. They are like the fire that warms the home, and they cast a clear light on big things: night and day, love and hate, war and peace, life and death.
>
> If a long word says just what you want, do not fear to use it. But know that your tongue is rich in crisp, brisk, swift, short words. Make them the spine and the heart of what you speak and write. Like friends, they will not let you down.

Threads

For information about a career as a writer, contact: National Writers Union, 13 Astor Place, 7th floor, New York, NY 10003

Encyclopedia of Associations

Gaining Writing Practice: Using Short, Familiar Words when Writing a Definition

EXERCISE 49

Write a short paragraph in which you define the term *writing style*. Make sure that you use short, familiar words. You are writing this definition for yourself and your classmates. Your purpose is to inform.

Gaining Writing Competence

USING SPECIFIC WORDS AND PHRASES

In the next writing task, you will write a story. When you write this story, you will need to avoid general or vague words. Good writers do not use such words in their writing. Rather, they use specific words and phrases. For instance, they do not use sentences like *Writing is nice.* The word *nice* is so general that it has lost its meaning. Instead, of using general words, good writers use sentences such as *I like to write to express my personal opinions and release my frustrations.* When you are writing your story, avoid using general words which have lost their meaning in English.

Gaining Writing Practice: Using Specific Words and Phrases

EXERCISE 50

The sentences below contain general words which describe something. These words are italicized. Replace these words and phrases with more specific words or phrases. Follow the examples given.

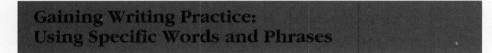

GENERAL SPECIFIC

1. I tried to write a *good* paper.

   I tried to write a paper which was not only neat and easy to read but also interesting.

2. I wanted my teacher to correct my paper *quickly*.

   I was so embarrassed about all the mistakes that I made that I wanted my teacher to take only a few seconds to correct my paper.

3. I wanted my papers to be *quite* interesting.

   _____

   _____

   _____

4. I didn't care *how much time I spent* writing my essay.

   _____

   _____

   _____

5. I wanted to write a *nice* essay.

   _____

   _____

   _____

6. I worked *long hours*.

_____

_____

_____

7. My elementary teacher did a *good* job correcting my errors.

_____

_____

_____

8. My teacher had a *long* history of offering constructive criticism.

_____

_____

_____

9. I wanted to make only a *small* number of errors.

_____

_____

_____

10. I wasn't willing to work *hard* on my writing.

_____

_____

_____

_____

LEARNING STRATEGY

Managing Your Learning: Keeping a list of new, meaningful words and expressions helps you remember and use them.

Gaining Writing Practice

KEEPING A FILE OF USEFUL WORDS AND EXPRESSIONS

Jot down memorable words and expressions from books, stories, articles, advertisements, posters, the newspaper—anything you read. Read them out loud and try to understand why they are effective. Are they entertaining? Do they refer to interesting ideas? Do they contain vivid words?

Gaining Writing Competence

SUGGESTIONS FOR WRITING A STORY

Explanation: In the next writing task, you will be asked to write a story. The following information is intended to help you complete this task.

A personal story may seem to be a casual retelling of a bygone event in your life, but it is actually much more than that. It can be a deliberate creation of an event which serves as a window into your life. One characteristic of a good story is the use of details. Details may concern sounds, smells, or sights, but they must provide the reader with an insight about your life. Another characteristic of a good story concerns the use of dialog. Dialog makes the characters of a story come to life.

Punctuation Explanation

USING QUOTATION MARKS

When writing a story, it is often useful to use dialog. This involves using quotation marks. Quotations seem to make the people in your story come alive. The following rules will help you use quotation marks properly.

1. Use quotation marks (" ") at the beginning and the end of the words spoken by the person you are quoting. The name of the person and a verb such as *said* are outside of the quotation marks.
2. Commas, periods, and question marks are put inside the quotation marks.
3. In writing the words of more than one speaker, new quotation marks and a new paragraph are used each time the speaker changes.

Punctuation Practice: Using Quotation Marks

EXERCISE 51

All the passages below contain indirect quotations. Rewrite these passages so that they contain direct quotations.

1. The bell rang. It was time to hand my midterm in. The teacher told me to give it to her. Slowly, I became aware that the other students had finished their midterms before me and were leaving the room.

2. I believed that my writing was good, reflecting ideas that I had been learning in my class. I was dismayed to find, therefore, that others could not understand my writing. My instructor confused me when she asked me what the topic of my essay was about. It turns out that I had failed to include a thesis statement. I thought these statements were unnecessary.

3. I wanted to write like my friend, Jane. Her writing seemed almost effortless. She would take out a notebook and fill out page after page of beautiful prose. Jane often told me not to become discouraged. Her encouragement was somehow reassuring.

4. My instructor told me that writing progress is difficult to measure. He said that he had observed improvement in my writing. Unfortunately, I knew that he was only being tactful. I felt that I had made no progress at all. I was tempted to ask him to spend more time helping me, but I didn't. I sat in the back of the class trying to do my best work. Then, one day, my writing suddenly came to life. Whereas on previous occasions I fumbled to find the right words, I now found them easily.

5. I had to overcome many obstacles. I was shy and withdrawn and didn't like to participate in class. My teacher would try to encourage me to participate, but I would always refuse. My language skills were worse than the other students'. I was embarrassed by my poor vocabulary and grammar skills. In addition to my language problems, my attitude towards writing was bad. I couldn't write well in my first language, and I was convinced that it would be impossible for me to learn to write in my second. Fortunately, my teacher told me not to give up, and finally one day I listened to him.

Writing Task: Writing a Story

Write a one to two page story about the obstacles which you overcame learning to write in English. You are writing this story for the general public. Your purpose is to inform readers of the difficulties involved in learning to write in a second (third, or fourth!) language.

BEFORE YOU WRITE

Consider this strategy:

LEARNING STRATEGY

Testing Hypotheses: Taking risks helps improve your writing skills.

Take a minute or two to think about several obstacles that you have overcome learning to write in English. Take another ten minutes to write about these obstacles. Don't worry about your writing. This is a good time to take some risks.

Find a partner. Discuss three obstacles which both of you have had to overcome to write in English.

Find a different partner. Write a list of six obstacles which most ESL students have to overcome to acquire English.

MAPPING

In this prewriting activity, called mapping, each student will need to take out a clean sheet of paper. You will draw a map of the story you will write shortly. Follow the example below.

1. Write the word OBSTACLES in the middle of the page. Draw a circle around it.
2. Draw three to five lines which radiate form the circle. On these lines, write the names of different types of obstacles that you have had to overcome.
3. Add additional ideas about the obstacles on lines which are connected to the radiating lines.

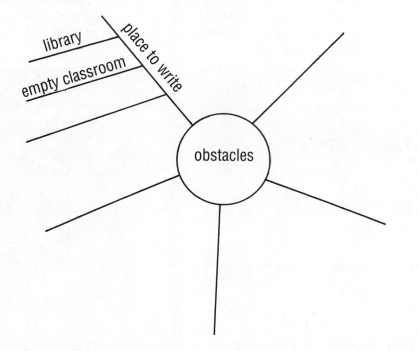

IT WORKS!
Learning Strategy:
Switching to Your
Native Language

IT WORKS!
Learning Strategy:
Asking for Help

WHILE YOU ARE WRITING YOUR FIRST DRAFT

Consider this strategy:

LEARNING STRATEGY

Managing Your Learning: Do not spend too much time thinking about the organization of your ideas; just write them down.

REVISE YOUR STORY

Read your story to a partner. Ask your partner to help you improve the content and organization of your story. Then, consider this strategy:

LEARNING STRATEGY

Managing Your Learning: Getting assistance from your teacher can provide you with valuable feedback and suggest outside activities to improve your writing.

Work out additional assignments with your teacher that will help you to improve your writing. Offer a cassette with your paper and ask your teacher to audiotape comments about your paper. Ask your teacher to go over your paper individually in a conference. To get the most from your teacher, write neatly and try to correct all your own mistakes before you hand in your final drafts. Ask your instructor to help you improve the organization and content of your story. The Instructor Feedback Form will help you.

INSTRUCTOR FEEDBACK FORM

1. Please put a straight line under those passages or words that you particularly liked. Please put a wavy line next to those passages or words that you think could be improved.
2. Please put a brief comment about that part of my writing that affected you.
3. Please comment on those parts of the essay which you think are unclear.

Here are some features of my writing that I especially want feedback on:

	STRONG	ADEQUATE	WEAK
liveliness of language	___	___	___
use of details	___	___	___
use of dialog	___	___	___
introduction	___	___	___
body	___	___	___
ending	___	___	___

4. What is the quickest, simplest change that I could make to improve this story?
5. What is one thing that I should try to work on to improve my next piece of writing?

REVISE YOUR STORY AGAIN

Use the feedback from your classmates and instructor to revise your story.

EDIT YOUR STORY

Edit each story in small groups. Read each paper aloud and try to correct the following types of mistakes:

EDITING CHECKLIST

1. *Punctuation*. Pay particular attention to the use of quotation marks.
2. *Verb Tense*. Make sure that each verb is in the correct tense.
3. *Sentence Fragments*. Make sure that all sentences are complete and that sentence fragments are not used.

Using a Language Learning Log

1. Vocabulary:

   Write down as many new words from the lesson as you can remember.

   _____
   _____
   _____
   _____

IT WORKS!
Learning Strategy:
Keeping Track of
Your Progress

2. Grammar:

   Note examples of any grammatical structures from the lesson learned or reviewed. Write a brief explanation of the grammar points that they illustrate.

   _____
   _____
   _____
   _____

3. Punctuation:

   Write down any new punctuation rules that you learned.

   _____
   _____
   _____
   _____

4. Techniques for Gaining Writing Competence:

List any new composition techniques that you learned. (Such techniques might include those for writing interesting introductions, bodies, and conclusions, or for composing different types of writing effectively.)

_____

_____

_____

_____

5. Learning Strategies:

Briefly describe any new learning strategies that you have applied in your writing.

_____

_____

_____

_____

6. Areas that Need More Work:

Note here in brief form any areas that you are still trying to improve. Try to be as specific as possible.

_____

_____

_____

_____

_____

Quick Write

MAKING AN ACTION PLAN

Write a one or two paragraph description of your major language learning objectives and your plan to accomplish these objectives. Be as specific as possible.

In this lesson, you examined professional writers' perspectives of good writing as well as your own perspectives. You wrote summaries, definitions, and narratives. In the next chapter, you will focus on persuasive language, the language of advertising.

QUICK REFERENCE TO LEARNING STRATEGIES

Overcoming Limitations: Using Familiar Words (p. 222)

Managing Your Learning: Keeping a List of New Meaningful Words (p. 224)

Testing Hypotheses: Taking Risks (p. 226)

Managing Your Learning: Don't Spend Too Much Time on Thinking (p. 227)

Managing Your Learning: Getting Your Teacher to Help You (p. 228)

Overview

In the last lesson, you investigated various views of writing. In this lesson, you examine one particular way in which writing is used—to deceive. You write an extended definition, a summary of survey findings, an analysis of an advertisement, and a business letter.

About the Reading

This reading focuses on the notion of *doublespeak,* the language of lies and irresponsibility. Doublespeak appears to communicate the truth, but actually expresses lies. It is to language pollution what a sewage plant is to fouling the environment. The author of the excerpts from *Doublespeak,* William Lutz, is Chair of the Committee on Public Doublespeak of the National Council of Teachers of English and edits the *Quarterly Review of Doublespeak.* He also teaches in the English Department at Rutgers University.

BEFORE YOU READ

To prepare you for the reading selections by Lutz, first think about some of the commercials you have seen on television. Then, find a partner. Discussing the answers to the following questions will help you understand Lutz's ideas.

1. Do you believe that commercials affect your buying habits?
2. In what specific ways do commercials influence you to buy their products?
3. What language do the commercials use?
4. Is the language truthful?
5. In which cultures are commercials most common? Why? Are commercials used in all cultures or only in consumer-oriented ones?

6. Americans living in the United States are often said to adhere to the following stereotypes. They:
- cherish change and novelty,
- give prominence to the young rather than the elderly,
- desire upward economic mobility,
- assume that natural problems can be overcome by technology,
- are competitive,
- believe in equality,
- stress individualism,
- are community-oriented,
- like to follow through on any promises they make,
- value a do-it-yourself approach to life.

While these are just stereotypes and not everyone adheres to them, many advertisements reflect them. First, discuss the stereotypes above with your partner. Then, consider the advertisements below. In what ways, if any, do they reflect the stereotypes listed above?

ADVERTISEMENTS

It's the Pepsi Generation.

It's not about fixing old windows. It's about opening new doors. Introducing IBM's OS/22.0.

Epson. Our lasers are aimed at everyone.

American Express Travelers Checques. Don't leave home without them.

People Magazine. We're these kind of people, too.

Mass Mutual. We help you keep your promises.

Toyota. Investing in the individual.

McDonald's. If you get something out of the community, put something back.

Consider this strategy:

LEARNING STRATEGY

Forming Concepts: Reading without looking up every single new word helps you read fluently and concentrate on the author's main ideas.

When you read the excerpts from *Doublespeak,* don't bother to look up every single word. Skip those words that you do not understand, or guess the meanings of these words from the contexts in which they occur.

DOUBLESPEAK (Excerpts)

William Lutz

Sometimes it seems as if the whole world is not just filled with advertising but dominated° by it. You can't get away from the ads. In the United States, every twenty-four hours, on the average, you are exposed to sixteen hundred commercial messages by one means of communication or another. Of these sixteen hundred ads, you notice eighty, but only twelve will get some kind of response from you. And it's not just radio, television, newspapers, and magazines that are filled with ads, but just about every part of your life. Ads are, of course, on all the products you buy. But then there are all the billboards, plus the signs on buildings, trucks, cabs, buses, subways, and anything else that moves or doesn't move. And don't forget all those coupons, flyers, and handbills, not to mention all the advertising junk mail.°

Advertising and Reality

2   Rosser Reeves, a famous ad man who worked for the Ted Bates advertising agency, once said that the basic problem advertisers had to solve was that most products were really the same: "Our problem is—a client° comes into my office and throws two newly produced half dollars onto my desk and says, 'Mine is the one on the left. You prove it's better.'" And that's the job of advertising: to make something out of nothing.

3   When Hicks B. Waldron was appointed president of Avon products in 1983, his previous experience had been with the Heublein Corporation, directing the sales of Smirnoff vodka and Kentucky Fried Chicken. Mr. Waldron said he saw little difficulty in moving from a job directing the sales of vodka and fried chicken to a job directing the sales of beauty-care products. As Mr. Waldron noted, it's not the product that's being sold, it's fashion and style. He cited the vodka business as an example, where a colorless, odorless, tasteless liquid is sold at a higher price that depends on its fashionability which is developed through advertising. "Advertising and positioning of the product are almost everything," Mr. Waldron was quoted as saying in an article in *The New York Times*. (All you vodka drinkers who insist on a special brand of vodka should read this paragraph three times.)...

4   In 1980 the Procter & Gamble and Colgate–Palmolive companies spent over $75 million to tout° "new" toothpastes that didn't make teeth any whiter than the toothpastes the companies currently sold. Nor did the new toothpastes prevent cavities any better, nor did they even have new names. But the new toothpastes did taste different and have new colors. Most competing brands° of everyday personal-care, household-cleaning, and food items are pretty much alike, according to *The Wall Street Journal* article that reported on this battle of the advertising giants. Therefore, manufacturers depend on minor changes in product appearances, packaging, scents, flavors, or other nonessential aspects of the product to sell it. . . . So Procter & Gamble spent $17.9 million to advertise Colgate on television and $16 million to advertise Aim. All this money was to promote products which were essentially the same. It didn't make much difference which toothpaste you bought because both cleaned your teeth the same. So if you bought one of these toothpastes because of the ads promoting it, the advertisers won.

5   De Beers, the company that runs the world's diamond cartel° and controls 80 percent of the world's supply in diamonds, learned long ago that making something out of nothing through advertising can create huge profits. Each year the world's diamond mines° produce over fifty times the number of gem diamonds (as opposed to industrial diamonds) needed for jewelry. . . . In short, there is and always was a glut° of diamonds in the world. Why, then, do diamonds cost so much?

6   Early on, the men who ran De Beers realized that diamonds had little value of their own and their price depended almost entirely on their scarcity. After gaining control over production of all the important diamond mines° in the world, they began a campaign to stimulate° the public's desire to buy diamonds. In 1938, De Beers hired the N. W. Ayer advertising agency to increase diamond sales in the United States. Ayer devised a campaign around the idea that diamonds were a gift of love, and the larger and finer the diamond, the greater

the expression of love. In 1948 Frances Gerety of Ayer came up with the saying, "A Diamond is Forever" on a picture of young lovers on a honeymoon—even though diamonds can be destroyed. Sales of diamonds in the United States went from $23 million in 1939 to more than $2.1 billion (wholesale prices) in 1979. . . . This campaign is considered one of the most successful in the history of advertising.

7   In 1976 the J. Walter Thompson advertising company began a campaign in Japan to popularize° diamond engagement rings. It seems that in 1968 fewer than 5 percent of Japanese women getting married received a diamond engagement ring. De Beers was determined to change this situation and increase diamond sales in Japan. By 1981 some 60 percent of Japanese brides had diamond rings and Japan was the second largest market for diamond engagement rings.

8   When small diamonds from Russian mines threatened to flood the market, De Beers changed its advertising campaign. Women were told they should no longer equate the status and emotional commitment° of an engagement with the size of the diamond. Instead, women were told that it was the quality, color, and cut of the diamond that were important, not the size. De Beers even invented the "eternity ring," which consisted of numerous small Russian diamonds and was advertised as the symbol of renewed love for married couples. Again, the campaign was successful, and a new market was created. Russia joined the De Beers cartel, and profits for everyone continue to be quite handsome, averaging about 40 percent of sales. Not a bad margin of profit° for selling a product for which there is a glut in the world. Remember this when you think about buying a diamond ring.

Puffing the Product and Truth in Advertising

9   It may come as a surprise to you, but advertisements do not have to be literally true. "Puffing" the product is perfectly legal. What is "puffing"? "Puffing" is an exaggeration about the product that is so obvious just about anyone is capable of recognizing the claim° as an exaggeration. The most common examples of "puffing" involve the use of such words as "exciting," "glamorous," "lavish," "perfect." However, when an advertising claim can be scientifically tested or analyzed, it is no longer "puffing.". . . The first rule of advertising is that nothing is what it seems, which brings us to the Rule of Parity.

The Rule of Parity

10   Products such as gasoline, cigarettes, toothpaste, soap, aspirin, cold remedies, cosmetics, deodorants, cereals, liquor, and others are called parity products. Parity products are simply products in which most if not all the brands in a class or category are pretty much the same. Most toothpastes, for example, are made the same way with pretty much the same formula. There is no essential difference among the dozens of toothpastes on the market today. Thus, all toothpastes are equal, which is what parity means. Now comes the interesting part. Follow this closely.

11   Since all toothpastes are equal, no one brand is superior to any of the others. Therefore, not only are all parity products "good" products, they are all the "best" products. Thus, you can advertise your toothpaste, gasoline, deodorant, or other parity product as the "best" and not have to prove your claim. However, if you claim your parity product is "better" than another parity product,you have to prove your claim because "better" is a comparative and a claim of superiority, and only one product can be "better" than the others in a parity class. Did you get that? In the world of advertising doublespeak, "better" means "best," but "best" means only "equal to." So the next time you see a parity product advertised as the best, the ad simply means that the product is as good as any other in its class. . . .

Weasel Words

12   . . . Advertisers use weasel° words to appear to be making a claim for a product when in fact they are making no claim at all. Weasel words get their name from the way weasels eat the eggs they find in the nests of other animals. A weasel will make a small hole in the egg, suck out the insides, then place the egg back in the nest. Only when the egg is examined closely is it found to be hollow. That's the way it is with weasel words in advertising: Examine the weasel words closely and you'll find that they're as hollow as any egg sucked by a weasel. Weasel words appear to say one thing when in fact they say the opposite, or nothing at all.

"Help"—The Number One Weasel Word

13   The biggest weasel word used in advertising doublespeak is "help." Now "help" only means to aid or assist, nothing more. It does not mean to conquer, stop, eliminate, end, solve, heal, cure, or anything else. But once the ad says "help," it can say just about anything after that because "help" qualifies everything coming after it. The trick is that the claim coming after the weasel word is usually so strong and so dramatic that you forget the word "help" and concentrate only on the dramatic claim. You read into the ad a message that the ad does not contain. More importantly, the advertiser is not responsible for the claim that you read into the ad, even though the advertiser wrote the ad so you would read the claim into it. . . .

14   Ads using "help" are among the most popular. One says, "Helps keeps you young looking," but then a lot of things will keep you "young looking," including exercise, rest, good nutrition, and a facelift. More importantly, this ad doesn't say the product will keep you young, only young looking. Someone may look young to one person and old to another. . . .

15   There are plenty of other weasel words used in advertising. . . . but in order to identify the doublespeak of advertising and understand the real meaning of an ad, you have to be aware of the most popular weasel words in advertising today.

Virtually Spotless

16   One of the most powerful weasel words is "virtually," a word so innocent that most people don't pay attention to it when it is used in an advertising claim. But watch out. "Virtually" is used in advertising claims that appear to make specific, definite promises when there is no promise. After all, what does "virtually" mean? It means "in essence or effect, although not in fact." Look at that definition again. Virtually means "not in fact." It does not mean "almost" or "just about the same as" or anything else. And before you dismiss all this concern over such a small word, remember that small words can have big consequences. . . .

New and Improved

17   If "new" is the most frequently used word on a product package, "improved" is the second most frequent. In fact, the two words are almost always used together. It seems just about everything sold these days is "new and improved." The next time you're in the supermarket, try counting the number of times you see these words on products. But you'd better do it while you're walking down just one aisle,° otherwise you'll need a calculator to keep track of° of your counting. . . .

18   What makes a product "new"? Some products have been around a long time, yet every once in a while you discover that they are being advertised as "new." Well, an advertiser can call a product new if there has been "a material functional change" in the product. What is "a material functional change," you ask? Good question. In fact it's such a good question it's being asked all the time.

It's up to the manufacturer to prove that the product has been changed. And if the manufacturer isn't challenged on the claim, then there's no one to stop it. Moreover, the change does not have to be an improvement in the product. One manufacturer added an artificial lemon scent to a cleaning product and called it "new and improved," even through the product did not clean any better with the lemon scent. The manufacturer defended the use of the word "new" since the artificial scent changed the chemical formula of the product and therefore constituted "a material functional change."

19   Which brings up the word "improved." When used in advertising, "improved" does not mean "made better." It only means "changed" or "different from before." So, if the detergent maker puts a plastic pour spout on the box of detergent, the product has been "improved," and away we go with a whole new advertising campaign. . . .

20   If there is a second edition° of this book, I'll just call it the "new and improved" edition. Wouldn't you prefer to have a "new and improved" edition of this book rather than a "second" edition?

Acts Fast

21   "Acts" and "works" are two popular weasel words in advertising because they bring action to the product and to the advertising claim. When you see the ad for the cough syrup that "Acts on the cough control center," ask yourself what this cough syrup is claiming to do. Well, it's just claiming to "act," to do something, to perform an action. What is it that the cough syrup does? The ad doesn't say. It only claims to perform an action or do something on your "cough control center." By the way, what and where is your "cough control center"? I don't remember learning about that part of the body in human biology class.

22   Ads that use such phrases as "acts fast," "acts against," "acts to prevent," and the like are saying essentially nothing, because "act" is a word empty of any specific meaning. The ads are always careful not to specify exactly what "act" the product performs. Just because a brand of aspirin claims to "act fast" for headache relief doesn't mean this aspirin is any better than any other aspirin. What is the act that this aspirin performs? You're never told. Maybe it just dissolves° quickly. Since aspirin is a parity product, all aspirin is the same and therefore functions the same. . . .

Like Magic

23   Whenever advertisers want you to stop thinking about the product and to start thinking about something bigger, better, or more attractive than the product, they use the very popular weasel word, "like." The word "like" is the advertiser's equivalent of a magician's use of tricks. "Like" gets you to ignore the product and concentrate on the claim the advertiser is making about it. "For skin like peaches and cream" claims the ad for a skin cream. What is this ad really claiming? It doesn't say this cream will give you peaches and cream skin. There is no verb in this claim, so it doesn't even mention using the product. How is skin ever like "peaches and cream?"

Can It Be up to the Claim?

24   Analyzing ads for doublespeak requires that you pay attention to every word in the ad and determine what each word really means. Advertisers try to wrap their claims in language that sounds concrete, specific, and objective, when in fact the language of advertising is anything but. Your job is to read carefully and listen critically so that when the announcer says that "Crest can be of significant value. . ." you know immediately that this claim says absolutely nothing. Where is the doublespeak in this ad? Start with the second word. . . .

25   It's so easy to miss the importance of those little words, "can be." Almost as easy as missing the importance of the words "up to" in an ad. These words are

very popular in sales ads. You know, the ones that say, "Up to 50 percent off!" Now, what does that claim mean? Not much, because the store or manufacturer has to reduce the price of only a few items by 50 percent. Everything else can be reduced a lot less, or not even reduced. Moreover, don't you want to know 50 percent off of what? Is it 50 percent off the "manufacturer's suggested list price,"° which is the highest possible price? Was the price artificially inflated° and then reduced? In other ads, "up to" expresses an ideal situation. The medicine that works "up to ten times faster," the battery that lasts "up to twice as long," and the soap that gets you "up to twice as clean" all are based on ideal situations for using those products, situations in which you can be sure that you will never find yourself."

Unfinished Words

26   . . .Unfinished words depend on you to finish them, to provide the words the advertisers so thoughtfully left out of the ad. Pall mall cigarettes were once advertised as "A longer, finer, and milder smoke." The question is, longer, finer, and milder than what ? . . .

27   Unfinished words are frequently used in advertising because they appear to promise so much. More importantly, they can be joined with powerful visual images on television to appear to be making significant promises about a product's effectiveness without really making any promises. In a television ad, the aspirin product that claims "fast relief" can show a person with a headache taking the product and then, in what appears to be a matter of minutes, claiming complete relief. This visual image is far more powerful than any claim made in unfinished words. Indeed, the visual image completes the unfinished words for you, filling in with pictures what the words leave out. And you thought that ads didn't affect you. What brand of aspirin do you use?

28   Some years ago, Ford's advertisements proclaimed: "Ford LTD—700% quieter." Now what do you think Ford was claiming with these unfinished words? What was the Ford LTD quieter than? A Cadillac? A Mercedes Benz? A BMW? Well, when the FTC asked Ford to substantiate° this unfinished claim, Ford replied that it meant that the inside of the LTD was 700% quieter than the outside. How did you finish those unfinished words when you first read them? Did you even come close to Ford's meaning?

Other Tricks of the Trade

29   . . .Since we like to think of ourselves as living in a technologically advanced country, science and technology have a great appeal° in selling products. Advertisers are quick to use scientific doublespeak to push their products. . . .

30   Shampoo, deodorant, mouthwash, cold medicine, sleeping pills, and any number of other products all seem to contain some special chemical ingredient that allows them to work wonders. "Certs° contains a sparkling drop of Retsyn." So what? What's Retsyn? What's it do? What's so special about it? . . .

ADVERTISING DOUBLESPEAK QUICK QUIZ

31   Now it's time to test your awareness of advertising doublespeak. (You didn't think I would just let you read this and forget it, did you?) The following is a list of statements from some recent ads. Your job is to figure out what each of these ads really says.

DOMINOS PIZZA. "Because nobody delivers better."

SINUTAB. "It can stop pain."

TUMS. "The stronger acid neutralizer."

MAXIMUM STRENGTH DRISTAN. "Strong medicine for tough sinus colds."

LISTERMINT. "Making your mouth a cleaner place."

CASCADE. "For virtually spotless dishes nothing beats Cascade."

NUPRIN. "Little. Yellow. Different. Better."

ANACIN. "Better relief."

SUDAFED. "Fast sinus relief that won't put you fast asleep."

ADVIL. "Advanced medicine for pain."

PONDS COLD CREAM. "Ponds cleans like no soap can."

MILLER LITE BEER. "Tastes great. Less filling."

PHILLIPS MILK OF MAGNESIA. "Nobody treats you better than MOM (Philips Milk of Magnesia)."

BAYER. "The wonder drug that works wonders."

CRACKER BARRELL. "Judged to be the best."

Source: William Lutz, 1989. *Doublespeak*. New York: HarperCollins Publishers, pp. 77–103.

VOCABULARY GLOSS

The definitions given will help you understand the readings. Words in the reading which have been marked (°) are defined below. Numbers in the parentheses to the right of the word refer to the paragraph in which the word appears. Not all words that you do not understand are glossed. Guess the meanings of those words in the reading selection which you do not understand.

to dominate (1) (v.)	to control
junk mail (1) (n.)	wasteful letters, usually advertisements
client (2) (n.)	person who pays for the services of another
to tout (4) (v.)	to praise a lot
brand (4) (n.)	make, name of group which makes product
cartel (5) (n.)	a group of business organizations which join together to eliminate competition from other organizations
mine (5) (n.)	a hole or pit dug in earth from which gems (such as diamonds) and minerals are taken
glut (5) (n.)	a large quantity; excessive in number
to stimulate (6) (v.)	to encourage the growth of
to popularize (7) (v.)	to make everyone like
commitment (8) (n.)	a promise to do something
margin of profit (8) (n.)	the difference between the amount of sale and the cost of producing something
claim (9) (n.)	something that is stated firmly
weasel (12) (n.)	a small, thin furry animal which is mostly brown and reddish in color, similar to a fox; considered tricky
aisle (17) (n.)	vertical row
to keep track of (17) (v.) (idiom)	to watch carefully
edition (20) (n.)	version

to dissolve (22) (v.)	to cause to disappear; to disintegrate; to divide into very small pieces
list price (25) (n.)	the price which is listed for sell
to inflate (25) (v.)	to increase the prices abnormally
to substantiate (28) (v.)	to establish by evidence
appeal (29) (n.)	attraction
Certs (30) (n.)	a type of breath mint

AFTER YOU READ

Consider this strategy:

LEARNING STRATEGY

Managing Your Learning: Rereading the material until you can understand it helps you develop language proficiency and form new concepts.

Reread the reading material. Several quick readings of the material will increase your comprehension of the main ideas more than one slow, careful reading.

Comprehension Workout

EXERCISE 52

Answer the following questions. If you have difficulty, refer to the number of the paragraphs (¶) given in parentheses.

1. How many commercial messages are you exposed to in the United States every twenty-four hours? (¶ 1)
2. Where do ads appear? (¶ 1)
3. According to Rosser Reeves, what is the basic problem of advertising? (¶ 2)
4. What does it mean "to make something out of nothing"? (¶ 2)
5. What percentage of the world's supply in diamonds does the De Beers company control? (¶ 5)
6. Why do diamonds cost so much? (¶ 6–8)
7. What is an "eternity ring"? (¶ 8)
8. How much profit does the De Beers cartel average? (¶ 8)
9. Why is this profit a good one? (¶ 8)
10. What is "puffing"? (¶ 9)
11. What is the first rule of advertising? (¶ 9)
12. What are "parity" products? (¶ 10)
13. What is the origin of the expression "weasel word"? (¶ 12)
14. What are three examples of "weasel words?" (¶ 13–23)
15. Why are "unfinished words" so common in advertising? (¶27)
16. Why do advertisers frequently depend on scientific terms to sell their products? (¶ 29–30)

Cooperative Learning

NUMBERED HEADS TOGETHER

Divide up into teams of four. Take Lutz's "Advertising Doublespeak Quick Quiz" on pages 238–239. Number off within groups (one, two, three, or four). Put your heads together to make sure that everyone in your group knows how each of the ads Lutz lists uses doublespeak to persuade readers to buy a specific product. Your team will have ten minutes to put your heads together to discuss the ads. At the end of this period, your instructor will call out a product from one of the ads. Then, your instructor will call out a number from one to four. Only students with that number can raise their hands.

Quick Write

WRITING AN EXTENDED DEFINITION

Write a one or two paragraph definition of the term *doublespeak*. In writing this definition, include several examples of the ways in which doublespeak is used to deceive others. Examples may come from the fields of science, government, business, and/or advertising.

Grammar Explanation

MODAL AUXILIARIES

Explanation: In the next writing activity, you will be asked to analyze a magazine advertisement. As Lutz points out in his essay, one way advertisements persuade readers to purchase products is through modal auxiliaries such as *can* and *must*. The following information is intended to help you understand the use of these modals. The modal auxiliaries are *can, could, had better, may, might, must, ought to, shall, should, will,* and *would*. Modal auxiliaries are special kinds of verbs which:

- generally express a writer's attitude and convey the strength of the attitude
- change the meaning of the verb that they precede
- have more than one meaning
- never have verb endings (*-s, -ing,* and *-ed*)
- are followed by a simple form of a verb (without an ending)

USING MODAL AUXILIARIES

1. Make a sentence with a modal auxiliary negative by adding *not* immediately after the modal.

   The advertisement <u>might</u> not influence anyone.

2. Make a modal auxiliary continuous with modal + *be* + verb + *-ing*.

   For a happier life, you <u>should</u> be drinking Kef's coffee.

3. Do not use *to* after a modal auxiliary.

   He <u>can</u> clean his house more quickly with Mean and Clean Cleanser.

   Exception: He <u>ought to</u> clean his house more quickly with Mean and Clean Cleanser.

4. In polite requests use the past tense verb form in "if clauses" following *would you mind*.

   Would you mind if I <u>edited</u> your paper?

5. *Cannot* is written as one word.

   You <u>cannot</u> eat just one Skipper's Potato Chip.

6. In American English, *shall* is normally reserved for very formal written English.

   He <u>shall</u> never write again.

DEGREES OF CERTAINTY: FUTURE

Modal auxiliaries are often used to express the extent of the writer's certainty.

100% certainty	Crest will reduce cavities.
90% certainty	Crest should reduce cavities. Crest ought to reduce cavities.
less than 50% certainty	Crest may reduce cavities. Crest might reduce cavities. Crest could reduce cavities.

THE MEANING OF MODALS

To review the meanings of modals, refer to the chart. Notice in the chart and in the example below that some modals (such as *may* and *might*) can express the same meaning. This pill *may* help you live longer = This pill *might* help you live longer. (possibility)

Chart of Modals and Related Idioms by Meaning

MEANING	PRESENT	FUTURE	PAST
Ability, physical	can be able to *This soap can clean.*	— be able to *This soap is able to clean.*	could could have + past part. be able to *This soap could clean.*
Ability, learned	can be able to know how to *He can cook.*	— be able to know how to *He knows how to cook.*	could be able to know how to *He was able to cook.*
Possibility, ability	can be able to *I can sing.*	can/could be able to *I could sing.*	could be able to *I was able to sing.*
Potential	—	can *John can receive good grades.*	could have + past part. (not realized) *John could have received good grades.*
Suggestion	—	can, could *Could you open the window?*	—
Permission	may be permitted to be allowed to *May I use this bathroom?*	may be permitted to be allowed to *Am I permitted to use this bathroom*	— be permitted to be allowed to *Was I allowed to use this bathroom?*
Necessity	must have to *Katy must buy this car.*	must have to *Katy will have to buy this car.*	— have to *Katy had to buy this car.*
Prohibition	must not *Jorgé must not sell that car now.*	must not *Jorgé must not sell that car next week.*	—
Lack of necessity	not have to *Today's consumers have to buy the products.*	not have to *Tomorrow's consumers will not have to buy the products.*	not have to *Yesterday's consumers did not have to buy the products.*
Advice	should ought to had better be supposed to *You should buy this product. today.*	should ought to had better be supposed to* *You should buy this product next week.*	should have + past part. ought to have + past part. — be supposed to + past part. *You should have bought this product last week.*

Chart of Modals and Related Idioms by Meaning (continued)

MEANING	PRESENT	FUTURE	PAST
Possibility (maybe)	may might *You may buy the milk here today.*	may might could *You may buy the milk here next week.*	may have + past part. might have + past part. could have + past part. *You may have bought the milk here last week.*
Preference	would rather *Jane would rather buy it now.*	would rather *Jane would rather buy it next week.*	would rather have + past part. *Jane would rather have bought it last week.*

*To use <u>be supposed to</u> in the future, use the verb <u>be</u> in the present tense: In the next three weeks, we <u>are supposed to</u> lose weight by taking Weight Loss Tabs.

Text Analysis: Modal Auxiliaries

EXERCISE 53

Read the following advertisements with a partner. Discuss the meanings of any modal auxiliaries used.

1. Winston. Winston tastes good like a cigarette should.
2. Crest. Using Crest can be of significant value.
3. Buick. This is one car you would sell to a friend.
4. Honda. A luxury car you can relate to.
5. Nikko Hotels International. A chain of hotels should reflect a city, not each other.
6. Chevy Trucks. The trucks you can depend on. The trucks that last.
7. Wrigley's Spearmint Chewing Gum. When you can't smoke, enjoy pure chewing satisfaction.
8. Express Mail. Express Mail will pick up unlimited packages for a single pick-up charge. With value like that, Express Mail could help any business have a banner year.
9. Bridgestone. Products and people you can count on.
10. Lever 2000. The deodorant soap that's better for your skin. It won't dry your skin like other deodorant soaps can.
11. Sony. Simply find the exact moment you want, and the Sony Color Video Printer will give you an amazing instant, instantly.

Look through magazines to find three more advertisement lines which use modal auxiliaries.

12. _____

_____

13. _____

_____

14. _____

_____

Grammar Practice: Modal Auxiliaries

EXERCISE 54

Fill in the blanks below with an appropriate modal auxiliary. There is no one "correct" answer.

If you travel by airline at all, you quickly become aware of the doublespeak used by airlines. Only airlines (1) _____ get away with calling four crackers and some artificial cheese spread or a package of twelve peanuts a "snack." Trans Florida Airlines provide s its passengers with a set of instructions to be followed "in case of a non-routine operation." Other airlines give you instruction s to follow in the event of a "water landing." The little paper sack is "for motion discomfort.". . .

The next really important doublespeak you learn (after the distinction between direct and nonstop flights) is that you do not fly in an airplane or a jet plane or even an airliner. Sometimes you (2) _____ fly in an aircraft, but far more often you fly in "equipment," as in, "The equipment has arrived and is now being serviced prior to our beginning the preboarding process." Or as in, "Ladies and gentlemen, because of a technical difficulty there (3) _____ be a change of equipment. (4) _____ you please deplane at this time." Of course, this last statement means the airplane is broken and won't fly so they have to get you off that plane and on to another—if there's some other "equipment" that works. If you want to know what kind of airplane you (5) _____ be flying on this trip, just as k the ticket agent, "What's the 'equipment' on this flight?" Without hesitation, you'll be told 727, L-1011, or something similar.

Before you ever make it to the equipment, however, you (6) _____ go through the "preboarding process," as in, "Ladies and gentlemen, in a few minutes we will begin the preboarding process." I live for the day when I (7) _____ see someone board the airplane before boarding it, and I want to see the process someone (8) _____ go through in order to preboard.

Airlines like to talk about "carry-on items," not baggage, as in "All carry-on items (9) _____ fit conveniently beneath the seat in front of you or in the overhead compartments." Airlines never speak of first class passengers, but always of "passengers in the first class section." And did you ever notice that, while there (10) _____ be a first class section, there's never a second class section? You probably ride in the "coach" section, as I do. American Airlines has even eliminated the first class section. On their planes it's the "main cabin." I wonder, where does that leave the rest of us?

Source: William Lutz. 1989. *Doublespeak.* New York: HarperPerennial, A Division of HarperCollins Publishers, pp. 23–24.

Quick Write

REPORTING SURVEY DATA

How do your classmates feel about ads? Do they justify their use? Do they believe that "doublespeak" is necessary in advertising, or do they think that it should be prohibited? Find out how your classmates feel by reviewing the survey data on page 212–214. You will write a brief report of the findings.

As a class, review the section of the survey entitled *The Language of Persuasion.* Analyze the results of this section by the first language backgrounds of the students in the class. Divide up into small groups. Try to identify two or three major trends in the data. Suggest several explanations for the trends. Write a one page report in which you identify two or three major trends in the survey data. Your report is for the general public. Your purpose is to inform.

Threads

In 1991, U.S. grocery stores sold $1,682 million of Marlboro cigarettes.

Information Resources, Inc.

Writing Task: Analyzing an Advertisement

In a four to six paragraph essay, analyze a magazine advertisement. Your purpose is to inform the general public of the subtle influences of advertising. In preparation for this task, it will be helpful for each student to bring five or six magazine advertisements to class.

BEFORE YOU WRITE

Consider some of the ways that advertising agencies highlight the best features of their products.

WEASEL WORDS WITH "AUDIENCE APPEAL"

When companies advertise, they highlight the best features of their products. If you study advertisements carefully, you will see that many of the same weasel words regularly appear in the various ads. These words have audience appeal. They help sell the product.

WORDS WITH AUDIENCE APPEAL

best	grand	perfect
better	greatest	professional
brand new	guaranteed	quality
choose	healthy	results
diet	hurry	safety
discovery	improved	satisfaction
easy	inexpensive	save
environmentally safe	introducing	simple
experience	love	special
free	money	successful
fresh	new	unique
gift	now	valuable

In small groups, discuss the advertisements below. Answer these questions:

1. How do the advertisements use "weasel words"?
2. What other ways do advertisers use to persuade readers to buy specific products?
3. What effect do the visual aspects of the advertisements have on the reader?

Share the magazine advertisements which you have brought to class with your group. With your group, identify five or six magazine advertisements which use "weasel words."

You are now ready to choose an advertisement which you would like to analyze. Each student should select one advertisement. Answer the prewriting questions on page 248 individually.

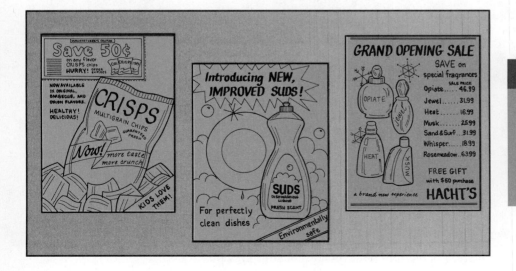

PREWRITING QUESTIONS

1. What is the name of the product or service advertised?
2. What are three positive features of it?
3. How would the customer benefit from the product?
4. What is the headline of the advertisement? How does it catch the reader's attention?
5. How does the advertisement use pictures and language to subtly influence the reader?

Consider this strategy:

LEARNING STRATEGY

Managing Your Learning: Writing in a comfortable place can improve your writing.

Find a comfortable place to write. When you are selecting a place, consider whether you prefer to work around others or by yourself, in a noisy or quiet location, or in a dimly lit or brightly lit room.

WRITE

You are ready to write. Try to get all your ideas on paper in a single sitting. Consider the following strategy:

LEARNING STRATEGY

Managing Your Learning: Asking your classmates and your instructor for help allows you to complete your first draft while simultaneously acquiring the language.

Ask others to help you express yourself. Use some of these expressions:

Excuse me. How do you say (*the word or expression in your native language*)?

What's another way of saying _____? Could you say this (*point to a part of the page*) in a better way?

AFTER YOU WRITE THE FIRST VERSION OF YOUR DRAFT

Read what you have written. Take ten minutes to cross out any parts of your essay that you do not like. Now, start over again. Write an entirely new version of the same essay. Write for forty minutes without stopping. Rewrite your essay. Use the best parts from both versions of your previous drafts.

Consider this strategy:

Forming Concepts: Focusing on one part of your writing at a time helps improve it and makes your writing more manageable.

Focus on the introduction and conclusion of your essay. Try to improve them. If you need to write a new introduction or conclusion, do so now.

REWRITE AGAIN

Make a clean draft of your paper that your classmates can read it.

MAKE YOUR FINAL REVISIONS

Consider this strategy:

Understanding and Using Emotions: Discussing your feelings about feedback with your instructor and classmates helps them understand how to provide you with constructive feedback.

Divide into small groups of three to four students. Discuss your feelings about feedback. Try to identify the types of feedback that you find most helpful. You may want to answer some of the following questions.

1. Do you like reviewers to provide you with a lot of feedback on each paragraph of your essay, or do you find this much feedback confusing?
2. Do you prefer reviewers to provide you with critical feedback, positive feedback, or a balance of both critical and positive feedback?
3. Do you prefer reviewers to provide you with written or oral feedback/ Why?
4. Do you mind it when reviewers discuss the negative aspects of your writing in front of you? What would you prefer?

Remain in the same groups. Read each student's essay aloud. Then, complete the Revision Checklist for each essay.

REVISION CHECKLIST

1. Does the essay contain a strong thesis statement?
2. Does the essay explain how the advertisement influences people to buy a specific product?
3. Does the essay stick together? Are their smooth transitions between the paragraphs?

4. Is the essay written in the correct tone? Is it too informal or too polite?
5. Is the introduction interesting?
6. Is the conclusion effective?
7. Which part of the essay do you like the most?
8. Which part of the essay needs to be improved?

Use the information you receive from your peers and instructor to revise your essay.

EDITING CHECKLIST

Use the Editing Checklist below to correct mechanical mistakes involving punctuation and grammar.

	YES	NO
1. Each sentence is complete.	____	____
2. Modal auxiliaries are used correctly.	____	____
3. Verb tenses are used correctly.	____	____
4. Definite articles are used correctly.	____	____
5. Nouns and verbs agree in number.	____	____

Gaining Writing Competence

REVIEW OF GUIDELINES FOR WRITING A BUSINESS LETTER

Explanation: In the writing task which follows, you write a formal business letter. The following guidelines will help you complete this task. (For more information about business letters, refer to pages 195–198.)

BLOCK STYLE—FORMAL BUSINESS LETTER

- Use the correct salutation. (In this case, the correct salutation would be *Dear Mr. Clarke*.)
- Use a colon (:) after the salutation.
- Single space.
- Do *not* indent paragraphs.
- Only skip lines between paragraphs
- Sign the letter.

Sample Letter

Your name
Your street
Your city, State, Zip

Name and Title of Addressee
Company Name
Street
City, State, Zip

Dear Mr./Ms. (Name of Person):

Paragraphs are not indented in the body. Do not skip lines.

Sincerely,

Your Name

Quick Write

WRITING A BUSINESS LETTER

Write a letter to a company about a product. Think of a product or service with which you are extremely satisfied or extremely disappointed. Write a letter to the company that made the product or provided the service and offer either praise or suggestions on how to improve it. If you have the address of the company, mail your letter.

Using a Language Learning Log

1. Vocabulary:

   Write down as many new words from the lesson as you can remember.

   _____

   _____

   _____

   _____

2. Grammar:

   Note examples of any grammatical structures from the lesson learned or reviewed. Write a brief explanation of the grammar points that they illustrate.

   _____

   _____

   _____

   _____

3. Punctuation:

Write down any new punctuation rules that you learned.

_____

_____

_____

_____

4. Techniques for Gaining Writing Competence:

List any new composition techniques that you learned. (Such techniques might include those for writing interesting introductions, bodies, and conclusions, or for composing different types of writing effectively.)

_____

_____

_____

_____

5. Learning Strategies:

Briefly describe any new learning strategies that you have applied in your writing.

_____

_____

_____

_____

6. Areas that Need More Work:

Note here in brief form any areas that you are still trying to improve. Try to be as specific as possible.

_____

_____

_____

_____

In this lesson, you examined *doublespeak,* the language of deception. You wrote an extended definition of this term, an analysis of an advertisement, and a business letter. In the next lesson, you will learn about the particular type of power which you can gain through the written word.

QUICK REFERENCE TO LEARNING STRATEGIES

Forming Concepts: Reading Without Looking Up All the Words (p. 233)

Managing Your Learning: Rereading the Reading Material (p. 240)

Managing Your Learning: Choosing a Comfortable Place to Write (p. 248)

Managing Your Learning: Asking Others for Help (p. 248)

Forming Concepts: Focusing on One Part at a Time (p. 249)

Understanding and Using Emotions: Discussing Your Feelings about Feedback (p. 249)

Overview

In the last two lessons, you examined how written language is acquired and how it is used to deceive others. In this lesson, you will focus on the use of language to empower. You will write a persuasive essay as well as a report of survey data.

About the Reading

This reading selection was written by a student at the University of California.

BEFORE YOU READ

Exploring your own knowledge of the topic helps you anticipate the content of a reading. To help you predict what the reading is about, answer the following questions with a partner. Try to find a partner who does not come from your same cultural background.

1. How do you use writing? Have you ever used writing to improve your personal, economical, or social status? In what ways?
2. Does writing determine academic success in the institute in which you are currently studying? Why? Does it determine academic success in institutes in other cultures? Why?
3. What are two ways in which writing can be used to improve one's own economic status?
4. What are three ways in which writing can be used to change society?
5. In the United States, writing is valued at least as much as speaking. However, in some cultures, speech is more valued than writing. How is writing valued in two different cultures?

Discuss your answers with the entire class. Consider this strategy:

LEARNING STRATEGY

Forming Concepts: Guessing the meanings of words that you don't know from the context in which they occur helps you read more fluently.

WHILE YOU READ

As you read, do not stop to look up every word you do not know in a dictionary. Instead, guess the meanings of the words that you do not know from the context in which they occur.

POWER THROUGH THE WRITTEN WORD

Stella Browning

1   What does it mean to gain power through the written word? Peter Elbow, a well-known writing expert, convincingly argues:[1] Writing with power means getting power over words and readers; writing clearly and correctly; writing what is true or real or interesting; and writing persuasively or making some kind of contact with your readers so that they actually experience your meaning or vision. . .But writing with power also means getting power over yourself and over the writing process; knowing what you are doing as you write; being in charge; having control; not feeling stuck or helpless or intimidated.

2   Dramatic changes can be realized° when individuals learn to write. Writing enables individuals to make significant changes in their lives. Such changes result when individuals use writing to fight against injustice. Changes also result when individuals use writing to redefine their roles within their daily lives, in the classroom, and in the community.

3   Writing provides a nonviolent means of fighting against injustice. Injustice occurs when individuals lose their freedom to worship the way that they like, to publish their writing, to run their own businesses, to receive fair pay for their work, or to participate in political meetings. Injustice occurs when the quality of education received by men and women differs, or when European-Americans are allowed to vote, but African-Americans are not.

4   Through writing, individuals are able to advertise the abuses of those in power, and they are able to inform those being abused of the abuses from which they suffer. This often means threatening the power of the dominant° group. For example, Brazilians who learned to read and then vote sometimes voted against their national leaders. African-Americans in the United States who learned to read and write, became educated lawyers who sought reforms in their communities. Thus, writing allows people to resist unfair political practices by soliciting° public opinion, initiating new laws, and monitoring the enactment of legal practices.

5   Another way in which writing helps people to fight against injustice is by enabling them to adopt a critical stance° in relation to the society in which they participate so that they do not become victimized° by it. For instance, through writing, individuals can analyze the pros and cons of nuclear warfare before they themselves experience it.

6   Not only can writing help individuals fight against injustice, it can also help individuals redefine their roles. In the classroom, writing explains why some students are defined as intellectuals while others are defined as dummies. Those students who are empowered through their writing feel a sense of control over their own lives and have the ability, confidence, and motivation to advance themselves academically. They are able to carry out successfully any academic task to which they are committed.° Writing, for these students, is not simply an exercise; it leads to learning and results in power.

7   Those students who are disempowered° through their writing are unable to affect positive changes in their own lives through the written word. Because of their weak writing skills, these students often fail academically. They have nothing important to say and no means to say it. No writing course can help

them overcome these obstacles.° Writing, for these students, is sheer drudgery which leads to failure and results in impotence.

8 Writing also allows individuals to redefine their roles in their own communities. Through writing, individuals are able to redefine their roles so that they do not reflect the existing societal power structure. Power and status relations can be negotiated° through writing. For instance, people can write persuasive letters to request new jobs, petitions to free prisoners and letters of complaint to change educational practices. There is no question that written language enables individuals to negotiate objectively° so that they can resist those who use their authority in unethical ways.

9 Significant changes can be realized when individuals learn to write. Personal changes result when individuals use writing to attain a sense of control over their own lives and the lives of others. Social changes result when individuals use writing to persuade decision makers of the importance of challenging institutional goals. Through the written word, personal and societal objectives are achieved, and individuals enable° themselves and others; in short, individuals attain power—through the written word.

[1]Peter Elbow. 1981. *Writing with Power: Techniques for mastering the writing process.* New York: Oxford Press. (In "Note to Reader.")

VOCABULARY GLOSS

The definitions given below will help you understand the essay. Numbers in the parentheses to the right of the word refer to the paragraph in which the word appears. Not all words that you do not understand are glossed. Either skip over the words that you do not understand, or guess the meanings from the context in which they occur.

to realize (2) (v.)	to make
dominant (4) (adj.)	characteristic of those with power
to solicit (4) (v.)	to approach with a request
stance (5) (n.)	position or view
to victimize (5) (v.)	to make a victim of
committed (6) (adj.)	characterized by doing something deliberately and with much motivation
disempowered (7) (adj.)	characterized by having lost all power
obstacle (7) (n.)	problem
to negotiate (8) (v.)	to bring about through discussion and compromise
objectively (8) (adv.)	involving the use of facts without personal feelings

Comprehension Workout

EXERCISE 55

Write a one paragraph reaction to the above reading selection. Explain what "writing with power" means to you. Your purpose is to explore your own ideas. You are writing this paragraph for yourself.

Grammar Explanation

PARALLEL STRUCTURE

Explanation: In the next writing task, you will be asked to write a description.

USING WORDS AND PHRASES
WHICH ARE PARALLEL IN FORM

Using words and phrases that are parallel in form can make your writing more sophisticated. Words in a pair or a series match in form.

WORDS IN PAIRS

	noun		*noun*
Writing empowers	women	and	men.

	noun		*noun*
Susana wants to be	a lawyer	or	a dentist.

	verb		*verb*
I want	to win,	but	not to lose.

SETS OF WORDS

	verb		*verb*
Hank	neither revises	nor	edits his essays.

	noun		*noun*
Neither	rain	nor	sleet could keep him from writing.

	adjective		*adjective*
Juan is	both friendly	and	smart.

	complete clause (containing subject and verb)		*complete clause (containing subject and verb)*
Not only	did she win the debate,	but she	also won the election.
Not only	does he like to read,	but he	also likes to write.

Grammar Practice: Parallel Structure

EXERCISE 56

Fill in the blanks with words that match in form.

1. Written language can be used to gain money, and to

_____

2. Dawn was ready to sever her relationship with her old lover and to

_____

3. Neither John nor _____ could write convincingly.

4. The boys could neither speak nor _____ well.

5. The politician promised not only to lower taxes, but also to

_____

6. The student not only failed to use commas appropriately, but also to

_____

7. Most people want the environment to be both healthy and

_____

8. Not only does Hyun Lee like revising, but she also likes

_____

Use *words in pairs* and *sets of words* to make two original sentences of your own.

9. _____

10. _____

Writing Task: Writing a Description

Write a three or four paragraph essay which describes the ways in which writing has helped you overcome an obstacle or obstacles.

You are writing for your classmates. Your purpose is to convince your readers of the importance of writing.

BEFORE YOU WRITE

Write a list of several obstacles which you overcame through the use of the written word. If you are having difficulty, consider the list below.

POSSIBLE OBSTACLES

- attaining a good grade in a course
- acquiring English more effectively
- breaking up a relationship with a friend
- consoling a friend about the death of a loved one
- completing an important job application
- understanding a difficult subject
- winning an important race or contest
- communicating effectively with an authority figure (such as a teacher, employer, or parent)

- dealing successfully with a disagreeable neighbor, family member, boss, or acquaintance
- returning a specific piece of merchandise
- obtaining important information (pertaining to travel, housing, jobs, or college)
- gaining entrance into an institute of higher education
- exploring your ideas about an important decision that you had to make

Find a partner. Discuss the obstacles which you have overcome through writing and explain how you overcame these obstacles. Describe the effect that these obstacles might have had on your life had you not overcome them. Consider this strategy:

LEARNING STRATEGY

Forming Concepts: When you ask your classmates about their writing topic, it helps them clarify their ideas.

Write two or three questions that you have about your partner's writing topic. Exchange questions with your partner and take turns answering these questions. Consider this strategy:

LEARNING STRATEGY

Managing Your Learning: Organizing your ideas before you write by using an outline helps you write more efficiently.

WRITE AN OUTLINE OF YOUR FIRST DRAFT

Before writing your outline, consider the information given below.

GUIDELINES FOR WRITING AN OUTLINE

Outlines can be used to guide your writing and to make sure that you have addressed the topic of your essay and no other topic.

1. Put your thesis at the top of the page.
2. Divide your paper into major categories. Label these categories I, II, III, etc.
3. Include subcategories under the major categories. Label these categories A, B, C, etc.
4. Provide supporting details under categories A, B, and C. Label these categories 1, 2, 3, etc.
5. Make sure that you express all ideas in parallel structures. For instance, you may want to have a complete sentence outline or a phrase outline. Don't use both.

6. Never have fewer than two categories or subcategories.

Outline your essay in the table below. If you need additional categories, add them. If you do not need categories, do not use them.

Thesis Statement:

_____

_____

I. Introduction

   A. _____

   B. _____

   C. _____

II. _____

   A. _____

   B. _____

   C. _____

III. _____

   A. _____

   B. _____

   C. _____

IV. _____

   A. _____

   B. _____

   C. _____

WRITE YOUR ESSAY

Try to write your essay in a single sitting. Do not worry about grammar, punctuation, or spelling. Just try to get all your ideas down on paper. It will be easier for you to revise your paper and edit it after you have written down all your ideas.

WHILE YOU ARE WRITING

Keep your outline close at hand. To prevent yourself from digressing, glance at your outline from time to time. To strengthen your writing, change parts of your outline or abandon parts of your outline as needed.

REVISE YOUR ESSAY

Use the Revision Checklist to revise your essay.

Threads

The bravest sight in the world is to see a great man struggling against adversity.

Seneca
c.5–65

REVISION CHECKLIST

1. Have you considered your reader's perspective? Try to anticipate the expectations of the reader to whom you are writing.
2. Are the obstacles which you discussed ones that others believe are important?
3. Have you provided enough examples and illustrations of the specific ways writing helped you?
4. Have you described what might have happened if you had not been able to write?
5. Have you convinced the reader of the importance of writing?

EDIT YOUR ESSAY

Use the Editing Checklist below when you correct the mechanical (grammatical and punctuation) errors in your writing.

Have you checked (✓) your essay for these aspects?

Subject/verb agreement   _____
Modal auxiliaries   _____
Verb choice (tense)   _____
Other (your choice)   _____

Grammar Explanation

INSERTING EXPRESSIONS OF OPINION TO MAKE YOUR WRITING LOOK SOPHISTICATED

Explanation: In the next writing task, you will write a persuasive essay. You can increase the complexity of your sentences by using expressions of opinion.

SOME USEFUL EXPRESSIONS OF OPINION

1. Those which generally come at the beginning of sentences:
   I agree with/disagree with. . .
   I strongly believe that. . .
   I support/reject the idea that. . .
   I am certain that. . .
   I am convinced that. . .
2. Those which can begin a sentence or which can be inserted in the sentence:

undoubtedly	in my opinion
unfortunately	in my perspective
fortunately	I think
luckily	in my view
indeed	in fact
clearly	certainly

Notice that commas are used to set off expressions of opinion when they are inserted in sentences.

EXAMPLE: I can, <u>I think</u>, write a persuasive essay.
                    ▲   ▲

PLACEMENT OF INSERTED EXPRESSIONS OF OPINION

1. At the beginning of the sentence:

    EXAMPLE: <u>In my perspective</u>, the purchase of guns should be illegal.

2. Between the modal auxiliary and the main verb:

    EXAMPLE: <u>modal</u>   <u>insert</u>

                I might,   <u>I think,</u>   be able to write this entire
                                                            essay in a single sitting.

Note: It is redundant to use two expressions of opinion which mean the same next to each other. <u>I think</u>, <u>in my perspective</u>, that war is bad. (This sentence is repetitive, since *I think* means the same as *in my perspective*.)

Gaining Writing Practice: Using Expressions of Opinion

EXERCISE 57

Use the expressions of opinion listed above to make sentences with the words below. Follow the example given.

EXAMPLE: smog—health
            I strongly believe that smog is bad for people's health.

1. alcoholic beverages—children

    _____

2. guns—necessity of making new laws

    _____

3. personal power—health, wealth, and knowledge

    _____

4. crimes—reduction

    _____

5. air pollution—reduction

    _____

6. women—equality

    _____

7. smoking—lung disease

_____

8. nuclear arms—reduction

_____

Grammar Practice: Expressions of Opinion

EXERCISE 58

Although expressions of opinion may not be grammatically necessary, they make your writing seem more sophisticated. In the following reading selection, written by Paul Lu, an UCI undergraduate student, the expressions of opinion have been underlined. Try taking each of the inserts out. What is lost if you do? What information do the inserts add? Discuss these questions with a partner.

DIFFERENCES BETWEEN SPOKEN AND WRITTEN ENGLISH

Paul Lu, Undergraduate Student, U.C.I.

1   Spoken English differs from written English in many ways. When you speak, you often use specific vocabulary words and grammatical structures. For example, you use such slang as "guy," "kid," and "ya know." Slang is, <u>in my view</u>, a useful means of making your language colorful and displaying friendliness. It gives a person's speech a casual appearance. That is why slang is not used in academic writing.

2   When you speak, but not write, hedges such as "a couple of," "kind of," "sort of," and "a little" are very useful. <u>In my perspective</u>, hedges make you less culpable for what you are saying. If your neighbors accuse you of borrowing their car too long, you can tell them, "Look. I told you that I'd just borrow your car for "a little while." "A little while" means about six hours to me. It must mean fewer hours to you." You would avoid using such hedges as "a little while" in written English, since they make your language seem imprecise.

3   Similarly, in spoken English you might use vague, general words such as "nice," "good," and "thing." In written English, you would not use these words. You would, <u>most likely</u>, replace these words with others such as "compassionate," "beneficial," and "item" which paint more vivid, accurate pictures for your readers.

4   Even your grammar would be different in written and spoken English. For instance, complex clauses are less characteristic of spoken English than written. In spoken English, sentences are frequently joined together with the word "and," as in, "<u>I think</u> we should stop fighting, <u>and</u> we should put down our guns, <u>and</u> we should live in peace." In contrast, written English contains a wide variety of sentence structures. You might, for instance, write, "Fighting is, <u>in my opinion</u>, never justified; we should therefore, put down our guns so that we can live in peace. Fighting is evil." Notice, in this example, that the writer uses both complex and simple sentence structures.

5   Yet another way in which spoken grammar differs from written grammar concerns subjects. In spoken English, you sometimes repeat subjects. Consider, for instance, the sentence: "The book, it is on the table." In this sentence, two subjects, *the book* and *it,* are placed next to each other. Although the repetition of subjects is very common in spoken English as well as in such languages as Japanese and Chinese, it is not permissible to repeat subjects in this way in written English.

6   Another grammatical difference between spoken and written English concerns the use of pronouns. In spoken English, you can use pronouns almost anywhere you like, as long as your addressee understands what the pronouns refer to. Hence, you can say, "John was the murderer. The murder happened last night. He murdered her with a knife." You would, <u>of course</u>, need to replace the pronouns, "he" and "her," in the last sentence with full noun forms (such as "John" and "his victim") in written English. Thus, you would have to state, "John was the murderer. The murder happened last night. John murdered his victim with a knife." This is because in written English, pronouns must always refer to specific nouns which occur in the previous sentence.

7   <u>Clearly</u>, the language you use to talk to a friend differs from the language you use to write to your professor. <u>In my perspective</u>, that is why written, though not spoken, English is so frequently taught in college classrooms.

Gaining Writing Competence

AVOIDING SPOKEN ENGLISH IN FORMAL WRITING

Unless you want to make your written English very informal, you should avoid using slang when you write.

INSTEAD OF:	USE:
guy	man, boy, adolescent
kid	child
kind of	somewhat, rather
sort of	somewhat, rather
a lot, lots of	a great deal, many
awesome	excellent

Gaining Writing Competence

AVOIDING COMMON FALLACIES

To write persuasively, you need to avoid making these common fallacies:

1. *Sweeping generalizations:* Sweeping generalizations are made when writers apply an assertion to an entire population. These mostly begin with words like *all* or *everyone*. Instead, use *most* or *some*.

   EXAMPLES: *Everyone* in this class is outstanding.
   No one will fail the class.
   All people are greedy.

2. *Quick judgments:* Quick judgments are made when writers jump to conclusions about an entire group based on very limited experience. For instance, an instructor who classifies a student as a bad writer on the basis of one essay is guilty of making a quick judgment.

3. *Rationalizing:* Rationalizing occurs when writers ignore facts or try to explain them by making excuses.

   EXAMPLES: Cutting down rain forests benefits the earth since it helps improve the global economy. (Just because cutting down rain forests improves the global economy does not mean that cutting down rain forests benefits the earth.)

4. *Non sequiturs* (Latin for "that which does not follow"): Nonsequiturs occur when writers jump from one topic to another without explaining their transition, or when writers arrive at a conclusion without explaining why. (Almost always the reaction to a nonsequitur is "Excuse me. I'm not following your reasoning.")

   EXAMPLES: John never learned to write persuasively. Therefore, he failed his speaking exam. (How is writing persuasively related to speaking well?)

5. *Oversimplifying:* Oversimplifying occurs when writers do not explain their position clearly with sufficient detail.

   EXAMPLES: Punishing children is wrong because it leads to child abuse. (It may be true that some parents punish their children too severely, but this does not necessarily mean that all punishment is bad.)

6. *Appeals to illegitimate authority:* Appeals to illegitimate authority occur when writers do not cite an appropriate source.

   EXAMPLES: Dr. Mary Jones, a well-known physician, supports the mayor. (Dr. Mary Jones's opinion of the mayor is irrelevant since her medical background does not qualify her to judge the mayor any better than other common citizen.)

7. *Appeal to people's fears:* When writers appeal to people's fears, they try to evoke strong emotions supporting their position.

   EXAMPLES: If you don't use Bright and Shiny Toothpaste, your teeth will decay, and you'll need to spend many hours in a dentist's chair.

8. *Begging the question:* When writers beg the question, they state an unproved assumption as though it were fact.

   EXAMPLES: Most people in the United States want to live in California.

9. *Circular argument:* When a circular argument is used, writers restate the initial assumption instead of supporting it with evidence.

   EXAMPLES: John Brown was a murderer because he killed.

   Jill was insensitive because she was unkind.

10. *Name calling:* When writers use name calling, they use insults to try to defeat an opponent. They define and label the opponent inaccurately (for example, they should use such terms as radical extremist; irresponsible tax spender; warmonger, etc.).

WRITING PERSUASIVELY

One of the reasons for writing is to argue in support of a theory, an opinion, a belief, or a solution to a problem. Writing with this purpose is called *persuasive writing*. Persuasive writing focuses on a position about which you can argue. It must have two sides, one for and one against something. In the previous lessons, you learned that a thesis statement expresses the main idea of an essay. In a persuasive essay, the main idea is considered a proposition of a position. The position is the idea which you want your readers to agree with. It should be clearly stated and supported by verifiable evidence (facts, examples, statistics, and details). When you write a persuasive essay, remember to show your position in its broad context rather than in isolation, to use logical evidence to support your position, and to avoid the propaganda techniques discussed in the previous lesson.

INTRODUCTION

The introduction should identify the issue and include a thesis that states the position the essay defends. Sometimes the introduction also briefly discusses the counterarguments.

BODY: PRESENTATION OF ARGUMENTS AND COUNTERARGUMENTS

The body of the essay presents the arguments (and counterarguments) logically, using verifiable evidence. Here are some ways to present arguments and counterarguments:

1. Present anticipated counterarguments to your views; address each in turn.
   a. Counterargument 1

Refutation of Counterargument 1
   b. Counterargument 2
   Refutation of Counterargument 2
   c. Counterargument 3
   Refutation of Counterargument 3
2. Present your own arguments with their counterarguments.
   a. Argument 1
   Counterargument 1
   b. Argument 2
   Counterargument 2
   c. Argument 3
   Counterargument 3
3. List all your own arguments first, then list the counterarguments.
   a. Arguments
      1. Argument 1
      2. Argument 2
      3. Argument 3
   b. Counterarguments
      1. Counterargument 1
      2. Counterargument 2
      3. Counterargument 3
4. List all counterarguments first, then all your own arguments.
   a. Counterarguments
      1. Counterargument 1
      2. Counterargument 2
      3. Counterargument 3
   b. Arguments
      1. Argument 1
      2. Argument 2
      3. Argument 3

CONCLUSION

The conclusion reexamines the position that you have taken, and asserts its correctness. It may end with a restatement, a warning, a prediction, or a value judgment. What follows are sample concluding statements for the essay topic, "Smoking is bad for your health."

Restatement:	In conclusion, smoking is wrong. It endangers your own life as well as the lives of others. In addition, it encourages the growth of the tobacco industry, an industry this country does not need.
Warning:	Do not smoke if you want to live a long, healthy life.
Prediction:	People who smoke may end their lives early.
Value Judgment:	When people light up their cigarettes, they are harming others.
Prediction:	People who . . .

AVOID EMOTIONALLY CHARGED LANGUAGE

While it is possible to write a convincing position with emotionally charged language, such language often makes the reader believe that the writer has not presented the information objectively and impartially. Read the following statements and identify the emotionally charged words and phrases.

1. The crazed politician led the violent demonstration.
2. The needless destruction of our forests has resulted in the terrifying devastation of our environment.
3. The sweet, innocent child, who was punished needlessly by his ill-mannered, boisterous father, wept pitifully.
4. As the villagers gazed in horror, the crazed soldiers followed their rabid leaders throught the war-torn village.
5. The disruptive crowd, refusing to uphold the law, incited further violence.
6. The mothers' children were torn from their arms, while the angry, hate-filled warmongers attacked the villagers.

Listening

PERSUASIVE ESSAYS: IS CAPITAL PUNISHMENT NECESSARY?

The audiotaped essays which correspond to this chapter concern capital punishment. Listen to the audiotape. Then, respond to the essays in your journal.

BEFORE YOU LISTEN

Write one paragraph in which you explain your own views of capital punishment. Take a stand. How do you feel about capital punishment? Do you believe that capital punishment prevents crime? Do you believe that capital punishment is immoral?

AFTER YOU LISTEN

Write a one page response to the essays in which you discuss whether your perspective of capital punishment has changed. Then fill in the blanks below.

Techniques which the writers used to persuade you to accept their views.

1. _____
2. _____
3. _____

Emotionally charged language used to persuade the reader to accept specific views:

_____

_____

Brief Description of the Organization of the Essay

Essay 1.

_____

_____

Essay 2.

_____

_____

Divide the class into two groups: those that support capital punishment and those that do not support it. Hold a debate in which four representatives of each side discuss the advantages and disadvantages of capital punishment. The debate should last twenty minutes. After the debate, analyze and evaluate the success of the points presented and the reasons for their success.

Additional Reading

ABOUT THE READING

Martin Luther King, Jr. (1929–1968), clergyman and civil rights leader, achieved national fame in 1955–1956 when he led the boycott against segregated bus lines in Montgomery, Alabama. In 1964, he was awarded the Nobel Peace Prize for his policy of passive resistance to racism.

NONVIOLENT RESISTANCE

Martin Luther King, Jr.

1   Oppressed° people deal with their oppression in three characteristic ways. One way is acquiescence:° the oppressed resign themselves to their problems. They tacitly adjust themselves to oppression, and thereby become conditioned to it. In every movement toward freedom, some of the oppressed prefer to remain oppressed. Almost 2800 years ago Moses set out to lead the children of Israel from the slavery of Egypt to the freedom of the promised land. He soon discovered that slaves do not always welcome their deliverers. They become accustomed to being slaves. They would rather bear those ills they have than flee to others that they know not of.

2   Some people are so worn down by the oppression that they give up. A few years ago in the slum areas of Atlanta, a Negro guitarist used to sing almost daily: "Been down so long that down don't bother me." This is the type of resignation° that often destroys the lives of the oppressed.

3   But this is not the way to overcome oppression. To accept passively° an unjust system is to cooperate with that system. The oppressed who accept injustice become as evil as the oppressor. Noncooperation with evil is a moral obligation. The oppressed must never allow the conscience° of the oppressor to sleep. Religion reminds every man that he is his brother's keeper. To accept injustice or segregation passively is to say to the oppressor that his actions are morally right. It is a way of allowing his conscience to fall asleep. At this moment the oppressed fails to be his brother's keeper. So acquiescence—while often the easier way— is not the moral way. It is the way of the coward. The Negro cannot

win the respect of his oppressor by acquiescing; he merely increases the oppressor's arrogance. Acquiescence is interpreted as proof of the Negro's inferiority. The Negro cannot win the respect of the white people of the South or the peoples of the world if he is willing to sell the future of his children for his personal and immediate comfort and safety.

4   A second way that oppressed people sometimes deal with oppression is to use physical violence. Violence often brings about momentary° results. Nations have frequently won their independence in battle. But in spite of temporary victories, violence never brings permanent peace. It solves no social problem; it merely creates new and more complicated problems.

5   Violence as a way of achieving racial justice is both impractical and immoral. It is impractical because it is a descending° spiral ending in destruction for all. The old law of an eye for an eye leaves everybody blind. It is immoral because it seeks to humiliate the opponent rather than win his understanding. Violence is immoral because it thrives on hatred rather than love. It destroys community and makes brotherhood impossible. It leaves society in monologue rather than in dialogue.

6   If the American Negro and other victims of oppression use violence in their struggle for freedom, future generations will be the recipients of a night of bitterness, and our chief present to these generations will be meaningless chaos.° Violence is not the way.

7   The third way open to oppressed people in their quest for freedom is the way of nonviolent resistance.° The principle of nonviolent resistance seeks to reconcile° the truths of two opposites—acquiescence and violence—while avoiding the extremes and immoralities of both. The nonviolent resister agrees with the person who acquiesces that one should not be physically aggressive toward his opponent; but he balances the equation by agreeing with the person of violence that evil must be resisted. He avoids the nonresistance of the former and the violent resistance of the latter. With nonviolent resistance, no individual or group need accept any wrongdoing, nor need anyone resort to violence in order to right a wrong.

8   It seems to me that nonviolent resistance is the method that must guide the actions of the Negro in the present crisis in race relations. Through nonviolent resistance the Negro will be able to rise to oppose the unjust system while loving those who support the system. The Negro must work passionately for his rights as a citizen, but he most not use inferior methods to gain these rights. He must never come to terms with falsehood, hate, or destruction.

9   Nonviolent resistance makes it possible for the Negro to remain in the South and struggle for his rights. The Negro's problem will not be solved by running away. He cannot listen to the suggestion of those who would urge him to leave the South and go to other sections of the country. By grasping his great opportunity in the South he can make a lasting contribution to the moral strength of the nation and set an example of courage for generations yet unborn.

10   By nonviolent resistance, the Negro can also enlist all men of good will in his struggle for equality. The problem is not a purely racial one, with Negroes set against whites. In the end, it is not a struggle between people at all, but a tension between justice and injustice. Nonviolent resistance is not aimed against oppressors but against oppression.

11   If the Negro is to achieve the goal of integration,° he must organize himself into a militant and nonviolent mass movement. The movement for equality and justice can only be a success if it has both a mass and militant character; the barriers to be overcome require both. Nonviolence is an imperative in order to bring about community.

12   A mass movement of militant quality that is not at the same time committed to nonviolence tends to create conflict, which in turn results in anarchy.° The support of the participants and the sympathy of the uncommitted are both

inhibited by the threat that bloodshed. This reaction in turn encourages the opposition to threaten and use force. When, however, the mass movement rejects violence while moving resolutely toward its goal, its opponents are revealed as the instigators° and practitioners of violence if it occurs. Then, public support is magnetically attracted to the advocates of nonviolence, while those who use violence are disarmed by overwhelming public sentiment against their stand.

13   Only through a nonviolent approach can the fears of the white community be lessened. A guilt-ridden white minority lives in fear that if the Negro should ever attain power, he would act without pity to get even for the injustices and brutality of the years. It is something like a parent who continually mistreats a son. One day that parent raises his hand to strike the son, only to discover that the son is now as tall as he is. The parent is suddenly afraid—fearful that the son will use his new physical power to repay his parent for all the blows of the past.

14   The Negro, once a helpless child, has now grown up politically, culturally, and economically. Many white men fear that the Negro will try to get even with them for the mistreatment which he has received from the white men. The job of the Negro is to show these white men that they have nothing to fear, that the Negro understands and forgives and is ready to forget the past. He must convince the white man that all he seeks is justice, for both himself and the white man. A mass movement exercising nonviolence is a lesson in power, a demonstration to the white community that if such a movement attained a degree of strength, it would use its power creatively and not vengefully.

15   Nonviolence can help the law. When the law regulates behavior it indirectly affects public sentiment. The enforcement of the law is itself a form of peaceful persuasion. But the law needs help. The courts can order desegregation of the public schools. But what can be done to lessen the fears, to end the hatred and the violence gathered around school integration, to take the initiative out of the hands of racial demagogues°? In the end, for laws to be obeyed, men must believe they are right.

16   Here nonviolence comes in as the ultimate form of persuasion. It is the method which seeks to carry out fair laws by appealing to the consciences of the great decent° majority who through blindness, fear, pride, or irrationality have allowed their consciences to sleep.

17   The nonviolent resisters° can summarize their message in the following simple terms: We will take direct action against injustice without waiting for other agencies to act. We will not obey unjust laws or submit to unjust practices. We will do this peacefully, openly, cheerfully because our aim is to persuade. We adopt the means of nonviolence because our end is a community at peace with itself. We will try to persuade with our words, but if our words fail, we will try to persuade with our acts. We will always be willing to talk and seek fair compromise, but we are willing to suffer when necessary and even risk our lives to become witnesses to the truth as we see it.

18   The way of nonviolence means a willingness to suffer and sacrifice. It may mean going to jail. If such is the case, the resister must be willing to fill the jail houses of the South. Nonviolence may even mean death. But if death is what a man must pay to free his children and his white brothers from the permanence of spiritual death, then nonviolent resistance is imperative.

VOCABULARY GLOSS

The definitions given below will help you understand the essay. Numbers in the parentheses to the right of the word refer to the paragraph in which the word appears. Not all words that you do not understand are glossed. Either skip over the words that you do not understand, or guess the meanings from the context in which they occur.

oppressed (1) (adj.)	the state of being held back by an authority
acquiescence (2) (n.)	acceptance of something (usually negative)
resignation (2) (n.)	the act of accepting something passively without rebelling
passively (3) (adv.)	not actively
conscience (3) (n.)	the idea of moral goodness
momentary (4) (adj.)	continuing only a moment, very brief
descending (5) (adj.)	downward
chaos (6) (n.)	a state of confusion
resistance (7) (n.)	the act of trying to stop or prevent something
to reconcile (7) (v.)	to restore to friendship
integration (11) (n.)	the treatment of different groups as equals
anarchy (12) (n.)	lack of government
instigator (12) (n.)	person who starts something
demagogue (15) (n.)	leader who lied in order to gain power
decent (16) (adj.)	good
resister (17) (n.)	person who fights against something

COMPREHENSION CHECK

What is nonviolent resistance? In answering this question, refer to King's use of the term as well as examples of nonviolent resistance from your own experience.

Writing Task: Writing a Persuasive Essay

Write a persuasive essay of approximately 250 words in which you support a specific position. You will define your own audience for this essay and your own purpose. Divide into groups of about four or five students. Discuss one of the positions below. Discuss reasons that support your side of the position.

Women should fight in the armed forces to protect their country.

Personal power leads to greed.

Rain forests should not be destroyed.

Pollution should be reduced.

Children should not be allowed to play with toy guns.

Violent TV shows should be eliminated.

Environmental concerns are less important than economic ones.

After your group has discussed one of the positions above, each member of the group should complete this form:

Position: In my perspective,

_____

There are several reasons for this:

1. _____

2. _____

3. _____

These reasons support my view that

_____

LEARNING STRATEGY

Understanding and Using Emotions: When you believe in your position, it helps you write with more conviction and interest.

Decide on the topic that you would like to write about. Choose a topic that you believe in and care about. In deciding on a topic, consider these questions:

GUIDELINES FOR CHOOSING A TOPIC

1. Do I care about my topic?
2. Is my topic an important one? Are others interested in my topic?
3. Is research on my topic available?
4. Is my topic too broad or too narrow to research effectively?

Take a strong stand on your topic. Consider these guidelines:

QUESTIONS

1. Do I really believe in my position?
2. Is there more than one side to my position?
3. Can I find evidence which supports my position?
4. Do I know who takes opposing views?

Describe the readers of your persuasive essay. Complete the following questions.

AUDIENCE CONSIDERATIONS

1. Who am I writing my essay for?
2. What are the characteristics of my readers?

3. Will my readers agree or disagree with my position? What arguments will they have which support their views of my topic?
4. How much background information do I need to provide my readers?

Role playing helps you to understand how other people see your position. Find a partner. Ask your partner to play the role of adversaries of your position. Then, consider this strategy:

LEARNING STRATEGY

Managing Your Learning: Using resources to support your position makes your writing more convincing.

Make sure that you obtain information from the library which provides statistics, facts, and quotations which support your position. Make sure that you research alternative positions. Once all your information is gathered, you are ready to write your essay.

REVISE YOUR ESSAY

Make whatever changes that you like to improve your essay. You may want to add, delete, combine, or move some details. Reread your paper. Make sure that you use a neutral tone in presenting your opinion. Before giving our essay to your classmates for paper review, consider these questions:

1. Is your position clearly stated?
2. Are all the facts which you presented written clearly in a neutral tone?
3. Are your opinions supported with evidence?
4. Is the position arranged in a logical order?

Find a partner. Read each other's essay. Then, complete the following Peer Revising Checklist.

PEER REVISING CHECKLIST

1. Does the author have specific facts which support and strengthen his or her position?
2. Are the sources of the author's facts credible?
3. Are the resources up-to-date?
4. Is the support for the authors position grounded in opinions or in facts?
5. Has the author established his or her knowledge of the topic?
6. Has the author presented his or her position in a broad context?
7. Has the author considered counterpositions and refuted these counterpositions fairly?

Use the information from the Peer Revising Checklist to revise your essay.

Threads

No man is good enough to be another man's master.

George Bernard Shaw
1856–1950

EDIT YOUR ESSAY

When you are finished revising your essay, edit it carefully. Copy your revised essay neatly before handing it in to your instructor or asking your instructor to help you edit.

REFLECT ON WHAT YOU LEARNED

Reflect on what you learned. Analyze the patterns of errors that you made in your essay. The following checklist may be helpful.

EDITING CHECKLIST	YES	NO
CONTENT		
Knowledge of Topic		
Am I knowledgeable of the topic?	___	___
Support for My Position		
Have I provided good support for my position?	___	___
Interest		
Is my essay interesting?	___	___
ORGANIZATION		
Introduction		
Does my introduction describe my position clearly?	___	___
Developing Paragraphs		
Is the organization of the developing paragraphs logical?	___	___
Supporting Facts		
Are there sufficient supporting facts?	___	___
Appropriate Transitions		
Are there smooth transitions across paragraphs?	___	___
Conclusion		
Does the conclusion provide closure to the essay?	___	___
VOCABULARY		
Word Choice		
Are the words appropriate? Have I avoided slang and general words?	___	___
Word Form		
Are word forms used accurately?	___	___
GRAMMAR		
Subject/Verb Agreement		
Do subjects and verbs agree in number?	___	___

EDITING CHECKLIST (continued)	YES	NO
Pronoun Agreement and Pronoun Reference Do pronouns agree with nouns in number and gender?	_____	_____
Are pronouns used consistently?	_____	_____
Articles Are articles used correctly?	_____	_____
Verb Choice (Tense) Are verbs used in the appropriate tense?	_____	_____
Appropriate Use of Parallel Structure Have I used parallel structures correctly?	_____	_____
Avoidance of Run-on Sentences and Sentence Fragments Have I avoided run-on sentences and sentence fragments?	_____	_____
MECHANICS **Spelling** Are my words spelled correctly?	_____	_____
Punctuation Have I used punctuation accurately?	_____	_____

List of Five of My Most Significant Mistakes

1. _____

2. _____

3. _____

4. _____

5. _____

Quick Write

Write one paragraph about what you learned in writing this persuasive essay. Include in this paragraph a description of three mistakes that you made when writing the essay and the ways you intend to avoid making these mistakes in the future.

REPORTING SURVEY DATA

Write a one page report of two or three major trends from the survey data collected earlier. Your purpose is to inform. The readers of this report are your classmates.

Using a Language Learning Log

1. Vocabulary:

   Write down as many new words from the lesson as you can remember.

   _____

   _____

2. Grammar:

   Note examples of any grammatical structures from the lesson learned or reviewed. Write a brief explanation of the grammar points that they illustrate.

   _____

   _____

   _____

   _____

3. Punctuation:

   Write down any new punctuation rules that you learned.

   _____

   _____

   _____

   _____

4. Techniques for Gaining Writing Competence:

   List any new writing techniques that you learned. (Such techniques might include those for writing interesting introductions, bodies, and conclusions, or for composing different types of writing effectively.)

   _____

   _____

   _____

   _____

IT WORKS!
Learning Strategy:
Keeping Track of
Your Progress

5. Learning Strategies:

   Briefly describe any new learning strategies that you have applied in your writing.

   _____

   _____

   _____

6. Areas that Need More Work:

Note here in brief any areas that you are still trying to improve. Try to be as specific as possible.

_____

_____

_____

_____

LEARNING STRATEGY

Managing Your Learning: Making definite action plans and taking appropriate steps neessary to accomplish specific language objectives helps you develop better language skills.

Quick Write

DESCRIBING AN ACTION PLAN

Write a one paragraph description of your language learning goals and the specific actions which you want to take to accomplish these goals. Try to describe realistic goals and actions. Explain when you will take the actions. You are writing this for your instructor and yourself. Your purpose is to inform.

SUMMARY OF LESSON 3: EMPOWERMENT THROUGH THE WRITTEN WORD

In this lesson, you examined some ways of influencing others through writing. You wrote an essay describing obstacles which you have overcome through the written word, a persuasive essay, and a report of survey data. All these activities were designed to give you the competence to complete the writing assignment contained at the end of this unit.

QUICK REFERENCE TO LEARNING STRATEGIES

Forming Concepts: Guessing Intelligently (p. 254)

Forming Concepts: Asking Your Classmates Questions (p. 259)

Managing Your Learning: Organizing Your Ideas by Using an Outline (p. 259)

Understanding and Using Emotions: Believing in Your Position (p. 273)

Managing Your Learning: Using Resources (p. 274)

Managing Your Learning: Making Definite Action Plans (p. 278)

Description of Writing Assignment

Write a two to three page essay which you believe will make a difference in someone's life—your own or someone else's. You might write a set of recommendations for obtaining personal power or a report on violence or pollution. You might want to revise one of the essays you wrote for a previous assignment. You will need to identify your own audience for this particular topic as well as your specific purpose for writing. Your general purpose is to make a difference in someone's life.

Prewriting Activities

GUIDED DISCUSSION

It is helpful to discuss your ideas before you write your essay. Find a partner and tell each other about the essay that you plan to write. The following questions may be helpful:

1. What is my essay about?
2. Why am I writing this essay?
3. How will this essay affect my audience?
4. What are the characterisitics of my audience?
5. What information do I need in order to complete this writing assignment?

BRAINSTORMING

Brainstorming involves thinking quickly so as to give as many different ideas as possible about a given topic. It is an especially good way to generate ideas and to get ideas organized before you start a writing assignment. With the same partner, generate as many ideas about the topic as you can.

LISTING

After you brainstorm, you may want to use listing, a technique writers use to generate ideas quickly. Because speed is important in this activity, it is best to limit your listing to ten minutes. Follow the directions on page 280.

LISTING DIRECTIONS

1. Write the main idea of your essay on the top of the page.
2. Make a list of all the topics related to your main idea as quickly as you can. Do not stop writing until you are finished. Do not bother to correct any mistakes that you make.
3. If you can not think of a word you need, use another one or write in your native language.
4. When you are finished with your list, use a dictionary or rely on your teachers to help you replace translated or incorrect words with correct English words.
5. Review your list. If there are topics which do not relate to your main topic, cross them out. Circle the most interesting topics.

REVISING ACTIVITIES

After writing your first draft, use the following peer review sheet and response form to provide your peers with encouragement and contructive criticism.

PEER REVIEW SHEET

Reviewers: _____

Paper which is being reviewed: _____

What do you believe the author's purpose was in writing this essay? (For example, the author wanted to show how. . .; the author wanted to describe an event which would cause us to change. . .; the author wanted to convince us that. . .; the author wanted to explain. . .)

Who will read this essay? What are their general characteristics?

On a scale from 1–5, rate the essay for content (with "5" indicating excellent content and "1" indicating poor content).
Rating for content _____

Reason for giving this rating:

What would you suggest? (Be specific. For instance, if a certain paragraph needs more detail, state which paragraph you are talking about.)

On a scale from 1–10, rate this essay for organization (with "10" indicating excellent organization and "1" indicating poor organization.)
Rating for organization: _____

Reasons for giving this rating:

What would you suggest? How could the author organize the essay better?

Did the essay make a difference in the way you think about a subject? Why or why not?

How could the author be more convincing?

REPONSE SHEET

I agree with the following comments:

These are the changes I plan to make as a response to the reviewers' suggestions:

This is the way I plan to make my essay more convincing:

I disagree with the following comments made by the reviewers:

I need help with the following parts of the essay:

introduction   _____
evidence which supports my argument   _____
writing persuasively   _____
conclusion   _____
transitions   _____
vocabulary   _____
grammar   _____
other (please describe)

_____
_____
_____
_____
_____

*This form is adapted and printed with the permission of the author Roni Lebauer, from a class handout, Unversity of California Irvine 1989.

Tear out this page and give it to your teacher.

Editing Activity

EDITING CHECKLIST

Use a checklist when you edit your final essay. Before turning in your final essay, check the following points.

CONTENT AND ORGANIZATION

Yes   No

Yes	No	
_____	_____	**1.** My thesis is clearly stated.
_____	_____	**2.** My writing is persuasive.
_____	_____	**3.** My introduction interests the readers.
_____	_____	**4.** My essay contains original ideas.
_____	_____	**5.** I have provided sufficient information (for instance, statistics, quotes, examples, etc.) to adequately support my statements.
_____	_____	**6.** My conclusion contributes to the overall unity of my essay.
_____	_____	**7.** The essay will make a differnece in someone's life.

LANGUAGE

Yes   No

Yes	No	
_____	_____	**1.** I have corrected grammar, punctuation, and spelling errors that were indicated by my teacher.
_____	_____	**2.** I have tried to use a variey of sentence structures and have avoided using the same structures again and again.

SHARING YOUR WRITING

In small groups, choose those writings which best illustrate what you have learned in this chapter. Then, share them with the rest of the class. There are many ways to share your writing. These include reading student work out loud in class, writing in student-produced class magazines or newsletters, photocopying compositions and sharing them with other students, and sharing writing with students in other classes. You might also consider submitting student writing to local newspapers and magazines that publish student writing.